vegetarian
pleasures

vegetarian
pleasures

a menu cookbook

jeanne lemlin

alfred a. knopf · new york · 1989

This Is a Borzoi Book published by Alfred A. Knopf, Inc.

Copyright © 1986 by Jeanne Lemlin
Illustrations copyright © 1986 by Rita Grasso Pocock
All rights reserved under International and
Pan-American Copyright Conventions.
Published in the United States by Alfred A. Knopf, Inc.,
New York, and simultaneously in Canada
by Random House of Canada Limited, Toronto.
Distributed by Random House, Inc., New York.

Library of Congress Cataloging-in-Publication Data
Lemlin, Jeanne.
Vegetarian pleasures.
Includes index.
1. Vegetarian cookery.   2. Menus.   I. Title.
TX837.L45   1986   641.5'636   85-45702
ISBN 0-394-54117-0
ISBN 0-394-74302-4 (pbk.)

Manufactured in the United States of America
Published May 14, 1986
Reprinted Once
Third Printing, January 1989

to ed

Many thanks to family and friends who have helped me along the way, and special thanks to my editor, Judith Jones, for her encouragement and invaluable editorial direction, and to my agent, Susan Lescher, for her unfailing support.

contents

introduction   page xiii

quick menus

menu one   page 4
braised tempeh napoletano
fine egg noodles with light garlic sauce
blueberry streusel cake

menu two   page 7
crudités with creamy garlic tofu dip
penne with eggplant sauce
apricot orange mousse

menu three   page 10
avocado and bathed bread vinaigrette
skillet bulghur and vegetables
with shredded basil
gingerbread

menu four   page 13
ricotta basil spread
(on crackers or french bread)
polenta puttanesca
sautéed apples and maple syrup
topped with yogurt

menu five   page 16
cucumber and grated carrot salad
in creamy dill dressing
bean tostadas
hot fudge pudding cake

menu six   page 19
tempeh in curried yogurt sauce
perfect brown rice
indian pudding

menu seven   page 21
mixed green salad
farfalle with broccoli di rapa
chocolate oatmeal bars or fresh fruit

menu eight   page 24
zucchini, tomato, and basil frittata
bulghur pilaf
stuffed peaches with fresh cherries
and almonds, or marinated oranges
in grand marnier sauce

menu nine   page 27
stuffed red pepper strips
with ricotta basil spread
pasta with swiss chard and garlic
bananas in ginger syrup

menu ten   page 29
crustless broccoli and cottage cheese pie
lemon-glazed broccoli stalks julienne
kasha pilaf
baked apples with honey and brandy

menu eleven   page 32
braised curried eggplant
fruited rice curry
(plain yogurt)
(vanilla ice cream topped with
maple syrup and walnuts)

menu twelve   page 34
spicy cucumber salad
stir-fried tempeh with hot pepper sauce
perfect brown rice
chocolate oatmeal bars

menu thirteen   page 36
salad with sesame ginger dressing
buckwheat noodles/soba and tofu
chocolate chocolate-chip cookies

menu fourteen   page 39
kasha topped with mushrooms
in sour cream sauce
sautéed cabbage with fennel seed
pear and apricot crisp

menu fifteen   page 42
stuffed mushrooms with feta and dill
spaghettini with garlic and hot pepper
winter fruit salad with apple cider glaze

informal menus

menu one   page 46
indonesian salad
with spicy peanut dressing
indonesian curried vegetable stew
with coconut milk
stuffed bananas with rum cream
and cashews

menu two page 49
watercress and jerusalem artichoke salad
with sweet mustard dressing
baked mexican-style beans
with sour cream and chilies
sautéed greens with garlic
sangria
chocolate-chip fudge brownies

menu three page 53
fresh pea salad rémoulade
stir-fried asparagus, tofu, and red pepper
perfect brown rice
rhubarb tart

menu four page 56
tamale pie
apple crisp

menu five page 59
simple salad with lemon soy dressing
szechuan braised bean curd
and vegetables
perfect brown rice
(fresh pineapple)

menu six page 61
spinach salad with creamy dill dressing
fragrant vegetable stew
with corn dumplings
maple pecan pie

menu seven page 64
mixed green salad
neapolitan pizza
carrot cake with cream cheese icing

menu eight page 67
baked eggplant stuffed
with curried vegetables
perfect brown rice
(plain yogurt)
strawberries and wine

menu nine page 69
salsa picante with hot pita triangles
mexican-style stuffed summer squash
sangria
fresh fruit with yogurt lime sauce

menu ten page 73
cheese and crackers
stir-fried noodles and vegetables
with sesame seeds
susanne's spice cake

menu eleven page 76
crudités with yogurt herb dip
vegetarian chili
cornbread
poached pears in red wine with raisins

menu twelve page 79
asparagus vinaigrette
baked eggplant, chickpeas, and tomatoes
(hot french bread)
apricot orange mousse

menu thirteen page 81
mixed green salad
braised tofu and vegetables with
white wine and tarragon
perfect brown rice with peas
sweet potato pie

menu fourteen page 84
arugula and boston lettuce salad
baked macaroni and cheese with
cauliflower and jalapeño peppers
poached pears in red wine with raisins

menu fifteen page 86
watercress and jerusalem artichoke salad
with sweet mustard dressing
celery root au gratin
kasha pilaf
honey bread pudding with apricot sauce

menu sixteen page 89
pesto on toasted french bread
tofu fra diavolo with spinach fettuccine
fresh fruit
or chocolate-chip walnut squares

menu seventeen page 91
mixed green salad
chalupas
apple crisp

menu eighteen page 93
mixed vegetable slaw
baked lima beans basque-style
chilled zabaglione with honey

menu nineteen   page 96
curried rice, tofu, and vegetables
banana raita
cowboy cookies

menu twenty   page 99
marinated shell bean and zucchini salad
polenta and pesto soufflé
sautéed grated beets and beet greens
fresh fruit or pear and apricot crisp

menu twenty-one   page 102
garden salad with creamy garlic
tofu dressing
baked chickpeas provençale
almond butter cookies

menu twenty-two   page 105
mozzarella, roasted pepper,
and black olive salad
risotto of brown rice and mushrooms
braised broccoli with wine and garlic
fresh fruit with honey zabaglione sauce

menu twenty-three   page 109
indian eggplant dip
cashew nut curry
curried cauliflower and peas
fried bananas
perfect brown rice
(plain yogurt)
ice cream sprinkled with espresso

menu twenty-four   page 113
crudités with yogurt herb dip
cuban black beans and rice
marinated oranges
in grand marnier sauce

menu twenty-five   page 115
baked stuffed artichokes with
pine nuts and lemon herb sauce
cauliflower and pasta soup
rhubarb cobbler

menu twenty-six   page 119
mixed green salad
cauliflower and cashew croquettes
green beans provençale
glazed pear cake

menu twenty-seven   page 123
spicy buddha's delight
(lo mein or linguine)
coconut macaroons

menu twenty-eight   page 125
mixed green salad
spaghetti squash with
broccoli butter sauce
brandied fruit compote

menu twenty-nine   page 128
mixed green salad
buttermilk herb and onion tart
sesame broccoli
chocolate-chip walnut squares

menu thirty   page 131
ricotta basil spread
(on crackers or french bread)
collards mornay
barley pilaf
ginger cookies

elegant menus

menu one   page 136
pâté de légumes
(french bread)
sautéed tofu in french sweet butter
and vinegar sauce
perfect brown rice with peas
maple custard with maple pecan sauce

menu two   page 140
arugula and boston lettuce salad
rolled stuffed lasagne with kale
in a tomato cream sauce
linzertorte

menu three   page 143
miso soup
moo shoo vegetables
with mandarin pancakes
chilled green beans with sesame sauce
maple-glazed baked stuffed apples
with crème fraîche

menu four   page 149
mango and avocado salad
with raspberry vinaigrette
spinach custard ring
with tomato cream sauce
bulghur almond pilaf
prune tart with orange almond crust

menu five   page 153
puris
vegetable kofta
red lentil dal
perfect brown rice
orange raita
raisin chutney
kheer

menu six   page 159
three-layered vegetable pâté
with herb mayonnaise
skillet tofu and vegetables
in brandy cream sauce
brussels sprouts with lemon soy glaze
fine egg noodles with light
garlic sauce
mocha walnut torte

menu seven   page 164
hummus
tabbouleh
spanakopita
honey-glazed sugar snap peas
with carrots
banana rum roll cake

menu eight   page 170
arugula and boston lettuce salad
noodle timbales with pesto cream sauce
zucchini, red pepper, and snow pea sauté
raspberry almond torte

menu nine   page 173
guacamole
black bean and cream cheese enchiladas
sautéed greens with garlic
sangría
pear tart with almond nut crust

menu ten   page 177
deep-fried cheese-filled polenta balls
tofu francese with artichoke hearts
rutabaga gratin
perfect brown rice pilaf
poached honey pears topped
with ginger custard

menu eleven   page 181
moroccan tomato and
roasted pepper salad
vegetarian b'stilla
braised celery
mocha walnut torte

menu twelve   page 184
stuffed mushrooms with blue cheese
leek timbales with white wine sauce
bulghur pilaf
pear tart with almond nut crust

menu thirteen   page 187
—a thanksgiving feast to serve six—
yogurt herb cheese
walnut loaf with burgundy sauce
chestnut purée
braised red cabbage with apples
roasted potatoes with rosemary
cranberry fruit tart

summer menus

menu one   page 194
tzadziki with pita bread
curried rice salad
with apples and cashews
peach almond torte

menu two   page 197
pasta with uncooked tomato and
fresh basil sauce
raspberry pie

menu three   page 199
iced plum soup
tempeh salade niçoise
fresh peaches with honey rum sauce

menu four   page 201
gazpacho
marinated pasta and vegetable salad
summer fruit tart

menu five   page 205
marinated bean curd, cucumber,
and radish salad
cold sesame noodles with broccoli
and cashews
ginger cookies
chocolate-dipped strawberries

menu six   page 208
cold cucumber and watercress soup
chilled tomatoes stuffed with white beans
and pesto
peaches marsala

menu seven   page 210
bulghur salad with tarragon
and vegetables
open-face tomato sandwiches
summer fruit salad

menu eight   page 212
cheese and onion boeregs
cacik
cantaloupe with strawberries and lime

menu nine   page 215
yogurt herb cheese
(french bread)
new potato and dill salad
marinated vegetables
with sesame dressing
summer pudding

menu ten   page 218
chilled summer borscht
wild rice and artichoke salad
(french bread)
strawberries with yogurt

breakfast and brunch menus

menu one   page 223
orange and grapefruit sections with kiwi
maple pancakes
coffee or tea

menu two   page 225
granola (with yogurt or milk)
blueberry muffins
coffee or tea

menu three   page 227
fresh fruit
french toast with orange and brandy
coffee or tea

menu four   page 228
(cape codder: vodka and cranberry juice)
egg and pepper croustades
sweet potato home fries
oatmeal scones
homemade prune butter
baked apples with honey and brandy
coffee or tea

menu five   page 233
orange lassi
samosa
bombay-style curried eggs
brown rice pilaf
brandied fruit compote

menu six   page 236
(fresh strawberries and sliced mango,
if in season) or winter fruit salad with
apple cider glaze
irish soda bread
mushroom quiche
home-fried potatoes and onions
coffee or tea

soups and breads
page 239

the basics
page 265

glossary of ingredients, etc.
page 280

index
page 289

key to symbols

G Indicates that more detailed information can be
found in the Glossary of Ingredients

( ) Food listed within parentheses indicates recipe not provided

introduction

There has been an unprecedented growth in the popularity of vegetarian cooking over the past twenty years, so much so that it is no longer seen as a fad but as an important part of this country's diverse culinary repertoire. Yet, although many people have discovered that meat is not necessary for creating an enticing and satisfying cuisine, they find that vegetarian cooking does offer its own unique challenges for menu planning. Traditionally, not only have we depended on meat for its high protein contribution, but it has also usually been the centerpiece around which the entire menu revolved. In the vegetarian cooking classes that I have given over the past seven years, my students, both vegetarians and non-vegetarians alike, have continuously raised such questions as: "What would you serve with...?" "Will the meal be nutritionally complete?" "What can I serve as the centerpiece?" "What dishes are quick so as to allow time for the more involved ones?"

I have written this menu cookbook with all those questions in mind, to offer you many tempting and varied menus that are both nutritionally and aesthetically balanced. To combine dishes harmoniously I encourage my students—as I have done in this book —to take into account flavor, richness, texture, color, nutritional makeup, the time demanded for preparation, and the seasonal availability of ingredients. Although vegetarians must be careful to provide themselves with, in particular, adequate protein and iron, I do not feel that nutritional concerns should dominate vegetarian cooking. Of course they must be a factor (something totally ignored in haute cuisine), but that does not mean that every menu must be meticulously calculated.

So much has been written about the need for vegetarians to maintain a balanced diet that many people panic when they decide to cut down on or eliminate their meat intake. Certainly we should be attentive to our dietary needs, but once you discover which foods are wholesome and should be eaten often, you can relax your concerns somewhat and assess your overall diet. Each meal doesn't have to be a model of nutritional perfection. If you eat plenty of fresh vegetables, fruits, whole grains, and a modest amount of dairy products, I believe you can include some white flour and sugar in your cooking without fear of damaging your health. When your diet draws primarily from the wealth of the plant kingdom, then an occasional rich and satisfying dessert, for example, will not only please the senses but will feed the spirit as well. Nothing hampers the pleasure and spontaneity of cooking more than absolute rigidity.

At an early age I discovered that I found real joy in an adventurous, personal approach to cooking; once I had learned the ground rules I was invigorated by the possibilities that unfolded as I broke them. When I became a vegetarian at the age of fifteen I had the good fortune of having a mother who was intrigued by and supportive of my choice. Being a latchkey child who was given free rein in the kitchen, I was encouraged to experiment with the many new and unusual ingredients that would eventually replace the standard meat and potato fare that I had been brought up on. I was already a rather daring cook (the way an impetuous fifteen-year-old can be), and I soon realized what an asset this was as I explored the new world of vegetarian cooking.

The majority of vegetarian cookbooks that were (and are) available have been of two types: either "health foodish" with a heavy, bland approach to "nutritious" cooking, or overly reliant on products such as cheese, cream, and eggs to compensate for the lack of protein usually derived from meat. Neither of these styles wholly appealed to me, and I found myself delving into numerous international cuisines and adapting and combining them with abandon.

In the U.S. we don't have a culinary tradition that reflects a love of fresh vegetables, fruits, and grains as do many other countries such as Italy, France, China, India, and the various countries of the Middle East. Meat has always played an excessively important role in our cooking. It is inspiring to discover the many versatile ways that other cultures use dried beans, grains, and soy products, for example, and to note how instinctively they combine them to form complete proteins. Whether this versatility stems from religious conviction, poverty, or just from a genuine love of plant foods, these cuisines have a lot to offer vegetarians.

Being an American with a melting-pot heritage, I have felt very comfortable borrowing from other culinary traditions—and excited by the possibilities inherent in combining them. The Tofu Francese with Artichoke Hearts dish that I developed (page 178) is an example of a compatible marriage of Italian and Chinese styles. Chunks of tofu are dipped in an egg batter and sautéed, then cooked in a luscious lemon, butter, and white wine sauce with artichokes. Tempeh, an Indonesian staple, is delectable when marinated in a garlicky vinaigrette, then tossed with mayonnaise and served in the French Tempeh Salade Niçoise you'll find on page 200. And jalapeño peppers add fire and contrast to the creamy Baked Macaroni and Cheese with Cauliflower recipe on page 85. These are just three examples where mingling traditions creates a new and exciting dimension.

Discovery adds zest to any endeavor, and so too with cooking. Once we cultivate an adventurous approach to the preparation of food and the eating of it, our appreciation of fine food is greatly enhanced.

why vegetarianism?

It is heartening to me to see how vegetarianism has gained in popularity. Once the choice of a very small minority, it is now common to meet vegetarians in all walks of life, though their reasons for adopting a meatless diet vary. As a teenager I became increasingly uneasy about the unquestioned acceptance of the slaughtering of animals for food. The typical answers that adults would give as to why this practice had remained so prevalent never quelled my misgivings. I discovered that in order to see the issue clearly it needed to be placed in a historical perspective.

It is easy to imagine people of former times depending on meat for survival. Harsh climatic conditions, scarcity of suitable vegetation, lack of refrigeration, all contributed to a harsh way of life in which they continually faced the challenges of survival. Animals were needed to play a vital and intricate role in that struggle, providing food, clothing, labor, transportation, and shelter.

Now, however, in a society that imports and exports food on a global scale, has dependable refrigeration and transportation to ensure a salubrious variety of foods, and shamelessly destroys "surplus" livestock to secure the highest of prices, the same justification can no longer suffice. For most people who live in developed nations the *need* for meat has been replaced by the *desire* for meat.

One problem with this seemingly harmless desire is that it is satisfied at the expense of an immeasurable amount of suffering inflicted upon animals. Few of us stop to think of the horrendous ways that animals are raised by factory farming. The meat is sold in the markets in neatly wrapped packages with no hint of its history. But when we take the time to explore the conditions under which the animals were raised through high-tech farming, it becomes very difficult to turn our backs on the gruesome reality. For those who would like to look into this in more detail, I highly recommend Peter Singer's book *Animal Liberation*.

But for many people the attraction to vegetarianism stems from health concerns. Current research has shown that not only is a meatless diet adequate in meeting our dietary needs, but, in fact, it has been found to be superior to the typical high-fat, low-fiber diet of most Americans. Vegetables, grains, fruits, and a small amount of dairy products can provide us with all the necessary nutrients, and, in addition, help us resist the risk of heart disease and cancer. Meat has been known to contain many toxins, carcinogens, excess fat, and no fiber, and the overabundance of protein ingested with a meat-centered diet has been linked to osteoporosis (softening of the bones) and some types of cancer.

It has been a popular misconception among vegetarians that the elimination of meat is sufficient to free them from any concern over high cholesterol and fat consumption. In an effort to get an adequate amount of protein, many vegetarians eat large amounts of dairy products, confident that they are eating well because they aren't eating meat. Recent studies have pointed out, however, that dairy products—in particular, cream, eggs, hard cheese, and whole milk—should be restricted in all types of diets because of their excessive fat and cholesterol content. They also contain many of the toxic additives that threaten us in meat. We should use low-fat products whenever possible, such as low-fat yogurt and milk, buttermilk, and part-skim ricotta cheese. Many of the menus in this book are low in fat, and I suggest that if you are concerned about your fat consumption—and you should be—then choose these menus the majority of the time, saving the richer menus for special occasions.

When I think of contemporary haute cuisine I am reminded of what someone said about modern medicine: it's like the Tower of Pisa—a great achievement but a little off center. Cooking and nutrition must coalesce, or else the enjoyment we get from eating indiscriminately will undermine our well-being.

The possibilities that healthful vegetarian cooking offer are endless, and I hope that these menus will inspire you to cook with a new perspective. Above all, I wish to help you discover the deep satisfaction that one can feel when health, pleasure, and a respect for life are harmoniously linked. Good cooking brings together those elements, and enriches both the cook and those who are fortunate enough to share that cook's creations.

a secret to relaxed cooking

• Read the entire recipe through beforehand.

• Take out all of the ingredients you need and place them nearby or in front of you.

• Do all of the advance preparation you can before you actually begin cooking, for example: chopping nuts, cutting vegetables, making coconut milk, measuring ingredients, etc.

• Take out and prepare any pans or dishes that you will be cooking with.

• Pour yourself a glass of wine.

vegetarian
pleasures

key to symbols

quick menus

Quickness and ease of preparation characterize the recipes in this section, but don't let that dissuade you from choosing one of these menus for a special occasion. The dishes are simple to prepare, yet are imaginative and interesting, and would be suitable for lunches, quick after-work dinners, as well as for pleasing guests.

menu one

braised tempeh napoletano
fine egg noodles with light garlic sauce
blueberry streusel cake

This is one of my favorite quick menus; it is very nutritious, and each dish is special in itself. Although when I cook I usually choose foods that are in season, this Blueberry Cake can be a welcome reminder of summer when it is served in the late fall or winter, so I sometimes make it with frozen blueberries.

braised tempeh napoletano

Tempeh is a delicious fermented soybean product made with ground soybeans. Unlike tofu it has a flavor of its own, and its firm, dry texture makes it very easy to work with. In this dish, tempeh is simmered in an aromatic tomato sauce with vegetables and herbs. I think it goes particularly well with brown rice. Because tempeh freezes well, I always keep some on hand so I can make this on a moment's notice.

serves 4

¼ cup olive oil
6 cloves garlic, minced
1 medium-size onion, diced
2 small zucchini, halved lengthwise
　　and thinly sliced
1 large green pepper,
　　diced (½-inch dice)
8 ounces tempeh, G
　　cut into ½-inch cubes

1½ cups (from 16-ounce can) finely chopped
　　peeled tomatoes with their juice
2 tablespoons dry vermouth
　　(or dry red or white wine)
¼ teaspoon basil
¼ teaspoon marjoram
¼ teaspoon oregano
¼ teaspoon salt
Liberal seasoning freshly ground pepper

1. Heat the olive oil in a large skillet over medium-high heat, then add the garlic and onion, and sauté for 2 minutes, tossing frequently. Add the zucchini and toss for 2 more minutes. Add the green pepper and tempeh, and cook, tossing occasionally, for 5 more minutes.

2. Add the tomatoes, vermouth, and all of the remaining ingredients, and stir well. Reduce the heat to a simmer and cook slowly for about 10 minutes, or until the sauce is fragrant and thickened. Do not overcook the vegetables; they should still retain a slight crunchiness. Serve immediately, or cover and chill up to 24 hours, then reheat slowly until piping hot.

fine egg noodles with light garlic sauce

serves 4

½ pound fine egg noodles
3 tablespoons butter, cut into pieces
1 clove garlic, minced
½ cup minced fresh parsley
¼ cup grated Parmesan cheese
Salt to taste

1. Bring about 2 quarts of water to a boil in a medium-size saucepan. Add the noodles and cook for about 5 minutes, or until al dente—that is, tender yet slightly firm to the bite. Drain thoroughly in a colander.

2. Immediately return the pot to the stove and melt the butter with the garlic. Cook for 3 minutes over medium heat. Add the drained noodles and parsley and toss. Add the cheese and salt to taste and toss again. Serve immediately. *May be prepared up to 8 hours in advance, covered, and refrigerated. To reheat, place in a buttered baking dish, cover, and cook in a preheated 350-degree oven for 15 minutes, or until hot and steamy. Toss occasionally. If the noodles look a little dry, sprinkle on a few drops of water to moisten while cooking.*

blueberry streusel cake

A moist blueberry-filled cake that has a crisp, flavorful topping. It is delicious plain, but is spectacular when topped with lightly sweetened whipped cream.

2 cups unbleached white flour
2 teaspoons baking powder
1/2 teaspoon salt
2 cups (1 pint) fresh blueberries, rinsed and patted dry, or *unthawed* frozen berries
4 tablespoons butter, softened
1 cup sugar
1 teaspoon vanilla extract
2 eggs
1 cup milk

streusel:
1/3 cup unbleached white flour
1/3 cup sugar
1/2 teaspoon cinnamon
4 tablespoons chilled butter, cut into bits

Lightly sweetened whipped cream

1. Preheat the oven to 375 degrees. Generously butter and flour an 8-by-8-inch pan and set aside. (If you are using a glass dish, then set the oven at 350 degrees.)

Try to time the baking so that the cake can come out of the oven about 30 minutes before you begin eating.

2. Combine the flour, baking powder, and salt in a large bowl and mix well. Add the blueberries and gently toss to coat.

3. Cream the butter with the sugar and vanilla in a medium-size bowl until well blended. Add the eggs and mix. Carefully add the milk and beat just until blended.

4. Add this wet mixture to the flour mixture and stir *by hand* just until blended. Pour into the prepared cake pan.

5. To make the streusel: Mix the flour, sugar, and cinnamon in a medium-size bowl. Cut the butter in with a pastry cutter or two knives until the mixture is evenly blended but still crumbly. Sprinkle evenly onto the cake batter.

6. Bake for 40–45 minutes, or until the top is evenly golden and a knife inserted in the center comes out clean. Cool on a wire rack for 10 minutes before removing from the pan. Invert onto a plate or platter and then flip again right side up onto another plate or platter. Serve warm or at room temperature plain or with lightly sweetened whipped cream.

menu two

crudités with creamy garlic tofu dip
penne with eggplant sauce
apricot orange mousse

Crudités is the French word for raw vegetables. You could serve thin raw asparagus (use the top third of each stalk), red peppers, carrots, endive, cauliflower, blanched broccoli (blanch it for one minute in boiling water for added color and flavor, then cool thoroughly in cold water), and zucchini, or any raw vegetables of your choice. The tofu in the dip adds protein to this meal. If you prefer to serve a salad rather than the crudités, why not turn the dip into a dressing and try Garden Salad with Creamy Garlic Tofu Dressing (p. 102).

creamy garlic tofu dressing or dip

The texture of tofu changes dramatically when it is puréed in the blender and makes an unusually smooth and flavorful salad dressing, dip, or sandwich spread.

makes 1 1/2 cups

1/2 pound firm or soft tofu,
    patted dry
2 tablespoons lemon juice
    (about 1/2 lemon)
1/4 cup oil
4 tablespoons water
    (use only 2 for the dip or spread)
1 tablespoon tamari soy sauce
2–3 cloves garlic, chopped

1. Place all of the ingredients in a blender or food processor and purée until very smooth. (Use more or less garlic depending on your taste.) You may need to turn off the machine and scrape down the sides a few times.

2. If too thick for salad dressing, then add a little more water until desired consistency is reached. *May be kept covered in the refrigerator for up to 4 days.*

penne with eggplant sauce

It's amusing to contemplate how much taste is inextricably linked to texture, and the best illustration of this is pasta. Although most pastas are made from the same ingredients, their various shapes will determine the character of the dish they're in. The ingredients in two sauces can be identical, yet if one is served with angel hair pasta and one is served with ziti, the two dishes will taste different. With a robust sauce such as this one with eggplant, garlic, and hot peppers, short, thick pasta is a good match. I love these quill-shaped penne, and I think you'll agree that they are worth searching for if you cannot get them in a supermarket.

serves 4

    1 pound penne (short tubular pasta
        with pointed tips)
    5 tablespoons olive oil
    1 medium-large eggplant
        (about 1½ pounds),
        peeled and diced (1-inch dice)
    4 cloves garlic, minced
    ¼ teaspoon dried red pepper flakes
    35-ounce can imported plum tomatoes,
        roughly chopped and drained
    ½ teaspoon salt
    Liberal seasoning freshly ground pepper
    1½ tablespoons minced fresh parsley

1. Set all of the ingredients in front of you near the stove.

2. Bring a large (6–8-quart) pot of water to a boil. Add the penne and cook until al dente—tender yet slightly firm to the bite, about 12–15 minutes.

3. While the water is being brought to a boil you can begin the sauce. In a large skillet heat 2 tablespoons of the oil over medium-high heat until hot but not smoking. Add *half* of the eggplant and cook until almost tender. Toss frequently and do not add any more oil; just keep tossing if the eggplant begins to stick. When done remove onto a platter. Add 2 more tablespoons of oil and repeat with the remaining eggplant.

4. Add the remaining tablespoon of olive oil to the pan. Add the garlic and red pepper flakes, and cook until the garlic is golden, about 2 minutes, tossing frequently.

5. Add the tomatoes, salt, and pepper, and bring to a boil. Add the eggplant and cook until the sauce has thickened and the eggplant is tender, about 7–10 minutes. Keep the sauce hot over low heat if the pasta is not done yet.

6. Drain the pasta in a colander. Return it to the pot or a warm serving bowl and add the sauce. Toss. Add the parsley and toss again. Serve immediately with a bowl of grated Parmesan cheese to pass at the table.

apricot orange mousse

serves 6

1 1/2 cups dried apricots
   (10 ounces)
1 cup water
1/2 cup honey
1/4 cup orange juice
   (juice from 1 large orange—
   reserve 3 thin slices for garnish)
1 tablespoon Cointreau, Grand Marnier,
   or Triple Sec
1/2 cup heavy or whipping cream,
   well chilled
2 egg whites, at room temperature
3 thin slices orange for garnish

1. Put the apricots, water, and honey into a medium-size saucepan. Partially cover, bring to a boil, then reduce to a simmer and cook for 10 minutes, or until the apricots are soft.

2. Pour the apricots and their liquid into a blender or food processor, add the orange juice, and puree until smooth. Spoon into a bowl and stir in the liqueur. Refrigerate until chilled.

3. Meanwhile in a medium-size bowl whip the cream until stiff. (For best results chill the bowl and beaters beforehand.)

4. Wash and dry the beaters well. In a separate large bowl whip the egg whites until stiff but not dry. (The bowl, beaters, and egg whites should be warm for best results.)

5. When the apricot purée is chilled check the consistency; it should be like thick oatmeal. If necessary thin with a little liqueur, orange juice, or milk.

6. Spoon the chilled apricot purée into the egg whites and gently fold in. Add the whipped cream and fold in until well blended. Spoon into custard cups or attractive goblets and garnish with half of an orange slice twisted. Chill at least 1 hour before serving or up to 48 hours.

menu three

avocado and bathed bread vinaigrette
skillet bulghur and vegetables with shredded basil
gingerbread

This is one of my favorite quick menus; everything is extremely flavorful and very easy to prepare. Herbs and spices are used generously in each dish and so your kitchen will become wonderfully aromatic.

---

avocado and bathed bread vinaigrette

The combined flavors of the perfectly ripe avocado and thin slices of toasted French bread in this garlicky vinaigrette are incomparable. Black pebbly-skinned avocados are the best variety because they are the creamiest.

serves 4

> 1/2 cup Vinaigrette (p. 268)
> 2 cloves garlic, minced
> 6 slices French bread, about 1/4 inch thick
> 2 ripe medium-size avocados
>   (preferably black pebbled-skin variety)

1. In a small bowl mix the vinaigrette with the minced garlic and set aside.

2. Toast the French bread slices until golden on both sides. Cut each slice into 1-inch strips, then into bite-size pieces.

3. Slice the avocado in half vertically and remove the pit. Insert the handle of a teaspoon between the skin and flesh of each avocado half and move it around the avocado until the flesh is released from the skin. Discard the skin.

4. Arrange 4 small serving plates in front of you. Allow half an avocado for each person. Slice each half into 6 slices and arrange them on the serving plate with equally divided pieces of toasted French bread.

5. Drizzle the vinaigrette equally over the 4 portions and let sit for 5 minutes before serving.

skillet bulghur and vegetables
with shredded basil

serves 4

1 1/2 cups bulghur G
1/4 cup oil
2 cloves garlic, minced
2 medium-size onions, diced
2 small to medium zucchini (1 pound),
   halved lengthwise and thinly sliced
2 tablespoons finely shredded fresh basil,
   or 1 teaspoon dried basil
2 medium-size carrots, grated
2 teaspoons tamari soy sauce
1/2 teaspoon salt
Liberal seasoning freshly ground pepper
1 tablespoon butter, cut into bits

1. Rinse the bulghur in a sieve under cold running water. Place in a medium-size bowl and pour boiling water over it to cover plus 1 inch. Let soak for 30 minutes, or until tender when tasted. Transfer small batches at a time to a large piece of cheesecloth or a clean kitchen towel and squeeze out all of the liquid, then place in a bowl and set aside.

2. In a large skillet heat the oil over medium-high heat until hot but not smoking. Add the garlic and onions and sauté for 5 minutes.

3. Add the zucchini and basil and cook for 5 minutes, tossing occasionally. Add the carrots and cook for a few more minutes, or until the zucchini is tender but crisp—not mushy.

4. Add the bulghur, soy sauce, salt, pepper, and butter, and cook for 2–3 minutes, or until the bulghur is hot. Taste to adjust the seasoning. This dish is delicious as is or served with plain yogurt on the side.

gingerbread

This is a spicy version, which is interlaced with minced fresh gingerroot. Although it is still delicious served the day after, I prefer to serve it freshly made and still warm from the oven (or at room temperature) because it has a softer texture. If you prefer it this way also, time your baking so that the gingerbread has finished cooking about 1 hour before serving.

½ cup (1 stick) butter
¾ cup molasses
½ cup honey
1 cup water
½ cup firmly packed
　　light brown sugar
1 egg
1¾ cups unbleached white flour
2 teaspoons baking soda
½ teaspoon baking powder
1 tablespoon ground ginger
2 teaspoons cinnamon
½ teaspoon salt
2 teaspoons minced gingerroot

Lightly sweetened whipped cream

1. Preheat the oven to 350 degrees. Butter a round 10-inch springform pan, or an 8-by-8-inch square pan. (If you are using glass set the oven at 325 degrees.)

2. In a medium-size saucepan combine the butter, molasses, honey, and water. Heat just until the butter melts and the mixture is blended. Stir occasionally. Remove from the heat.

3. In a small bowl beat the brown sugar and egg together until blended.

4. In a large bowl combine the remaining dry ingredients and gingerroot and mix well.

5. Alternately add the molasses mixture and the egg mixture to the dry ingredients. Beat until well blended, but do not overbeat.

6. Pour into the prepared pan. Bake for 30–40 minutes, or until a knife inserted in the center comes out *almost* clean. (It continues to cook while cooling.) Cool on a wire rack.

7. Serve warm with lightly sweetened whipped cream, or dust with confectioners' (powdered) sugar.

menu four

ricotta basil spread (on crackers or french bread)
polenta puttanesca
sautéed apples and maple syrup topped with yogurt

Polenta is a wonderful grain dish to become familiar with because it is so quick to make, and it goes well with most vegetables and sauces. It is a good idea to keep some cornmeal, canned tomatoes, and Parmesan cheese on hand so you can put this polenta together on a moment's notice. If you want to improvise, for the green peppers and olives you could substitute zucchini, green beans, mushrooms, or a mixture of vegetables.

---

ricotta basil spread

makes 1½ cups

1 cup ricotta cheese
  (preferably part-skim)
¼ cup grated Parmesan cheese
1 tablespoon milk
1 clove garlic, minced

1 tablespoon minced fresh basil,
  or 1 teaspoon dried basil
¼ cup minced fresh parsley
Salt to taste
Freshly ground pepper to taste

Beat all the ingredients together by hand—except 1 teaspoon of minced parsley—in a medium-size bowl until very smooth. Scrape into a serving bowl and garnish with the remaining parsley. Cover and chill at least ½ hour before serving. Use as a spread on toasted French bread or crackers, or as a stuffing in raw pepper strips.

note:
If you would like to make this into a dip, increase the milk to 3 tablespoons and the parsley to ½ cup. Put all ingredients in the blender and blend until smooth. It will make an attractive jade-colored dip.

polenta puttanesca

Polenta is a type of cornmeal mush that is a staple in parts of northern Italy. It is so delicious and satisfying, and is so quick to prepare, it is regrettable that it isn't more popular in this country. The puttanesca sauce is a robust, brazen tomato sauce (*puttana* means whore) and it balances the subtle flavor of the polenta nicely.

serves 4

sauce:
1/3 cup olive oil
8 cloves garlic, minced
1/4 teaspoon dried red pepper flakes
2 large green peppers, cored and cut into
    1/2-inch strips
Two 28-ounce cans imported plum
    tomatoes, chopped and well drained
1 1/2 tablespoons tomato paste
10 imported black olives (1 1/2 ounces,
    preferably Kalamata), pitted and halved
2 teaspoons capers
1/2 teaspoon salt
Freshly ground pepper to taste

polenta:
4 cups water
1 1/4 cups cornmeal
    (either coarse or regular)
1/2 teaspoon salt
2 tablespoons butter, cut into bits
1/3 cup grated Parmesan cheese

1. In a large skillet heat the oil over medium heat until hot but not smoking, then add the garlic and red pepper flakes. Cook for 3 minutes, or just until the garlic begins to get golden and the oil is fragrant. Be careful not to burn it.

2. Add the green peppers and sauté for 10 minutes, stirring frequently.

3. Raise the heat to medium high and add the drained chopped tomatoes, tomato paste, olives, capers, salt, and pepper. Cook until the peppers are tender and the sauce is thickened, about 10 minutes. Stir frequently.

4. Meanwhile, make the polenta. In a medium-size heavy-bottomed saucepan bring the water to a boil. *Very slowly* drizzle in the cornmeal, whisking continuously with a wire whisk all the while it is being sprinkled in. Add the salt and reduce the heat to low. Continue to whisk the polenta until a thick mass develops. (At this point it is better to switch to a wooden spoon.) Stir continuously until the polenta pulls away from the sides of the pan, about 5–7 minutes.

5. To serve: Spoon equal portions of the polenta onto the center of each serving plate. Top with bits of butter and sprinkle on the Parmesan cheese. Finally top with the sauce. Serve immediately.

note:
If for some reason the polenta cannot be served immediately and it begins to harden in the saucepan, add a small amount of water and, over low heat, whisk the polenta until it is smooth and hot.

sautéed apples and maple syrup topped with yogurt

serves 4

6 medium-size apples
 (any kind except Delicious),
 peeled, quartered, and cored
1 tablespoon butter
6 tablespoons pure maple syrup
1/2 teaspoon cinnamon
1/8 teaspoon ground cloves
1 cup yogurt (preferably low-fat)
2 tablespoons finely chopped walnuts,
 toasted

1. Cut each apple quarter into 4 slices. Melt the butter in a large skillet over medium heat, add the apples and cook, stirring frequently, for 5 minutes.

2. Add 4 tablespoons of the maple syrup, 1/4 teaspoon of the cinnamon, and the cloves, and toss to coat. Cook for 7 minutes more, or until the apples are tender, not mushy, and the syrup is thickened. Scrape into a medium-size bowl and chill at least 1 hour. (Cover the bowl if you are going to chill it longer.)

3. In a medium-size bowl combine the yogurt, 1 tablespoon of the maple syrup, and the remaining 1/4 teaspoon of cinnamon. Chill at least 1 hour. *May be prepared up to 24 hours in advance to this point, covered, and chilled.*

4. When ready to serve, toss the apples with the remaining tablespoon of maple syrup. Spoon equal portions of the apples into decorative goblets or small serving dishes. Spoon the yogurt over the top of each serving and garnish with the walnuts.

note:
To toast the walnuts put them in a medium-size saucepan over medium heat and gently shake the pan until they are fragrant and lightly toasted, about 5 minutes. Cool thoroughly before serving.

menu five

cucumber and grated carrot salad
in creamy dill dressing
bean tostadas
hot fudge pudding cake

This is a great menu for kids—both to make and to eat. Everything is simple to prepare and tastes delicious. It is bound to please even the most finicky eaters. Try this the next time you have company, and, to add to the festive atmosphere, present an assortment of toppings at the table so everyone can assemble his or her own tostadas.

cucumber and grated carrot salad
in creamy dill dressing

serves 4

2 medium-size cucumbers
2 medium-size carrots
Creamy Dill Dressing (p. 268)

1. Peel the cucumbers and slice them in half lengthwise. Scoop out the seeds with a spoon and discard them. Slice the cucumbers into 1/4-inch-thick slices and divide them equally among serving plates.

2. Peel the carrots and grate them.

3. Drizzle the dill dressing over the cucumbers and top each serving with grated carrot.

bean tostadas

These make a quick meal if you use canned beans, store-bought tortillas, and store-bought salsa; you can also make the tortillas and salsa on a rainy day and have them on hand. In either case try experimenting with toppings such as avocado slices, shredded lettuce, or crumbled fried tofu, just to name a few.

serves 4

>   5 tablespoons oil
>   2 cloves garlic, minced
>   2 medium-size onions, finely diced
>   Two 15-ounce cans
>   (approximately 4 cups cooked)
>   kidney beans or black beans,
>   drained, rinsed, and drained again
>   1 cup water
>   Eight 6-inch wheat (flour) tortillas,
>   homemade (p. 277) or store-bought
>   4 cups grated Monterey jack cheese
>   (1 pound)
>   ½ cup sour cream
>   Salsa Picante (p. 70), or store-bought salsa

1. Heat 2 tablespoons of the oil in a large skillet over medium heat. Add the garlic and onions and sauté until the onions are tender, about 10 minutes.

2. Add the beans and water and simmer for 5 minutes. Mash half of the beans with the back of a spoon and stir to mix. Keep warm over low heat while preparing the tortillas.

3. Turn the oven on "broil." Brush the tortillas on both sides with the 3 remaining tablespoons of oil. Lay them on a cookie sheet (do this in batches) and broil on both sides until lightly golden.

4. Divide the beans equally and spread on each tortilla. Top with equal amounts of grated cheese.

5. Return to the broiler and broil until the cheese is melted and bubbly.

6. Remove from the oven and spread an equal portion of sour cream in the center of each. Serve immediately and let each person spoon on salsa to taste.

hot fudge pudding cake

This is a most unusual "cake" in which part of the batter rises to the top to form the cake layer, and a thick, creamy pudding develops on the bottom to serve as a sauce. Serve it warm, and for an outrageously good combination try it with vanilla ice cream.

serves 6

1¼ cups unbleached white flour
1¾ cups firmly packed light
   brown sugar
½ cup cocoa
2 teaspoons baking powder
¼ teaspoon salt
⅔ cup milk
½ teaspoon almond extract
2 tablespoons melted butter
2 cups hot water

1. Preheat the oven to 350 degrees. Set out an 8-by-8-inch baking pan. (If the pan is glass then use a 325-degree oven.)

2. In a medium-size bowl mix together the flour, ¾ cup of the brown sugar, ¼ cup of the cocoa, the baking powder and salt. Add the milk, almond extract, and melted butter, and mix again until blended. Do not overbeat. Spoon into the baking pan and spread evenly.

3. Combine the remaining ¼ cup of cocoa and 1 cup of brown sugar until well blended. Sprinkle evenly over the top of the batter.

4. Pour on the hot water but do *not* stir.

5. Bake for 35 minutes. Serve warm with some of the sauce spooned on each serving.

menu six

tempeh in curried yogurt sauce
perfect brown rice (p. 266)
indian pudding

The Tempeh in Curried Yogurt Sauce was inspired by the cuisine of India, and the Indian Pudding is related to American Indian cooking, yet their harmonious flavors could easily belie their unrelated origins.

You could finish the meal with a cup of apple cider heated with a cinnamon stick and a few cloves, for a delightful treat.

---

tempeh in curried yogurt sauce

"Woe to the cook whose sauce has no sting." We don't have to fear Chaucer's warning here where tempeh is braised in a spicy, gingery yogurt sauce. Try this served on rice.

serves 4

¼ cup oil
2 medium-size onions, finely diced
5 cloves garlic, minced
4 cups (about 12 ounces)
    quartered mushrooms
2 teaspoons minced gingerroot
1 teaspoon turmeric
1 teaspoon ground cumin
1 teaspoon ground coriander

½ teaspoon ground cardamom
⅛ teaspoon cayenne pepper
8 ounces tempeh, cut into ¾-inch cubes G
1 cup peas (fresh or frozen)
1½ cups chopped canned peeled
    tomatoes with their juice
1 cup yogurt (preferably low-fat)
½ teaspoon salt
Fresh coriander or parsley sprigs for garnish

1. In a large skillet heat the oil over medium heat. Add the onions, garlic, mushrooms, and gingerroot, and cook about 7 minutes, or until the onions are tender.

2. Add the spices, cook 1 minute, then add the tempeh (and fresh peas if you are using them), and cook 3 minutes more, stirring occasionally.

tempeh in curried yogurt sauce (continued)

3. Add the tomatoes, yogurt, frozen peas, and salt. Reduce the heat to a simmer and cook for 5 minutes, stirring often. *May be prepared in advance to this point, chilled, and reheated within 4 hours. If the sauce is too thick after reheating, add a few teaspoons of water.*

4. Serve over brown rice and garnish with fresh coriander or parsley sprigs.

indian pudding

The unique mingling of cornmeal, molasses, and ginger makes this classic American dessert one of my favorites. It's quick to put together, nutritious, and so delicious, and it's best served warm; therefore, time it so that it comes out of the oven about one hour before you plan to serve it.

serves 6

> 4 cups milk
> ¾ cup cornmeal
> 4 tablespoons butter,
>   cut into bits
> 1 egg, lightly beaten
> ½ cup firmly packed light or
>   dark brown sugar
> ½ cup molasses
> ½ teaspoon salt
> 1 teaspoon ground ginger
> 1 teaspoon cinnamon

1. Preheat the oven to 325 degrees. Butter a 1½-quart baking dish.

2. In a medium-size saucepan bring the milk to a boil. Lower the heat and very slowly add the cornmeal, whisking it with a wire whisk all the while. Whisk until the mixture is smooth and has thickened, about 5 minutes. Remove from the heat and add the butter. Let cool for 10 minutes.

3. Beat in all the remaining ingredients until well blended. Pour into the prepared dish. Place this dish in a larger baking dish and fill the outer dish with enough hot water to reach halfway up the sides of the inner dish.

4. Bake for 1 hour and 45 minutes, or until a knife inserted in the center comes out *almost* clean. Let cool on a wire rack and serve warm as is, or with heavy cream poured on each serving, or try it with vanilla ice cream for a superb combination.

note:
To reheat leftover pudding cut it into a few pieces and pour on a little milk to moisten. Place in a preheated 350-degree oven and turn it off. Heat for 15 minutes or so, or until it is warm throughout.

menu seven

mixed green salad
farfalle with broccoli di rapa
chocolate oatmeal bars or fresh fruit (p. 279)

The salad and pasta would be adequate for most appetites; however, if you feel you should add to this menu, you could serve some hot, crusty French or Italian bread with the salad course.

---

mixed green salad

Let your imagination and what's in the market (or garden) determine what will be put into this salad.

Try the less known greens, such as Belgian endive, watercress, arugula, radicchio, and alfalfa sprouts.

serves 4

8 cups mixed salad greens
    (such as red and green leaf lettuces,
    romaine lettuce, spinach, watercress,
    and arugula), rinsed, dried, and torn
    into bite-size pieces
1/2 cup slivered red onion
1 large carrot, grated
A combination of any of the following:
    thinly sliced zucchini
    Belgian endive, separated into leaves
    radicchio, leaves torn in half
    alfalfa sprouts
Vinaigrette (p. 268)
1/4 cup crumbled blue cheese (optional)

1. Put the greens in a large salad bowl and add the onion, carrot, and whatever else you choose.

2. Just before serving pour on half of the vinaigrette dressing and toss well. If more is needed add some more, but be sure not to overdo it or you will have a soggy salad.

3. Sprinkle on the blue cheese if desired. Serve immediately on individual salad plates.

farfalle with broccoli di rapa

Broccoli di rapa, also called broccoli rabe, is a leafy vegetable with small flower clusters resembling broccoli florets. I like to cook it with onions because their natural sweetness balances its slight bitterness. The bow-shaped pasta is worth going out of your way to get; it is delicious, and its bulky shape is a good match for the broccoli di rapa sauce.

serves 4

> 1 large bunch broccoli di rapa
>   (about 1 1/4 pounds untrimmed)
> 4 tablespoons butter
> 1/2 cup olive oil
> 2 large onions, diced
> 3 cloves garlic, minced
> 1 pound farfalle (bow-shaped pasta)
> 1/2 teaspoon salt
> Freshly ground pepper to taste
> 1/2 cup grated Parmesan cheese

1. Bring a large pot of water to a boil.

2. Meanwhile chop the coarse stems off the broccoli di rapa and discard them. (The remaining stems shouldn't be any thicker than the diameter of a pencil.) Clean it very well by dunking it in a pan of cold water several times. Drain thoroughly, then coarsely chop it. You should have about 6 cups.

3. Melt the butter with the olive oil in a large skillet over medium heat, then add the onions and garlic and sauté, tossing regularly, for 10 minutes. Add the broccoli di rapa and cook it, tossing from time to time, until it is tender — this will take about 10 minutes.

4. Meanwhile drop the farfalle into the boiling water and cook al dente — that is, tender yet slightly firm to the bite. Taste to make sure.

5. Season the broccoli di rapa with salt and pepper. When the farfalle is done, drain it thoroughly in a colander. Return it to the pot or a warm serving bowl and spoon on the greens and their sauce. Toss, sprinkle on the cheese, and toss again. Serve immediately.

chocolate oatmeal bars

These bars have a rich brown sugar and oatmeal flavor and are covered with melted chocolate and chopped walnuts. They'd make a wonderful holiday gift wrapped individually in plastic wrap and neatly arranged in a decorative tin.

makes 24 bars

> 1 cup (2 sticks) butter, softened
> 3/4 cup firmly packed light brown sugar
> 1 egg yolk
> 1 teaspoon vanilla extract
> 1 cup rolled oats (non-instant oatmeal)
> 1 cup whole wheat pastry flour
>   (or 1/2 cup whole wheat flour
>   and 1/2 cup unbleached white flour)
> 1 cup finely chopped walnuts (not ground)
> 1 1/2 cups (9 ounces) semisweet
>   chocolate chips

1. Preheat the oven to 350 degrees. Butter and flour a 12-by-2-by-7-inch pan or dish. (If it is glass, then preheat the oven to 325 degrees.)

2. In a large bowl beat together the butter, sugar, egg yolk, and vanilla until smooth and creamy.

3. Add the oats, flour, and half of the walnuts. Beat just until blended; do not overwork the dough. (You may have to do this step by hand.)

4. With a rubber spatula or your fingers spread this mixture into the prepared pan and smooth the top. Bake for 25 minutes, or until it is a rich golden color.

5. Remove the pan from the oven and sprinkle on the chocolate chips. Return to the oven for 3 minutes, or until they are soft. With a spatula spread the chocolate evenly over the surface. Sprinkle on the remaining nuts and press them lightly into the surface.

6. Cool on a wire rack for 30 minutes, then chill for 1 hour, or until the chocolate is firm but not hard. Cut into 24 bars and serve when the chocolate is hard. To store, wrap them in pairs in foil, or store in a tightly covered tin.

menu eight

zucchini, tomato, and basil frittata
bulghur pilaf
stuffed peaches with fresh cherries and almonds,
or marinated oranges in grand marnier sauce (p. 114)

If peaches are in season, then by all means try these simple yet striking Stuffed Peaches for dessert. They are beautiful to look at, are very quick to prepare, and are sweet and juicy. Otherwise the Marinated Oranges in Grand Marnier Sauce would be a nice light ending.

zucchini, tomato, and basil frittata

A frittata is a type of omelet in which the filling and the eggs are cooked together slowly, and then served cut into wedges. As with most egg dishes, in order for a frittata to be tender and delicate you must not overcook it.

serves 4

6 eggs
1/4 cup milk
1/4 cup grated Parmesan cheese
1/2 teaspoon salt
Liberal seasoning freshly ground pepper

3 tablespoons olive oil
2 medium-size onions, diced
4 medium-size tomatoes, peeled,
    seeded, and diced (fresh or canned
    and thoroughly drained)

1 tablespoon minced fresh basil,
    or 1 teaspoon dried basil
1 small zucchini, halved lengthwise and
    thinly sliced

1. Preheat the oven to 325 degrees. Butter a pie plate. (If your plate is glass set the oven at 300 degrees.)

2. In a large bowl beat together the eggs, milk, Parmesan cheese, salt, and pepper.

3. Heat the oil in a large skillet over medium heat. Add the onions and sauté for 5 minutes. Add the drained tomatoes and basil, and sauté for 10 more minutes (no less), tossing frequently.

4. Add the zucchini and cook until tender yet still slightly crisp, about 5 more minutes.

5. Add this mixture to the eggs and stir to blend. Pour into the prepared pie plate and bake for 15–17 minutes, or just until the frittata is set. (Test by inserting a knife.) Don't overcook it because it continues to cook on its way to the table. Cut into wedges and serve immediately.

bulghur pilaf

Tossing and cooking the bulghur with a beaten egg ensures light, fluffy results, and heightens the nutty taste of the bulghur. This pilaf is so tasty that I don't hesitate to serve it with just a steamed vegetable when I want a simple, extra-quick meal.

serves 4

1 cup bulghur G
1 egg, beaten
1 tablespoon butter
1/3 cup fine egg noodles
   (or 1-inch broken spaghetti strands)
1 medium-size carrot, grated

1 medium-size onion, minced
2 cups strong-flavored Vegetable Stock,
   homemade (p. 267) or store-bought*
1/2 teaspoon salt

* If you are making your stock out of a commercial vegetable powder base, use more powder in this case to make the stock stronger.

1. In a medium-size saucepan combine the bulghur and beaten egg. Toss well. Place over medium heat and stir continuously until the bulghur becomes dry and the grains are separate.

2. Make a well in the center and add the butter. When melted, add the noodles, carrot, and onion, and sauté for 2 minutes, stirring constantly to avoid burning.

3. Add the stock and salt, cover, and bring to a boil. Reduce the heat to a simmer and cook for 20 minutes, or until all of the stock is absorbed and the bulghur begins to stick to the pan. Do *not* stir or the bulghur will become mushy.

4. When all of the liquid is absorbed, remove the pan from the heat and gently fluff the bulghur with a fork. Cover the pan again and let sit for 5 minutes. Serve immediately.

note:
To reheat add 1 tablespoon water and heat over low heat. Fluff with a fork occasionally. Or turn into a

bulghur pilaf (continued)

buttered baking dish with 1 tablespoon water and reheat in a 350-degree oven for about 20 minutes, or until hot. Toss after 10 minutes.

bulghur almond pilaf:

Substitute 1/3 cup slivered almonds for the noodles and cook in the same manner.

---

stuffed peaches
with fresh cherries and almonds

This is an exquisite-looking dish that is easy to prepare. The dark red color of the cherries contrasts beautifully with the golden peaches. When served they sit on a bed of almond-flavored whipped cream.

serves 4

> 5 ounces fresh dark cherries (Bing),
>   about 1 cup whole cherries
> 1/3 cup finely chopped almonds
>   (not ground)
> 2 teaspoons sugar
> 4 large ripe peaches (preferably freestone)
> Juice of 1/2 lemon
> 2/3 cup chilled heavy or whipping cream
> 1 1/2 tablespoons powdered
>   (confectioners') sugar
> 1/2 teaspoon almond extract

1. Slice each cherry in half and remove the pit. Slice each half in half again, and mix in a small bowl with the almonds and sugar.

2. Peel the peaches and carefully cut them in half vertically. Remove the stones and discard. If necessary scoop out a little of the center of each peach half to make it large enough to hold some filling.

3. Put the lemon juice in a small dish and one at a time toss each peach half in it. Use your hands to coat the peaches evenly with the lemon juice. (This will prevent discoloration.)

4. Fill each peach half with an equal portion of the cherry filling and press it in gently but firmly. Arrange the stuffed peaches in a shallow dish. *May be prepared in advance to this point, covered, and chilled for up to 24 hours. Remove 20 minutes before serving to take off chill.*

5. Cream will whip better if you chill the beaters and bowl beforehand. Beat the cream in a medium-size bowl for a few minutes. When it begins to thicken add the powdered sugar and almond extract. Continue to beat until it has a nice whipped-cream consistency. (You can prepare the cream and chill it a few hours beforehand, but don't assemble the dish until you are ready to serve it.)

6. To serve, spread equal portions of whipped cream on 4 serving dishes. Place 2 stuffed peach halves on each bed of cream. Voilà!

menu nine

stuffed red pepper strips with
ricotta basil spread (p. 13)
pasta with swiss chard and garlic
bananas in ginger syrup

Red Swiss chard, also known as rhubarb chard, has become more and more visible in the markets lately, and although it has an almost identical flavor to green Swiss chard, I don't think it looks attractive in this pasta dish. You could substitute spinach for the Swiss chard with good results, if you like.

If you have all the ingredients on hand, this is an easy menu to put together at a moment's notice.

stuffed red pepper strips with ricotta basil spread

I love the vivid, contrasting colors of red, white, and green in this appetizer. It is very simple to prepare yet looks stunning. If red peppers at the market aren't firm and glossy, substitute green or yellow bell peppers.

serves 4

    1 recipe Ricotta Basil Spread (p. 13)
    2 large red bell peppers

1. Prepare the Ricotta Basil Spread and reserve 2 teaspoons of minced parsley for garnish.

2. Core the peppers and slice each into 6 vertical strips. Spread the inside of each strip with an equal portion of the spread, then garnish each strip with some minced parsley. Arrange the strips on a serving plate in a circular pattern to resemble a flower. Serve at room temperature for maximum flavor.

pasta with swiss chard and garlic

Swiss chard, which is an excellent source of vitamin A, is also listed on vegetable charts as being abundant in iron and calcium. Unfortunately this is of no avail to us because oxalic acid is also present, which inhibits the body's absorption of calcium and iron. Nonetheless, it is delicious and has a mild beet flavor (it is a member of the beet family). Both the leaves and the ribs are used, and, if you are a gardener, you'll find that it is one of the easiest vegetables to grow.

serves 4

> 1 pound pasta (such as vermicelli,
>   linguine, or spaghetti)
> 1–1 1/2 pounds Swiss chard
>   (about 8–10 cups chopped)
> 1/2 cup olive oil
> 2 tablespoons butter
> 8 cloves garlic,
>   finely chopped
> 1/4 teaspoon dried red pepper flakes
> 1/2 teaspoon salt
> Freshly grated Parmesan cheese

1. Bring a large (6-quart) pot of water to a boil, add the pasta, and cook until al dente — that is, tender yet slightly firm to the bite.

2. Meanwhile rinse the Swiss chard under cold running water until it is very clean, then pat very dry with cotton or paper towels. If the ribs are more than 1/2 inch wide, string them by making a shallow slit in the bottom of each rib and pulling the strings until they are released. Chop the ribs into 1-inch pieces and keep them in a separate pile from the leaves. Chop the leaves into 1-inch pieces.

3. Heat the oil and butter in a large skillet over medium heat, then add the garlic and red pepper flakes, and cook for 2 minutes, stirring often.

4. Raise the heat to medium high, add the chopped Swiss chard ribs, and cook for 2 minutes, continuing to stir often. Add the leaves and cook for 3–5 minutes more, or until the leaves are wilted and tender. Do not overcook; they should retain their bright green color. Add the salt and stir to blend.

5. When the pasta is done drain it thoroughly, then return it to the pot or a warm serving bowl and toss on the chard and its sauce. Serve immediately. Pass a bowl of grated Parmesan cheese at the table and use liberally.

bananas in ginger syrup

Ginger is a flavor I cannot get enough of; its potent spiciness renders it almost hypnotic. In both its fresh and dried (ground) form it enhances all types of dishes—in this case sweet, warm bananas with vanilla ice cream. Simplicity at its best.

serves 4

> 2 tablespoons butter
> 1 teaspoon ground ginger
> 3 tablespoons honey
> 4 medium-size ripe but slightly
>   firm bananas
> 1 tablespoon lemon juice
> 1 1/2–2 pints rich vanilla ice cream

1. In a large skillet over medium heat melt the butter. Add the ginger and honey and stir with a spatula to blend. Cook 30 seconds, or just until the syrup bubbles.

2. Peel the bananas and slice each one into 1/2-inch-thick slices, letting the slices fall carefully into the skillet. Toss the bananas in the syrup to coat.

3. Sprinkle on the lemon juice, toss again, and let cook for 30 seconds, or just until heated through. Remove from the heat and let sit for 5 minutes to cool off a bit. Serve over scoops of vanilla ice cream.

---

menu ten

crustless broccoli and cottage cheese pie
lemon-glazed broccoli stalks julienne
kasha pilaf (p. 88)
baked apples with honey and brandy

Serving broccoli in both the main dish and as a side vegetable isn't as repetitive as it seems. The broccoli stalks have a distinct texture and peppery flavor, which makes them pleasantly different from their florets. If you don't have any kasha on hand, you could instead serve Perfect Brown Rice (p. 266) with a little butter and Parmesan cheese on each serving.

crustless broccoli and cottage cheese pie

I love pies or tarts for a main course; they are so substantial and inviting. But they do take time to prepare, so I make this quick version with a bread crumb "crust" when I am in a hurry. Try substituting kale, spinach, or cauliflower with some minced parsley for color if broccoli is not a prime choice at the market.

serves 4

> 3 tablespoons grated Parmesan cheese
> 1/4 cup bread crumbs
>   (preferably whole wheat, p. 278)
> 1 1/2 cups cottage cheese
> 1/4 cup milk
> 1 cup cubed Monterey jack or
>   Muenster cheese
> 3 eggs, well beaten
> 2 cups chopped cooked broccoli florets*
> 1/4 teaspoon basil
> Dash cayenne pepper
> 1/4 teaspoon salt
> Freshly ground pepper to taste
> 1 tablespoon butter, cut into bits

*Use the raw broccoli stalks in Lemon-Glazed Broccoli Stalks Julienne (next recipe).

1. Preheat the oven to 350 degrees. Generously butter a 9-inch pie plate or quiche pan. Mix the Parmesan cheese and bread crumbs together and pat onto the bottom and sides of the dish—this will form the crust.

2. Mix the cottage cheese, milk, Monterey jack or Muenster cheese, and eggs together well, then stir in the remaining ingredients (except the butter). *May be prepared up to 8 hours in advance to this point. Cover and chill the crust and filling separately.* Pour into the pie crust and smooth over the top then dot with the butter.

3. Bake for 40 minutes, or until a knife inserted in the center comes out almost dry. Serve immediately.

lemon-glazed broccoli stalks julienne

Here is a wonderful way to use broccoli stalks, which you may have around if you have used only the florets. I like to peel them because they cook more evenly and become very tender. Of course, there is some vitamin loss from removing the skin, but much of that is redeemed by using the entire stalk, part of which would be otherwise inedible.

serves 4

2 large broccoli stalks (or the stalks from
   1 large bunch broccoli)
1½ tablespoons butter
1 tablespoon lemon juice
¼ teaspoon sugar

1. Peel the skin off the broccoli stalks by making a slit in one end and pulling the skin downward. Cut the stalks in half, then slice them lengthwise into ¼-inch-thick slices. Cut each slice into matchsticks (julienne).

2. Melt the butter in a large skillet over medium heat. Add the broccoli stalks and cook, tossing frequently, for 3–5 minutes, or until tender yet still crisp.

3. Add the lemon juice, toss, then sprinkle on the sugar. Toss again and cook for 15 seconds. Serve immediately.

baked apples with honey and brandy

serves 4

4 large tart apples
   (such as Cortland or McIntosh)
½ cup honey
¼ cup brandy
2 tablespoons water
½ teaspoon cinnamon
Pinch nutmeg
Pinch allspice
⅓ cup chopped walnuts
1 tablespoon butter

Lightly sweetened whipped cream
   (optional)

1. Preheat the oven to 425 degrees. Butter a baking dish just large enough to fit the apples comfortably— an 8-by-8-inch pan works well.

2. Peel one-third of the top of each apple and keep the remaining skin intact. Core the apples.

3. Put the honey, brandy, water, cinnamon, nutmeg, allspice, and walnuts in a small saucepan, and heat just until the liquids have blended, about 1 minute. Remove from the heat, then one by one roll the apples in the mixture to coat well. Place them in the baking dish and pour the remaining liquid over them. Cut the butter into bits and place on top of the apples.

4. Bake, basting occasionally, for 30 minutes, or until an apple is tender when gently pierced with a sharp knife or cake tester. Do not overcook, or the apples will burst. Serve warm or at room temperature with the remaining syrup poured over them. They are especially good served with a spoonful of lightly sweetened whipped cream.

menu eleven

braised curried eggplant
fruited rice curry
(plain yogurt)
(vanilla ice cream topped with
maple syrup and walnuts)

The simple and delicious ice cream dessert recommended here is a nice finale to this spicy Indian meal. Pure maple syrup is a luscious topping on ice cream, and is a natural match with walnuts.

braised curried eggplant

When we were in college my sister Jacqueline and I would oftentimes spend days delving into cookbooks to plan some exotic feast, which we would then cook that weekend for friends. Our favorite cuisine was Indian, and the surprises it offered were seemingly endless. She created this dish on the spur of the moment one day, and it has proven to be an enduring favorite.

serves 4

2 tablespoons Ghee (p. 272) or butter
1 onion, diced
2 cloves garlic, minced
1 teaspoon turmeric
2 teaspoons ground coriander
½ teaspoon cumin seed
¼ teaspoon cayenne pepper
   (or more to taste)

1 medium-large eggplant (1½ pounds),
   peeled and cubed (1-inch cubes)
3 cups (from 28-ounce can)
   finely chopped canned tomatoes
   with their juice
½ teaspoon salt
1 cup frozen peas
1 tablespoon lemon juice

1. Heat the ghee or butter in a medium-size saucepan over medium heat. Add the onion and garlic and sauté for 10 minutes, or until very tender.

2. Add the turmeric, coriander, cumin seed, and cayenne, and cook for 2 minutes.

3. Add the eggplant, toss well, and cook for 2 minutes. Add the tomatoes and salt and toss again. Cover the pan and simmer for 25 minutes, or until the eggplant is very tender and some of it is mushy. Remove the cover the last 5 minutes of cooking. The mixture should be somewhat soupy though not watery. If it is slightly watery then raise the heat and cook uncovered until thickened. *May be prepared to this point up to 24 hours in advance and chilled.*

4. Add the peas and lemon juice and cook 2 minutes more, or until the peas are heated through. They should still retain their bright green color.

---

fruited rice curry

serves 4

3 tablespoons oil
1 medium-large banana,
    sliced 1/2 inch thick
2 teaspoons minced gingerroot
1/2 teaspoon turmeric
1 teaspoon ground cumin
1 teaspoon ground coriander
1/8 teaspoon cayenne pepper
1 medium-size apple, peeled, cored,
    and diced (1/2-inch dice)
8 dried apricots, cut with scissors into
    1/4-inch dice (1/3 cup diced)
2 tablespoons raisins
Grated rind of 1 orange
1/3 cup coarsely chopped pecans
    or dry-roasted cashews
2 1/2–3 cups *cold* cooked brown rice
    (p. 266), made from 1 cup dry rice
1 tablespoon butter, cut into bits
1/2 teaspoon salt

1. In a large skillet heat 1 tablespoon of the oil over medium heat. Sauté the banana for 1 minute, or just until lightly golden. Do not allow it to get mushy. Remove and set aside.

2. Heat the remaining 2 tablespoons of oil. Add the gingerroot and spices and cook for 1 minute. Add the fruit, orange rind, and nuts, and sauté for 5 minutes, stirring often.

3. Add the cold rice, toss well, and cook, stirring frequently, until hot, about 7 minutes. Dot with the butter and add the salt. Add the reserved banana just before serving.

note:
You can prepare this up to 24 hours in advance and reheat in a skillet on the stove, or reheat in a covered baking dish in a 350-degree oven. Add the banana just before serving.

menu twelve

spicy cucumber salad
stir-fried tempeh with hot pepper sauce
perfect brown rice (p. 266)
chocolate oatmeal bars (p. 23)

Because the salad and main dish in this menu are low in fat, I can savor the Chocolate Oatmeal Bars for dessert with a minimum amount of guilt. Each recipe is quick and simple to execute, and it would be a good menu to prepare on a moment's notice.

---

spicy cucumber salad

This is a very simple salad with a delicious, piquant sauce. You could improvise by substituting for one of the cucumbers a red bell pepper or some crisp snow peas, if you'd like.

serves 4

dressing:
1 tablespoon tamari soy sauce
1 tablespoon Chinese rice vinegar
   (or white vinegar)
1 tablespoon peanut oil
1 teaspoon sugar
2 teaspoons Oriental sesame oil G
Dash Tabasco

3 medium-size cucumbers

1. Mix the dressing ingredients together in a medium-size bowl.

2. Peel the cucumbers. Cut in half lengthwise and scoop out the seeds with a spoon. Discard the seeds. Slice the cucumbers 1/2 inch thick.

3. Add to the dressing and toss very well. Serve immediately, or chill and let marinate for up to 2 hours. Don't marinate any longer or the cucumbers will get soggy.

stir-fried tempeh
with hot pepper sauce

Many people are surprised to learn that chili peppers do not harm the lining of the stomach—in fact, they aid digestion. Studies were made on various winners of chili-pepper-eating contests in Mexico and no adverse effects were discovered—and the winners had eaten thousands of them! It is true that one must build up a tolerance for hot foods; then somewhere along the line that tolerance turns into a craving, and that once-unbearable fiery sensation becomes a delight. Neophytes claim that the flavor of food is overpowered when it is too hot, but a veteran lover of spiciness can appreciate flavor and fieriness simultaneously. This tempeh dish, like other hot dishes in this book, will not scald your palate. It is moderately hot, but you can adjust the spiciness to your liking by cutting down or adding to the amount of red pepper flakes. De gustibus.

serves 4

    3 tablespoons Chinese rice wine
       (or dry sherry)
    1/4 cup tamari soy sauce
    1/2 teaspoon salt
    1/4 cup ketchup
    1 bunch broccoli
    3 tablespoons peanut oil
    1 tablespoon minced gingerroot
    2 cloves garlic, minced
    1/2 teaspoon red pepper flakes
    4 cups (12 ounces) sliced mushrooms
    8 ounces tempeh,G
       cut into 1-inch cubes

1. Mix together the rice wine, soy sauce, salt, and ketchup in a cup or small bowl. Set out all of the remaining ingredients before you to ensure relaxed cooking.

2. Cut off the broccoli florets just beneath the flower. Peel the stalks and cut into 1-inch logs. Put the florets and stalks in a wok or large skillet with 1/2 cup of water and steam, covered, just until they turn bright green, about 1 minute. Remove from the pan and set aside on a plate. Pour out any remaining water in the pan and wipe it dry.

3. In the same pan heat the peanut oil over high heat until hot but not smoking. Add the gingerroot, garlic, and red pepper flakes, and cook, stirring constantly, for 1 minute. Add the mushrooms and stir-fry for 3 minutes. Add the tempeh and stir-fry for 2 minutes. Add the broccoli and stir-fry for 2 more minutes.

4. Give the soy sauce mixture another stir, then pour over the tempeh and vegetables. Toss to coat, and serve immediately over rice.

note:
You can begin cooking this dish 10 minutes before the rice is done, or you can cook the rice in advance and keep hot in the oven (325 degrees).

menu thirteen

salad with sesame ginger dressing
buckwheat noodles/soba and tofu
chocolate chocolate-chip cookies

Don't hesitate to freeze some of these Chocolate Chocolate-Chip Cookies, so you can have them on another occasion without any fuss. They retain their delicious flavor and crisp texture, and very few people can resist rich homemade cookies. Freeze them double-wrapped in plastic bags.

salad with sesame ginger dressing

A very simple salad with a distinctive flavor.

serves 3

dressing:
1/2 cup peanut oil
2 teaspoons Oriental sesame oil G
3 tablespoons Chinese rice vinegar
    (or 2 1/2 tablespoons red wine or
    apple cider vinegar)
1 teaspoon minced gingerroot
1/4 teaspoon salt
Freshly ground pepper to taste

3/4 pound romaine lettuce (1 small head)

1. Put all the ingredients for the dressing into a medium-size jar with a cover. Shake vigorously. Chill for at least 30 minutes. Shake again before serving.

2. Wash the lettuce and spin it dry or pat very dry with paper towels. Tear into bite-size pieces and put in a large bowl. Pour on two-thirds of the dressing and toss well. Taste to see if more is needed. (If there is any leftover dressing, then chill it for future use.) Serve immediately.

buckwheat noodles/soba and tofu

Buckwheat and tofu are both very good sources of protein and iron, and both are very low in fat. This noodle dish is prepared Japanese-style—in a broth—like the popular dish ramen.

serves 3

       8 ounces buckwheat noodles/soba G
       1/4 cup oil
       1 pound firm tofu, cut into 1-inch cubes
          and patted very dry
       3 cups thinly sliced mushrooms
          (8 ounces)
       1 1/2 teaspoons minced gingerroot
       2 cups Vegetable Stock, homemade
          (p. 267) or store-bought
       1/4 cup tamari soy sauce
       3 small scallions, thinly sliced

1. Bring a large (6-quart) pot of water to a boil and drop in the buckwheat noodles. Cook until al dente—that is, tender yet slightly firm to the bite—about 10 minutes. Drain well.

2. Meanwhile, heat the oil in a large skillet over high heat until hot but not smoking. Add the tofu and stir-fry until golden, about 10 minutes. Remove from the pan and set aside.

3. Reduce the heat to medium and add the mushrooms. Stir-fry until the mushrooms are brown and tender, about 7 minutes.

4. Return the tofu to the pan and add the ginger. Stir-fry 1 minute. Add the vegetable stock and tamari and boil 2 minutes.

5. Place some noodles in each soup bowl. Spoon equal portions of the tofu mixture and broth over each serving. Garnish with the sliced scallions.

chocolate chocolate-chip cookies

These are my idea of a great chocolate-chip cookie—crisp, buttery, and very chocolaty. You had better hide some of these if you don't want them all eaten in one sitting.

makes 4–5 dozen

12-ounce package (2 cups) semisweet chocolate chips
1 cup (2 sticks) butter, softened
1/2 cup white sugar

1/2 cup firmly packed light brown sugar
1 teaspoon vanilla extract
2 1/4 cups unbleached white flour
1/4 teaspoon baking soda

1. Preheat the oven to 350 degrees. In a double boiler melt 1 cup of the chocolate chips. Set aside to cool slightly.

2. In a large bowl cream the butter with both sugars until smooth and fluffy. (Use an electric beater.) Beat in the melted chocolate and vanilla until well blended.

3. Beat in 1 cup of the flour and the baking soda until blended. Beat in the remaining flour; you might have to do it by hand at this point. Stir in the remaining chocolate chips until well mixed.

4. To get nicely shaped cookies drop by teaspoonfuls onto an ungreased cookie sheet about 2 inches apart from each other, and use the teaspoon to push the edges into a circle.

5. Bake for 15–17 minutes. Do not let burn. Let the cookies sit on the cookie sheet for a minute before removing. Cool on a wire rack. When thoroughly cooled store in a covered tin.

menu fourteen

kasha topped with mushrooms in sour cream sauce
sautéed cabbage with fennel seed
pear and apricot crisp

Here is a light menu that is very nutritious and simple to prepare. I associate fall and winter with these flavors, although everything is available year round.

You can make the Pear and Apricot Crisp in advance, but the kasha and cabbage dishes should be made just before serving.

kasha topped with mushrooms in sour cream sauce

Kasha (buckwheat groats) is an interesting and delicious grain to become acquainted with. It is very quick to prepare, has a tender, fluffy texture, and is high in protein and iron. The mushrooms in this lightly spiced sauce complement the nutty, roasted flavor of the kasha superbly.

kasha topped with mushrooms in sour cream sauce (continued)

serves 4

    1 1/4 cups kasha ^G
      (medium granulation)
    1 egg, lightly beaten
    1 tablespoon butter
    2 1/4 cups hot Vegetable Stock,
      homemade (p. 267) or store-bought
    1/4 teaspoon salt

sauce:
3 tablespoons butter
1 large onion, diced
1 pound sliced mushrooms (6 cups sliced)
1/4 teaspoon thyme
Dash cayenne pepper
Liberal seasoning freshly ground pepper
1 cup sour cream
Minced parsley for garnish

1. Combine the kasha and egg in a medium-size saucepan and stir over medium heat until the kasha is well coated then begins to look dry, about 3 minutes. Make a well in the center of the pan and melt the butter. Toss it with the kasha, then pour in the hot stock and salt. Reduce the heat to a simmer and cook, covered, until the stock is completely absorbed, about 10 minutes.

2. Meanwhile make the sauce. Melt the butter in a large skillet over medium-high heat, then add the onion and sauté for 3 minutes. Add the mushrooms, thyme, cayenne, and freshly ground pepper, and cook, stirring occasionally, for 10 minutes, or until the mushrooms are brown and juicy.

3. Add the sour cream, stir, and cook 2 more minutes, or until hot and bubbly. Spoon some kasha onto each dinner plate and top with the sauce. Garnish with the parsley and serve immediately.

---

sauteed cabbage with fennel seed

serves 4

    1 tablespoon butter
    1 tablespoon oil
    1/2 teaspoon fennel seed

6 cups chopped cabbage
    (about 1 1/4 pounds)

Melt the butter with the oil in a large skillet over medium heat. Add the fennel seed and cook for 1 minute. Add the cabbage and sauté for 5 minutes, tossing frequently. Cover the pan, reduce the heat a little, and cook 10 minutes more, or until tender, stirring occasionally. Serve immediately.

pear and apricot crisp

Here is a nutritious dessert with a distinct fruit flavor. The apricots provide an interesting tartness, and the oatmeal and walnuts give it a deliciously crunchy topping.

serves 4–6

6 ripe but slightly firm pears
  (preferably Bosc)
1/2 cup diced dried apricots
1 tablespoon unbleached white flour
1/3 cup honey

topping:
1/2 cup rolled oats (non-instant oatmeal)
1/4 cup whole wheat pastry flour
  (or 2 tablespoons whole wheat flour
  and 2 tablespoons unbleached
  white flour)
1/2 teaspoon cinnamon
1/4 cup firmly packed light brown sugar
3 tablespoons butter, cut into bits
1/4 cup finely chopped walnuts

Lightly sweetened whipped cream
  (optional)

1. Preheat the oven to 400 degrees. Butter an 8-by-8-inch baking pan or other shallow pan of comparable size.

2. Peel and core the pears, then slice them into bite-size pieces and put them in a medium-size bowl with the apricots. Add the flour and toss to coat, then pour on the honey and toss again until blended. Scrape this mixture into the prepared pan and smooth over the top.

3. In the same bowl combine the oats, flour, cinnamon, and brown sugar, and mix well. Blend in the butter with the tips of your fingers until the mixture resembles coarse meal, then stir in the walnuts. Sprinkle this crumb mixture evenly over the pears.

4. Bake for 30–40 minutes, or until the fruit is tender and the top is golden. Serve warm or at room temperature. It is delicious as is or with lightly sweetened whipped cream.

menu fifteen

stuffed mushrooms with feta and dill
spaghettini with garlic and hot pepper
winter fruit salad with apple cider glaze

This is a light menu, and it is a good one to have in the evening after you have had a heavy lunch. If you want to add to it, then serve some crusty French bread and/or a green salad such as Mixed Green Salad (p. 21). The Winter Fruit Salad with Apple Cider Glaze is most flavorful when prepared with fresh apple cider. If it is not in season, you could serve another fruit dessert, such as Marinated Oranges in Grand Marnier Sauce (p. 114) or a quick cake such as Susanne's Spice Cake (p. 75).

stuffed mushrooms with feta and dill

serves 4

½ cup walnuts, finely chopped
½ cup bread crumbs
   (preferably whole wheat, p. 278)
1 heaping tablespoon finely chopped
   fresh dill
¾ cup finely crumbled feta cheese
2 tablespoons milk
Freshly ground pepper to taste
16 large mushrooms
2½ tablespoons olive oil

1. Preheat the oven to 375 degrees. Mix the walnuts, bread crumbs, dill, feta, milk, and pepper together in a medium-size bowl.

2. Wipe the mushrooms very clean with a damp cloth, then remove the stems and reserve for another use. Divide the mixture evenly and stuff each mushroom cap, pressing in the stuffing firmly.

3. Generously butter a baking dish that will hold all of the mushrooms and place them in it, then drizzle the olive oil over each one. *May be prepared up to 24 hours in advance to this point, covered, and chilled.* Bake for 20 minutes, or until the mushrooms are juicy and the tops are lightly browned. Serve immediately.

spaghettini with garlic and hot pepper

This is a hot and spicy pasta dish that is rather light and is usually served as is, though one may add a light sprinkling of Parmesan cheese if desired. If you prefer a milder version, chop the garlic and chili into large pieces and remove before adding the butter sauce to the pasta, although I highly recommend enjoying this full-strength.

serves 4

1 teaspoon salt
1 pound spaghettini
1 tablespoon butter
1/3 cup olive oil
5 cloves garlic, minced
1 small red chili pepper, minced, G or
    1/3 teaspoon dried red pepper flakes
2 tablespoons minced parsley

G See Glossary of Ingredients about handling chilies.

1. Bring a large pot of water to a boil. Add the salt and cook the spaghettini until al dente — that is, tender yet slightly firm to the bite.

2. Meanwhile, melt the butter with the olive oil in a medium-size skillet; then add the garlic and chili pepper, and cook gently until the garlic is lightly golden, about 3 minutes. Be careful not to burn it.

3. Drain the pasta well, return to the pot or a warm serving bowl, pour on the sauce, and toss well. Add the parsley, toss again, and serve immediately.

winter fruit salad with apple cider glaze

This is a quick and delicious fruit salad with no added sugar; it works well for dessert or breakfast. Try to get good-quality unfiltered apple cider for best results. If your fruit is very attractive, you can leave the skin on, although I prefer the delicate texture of peeled fruit in this case.

serves 4

3 ripe pears (preferably Bosc, Anjou, or Comice), peeled, cored, and diced (1-inch dice)
1 tart apple (such as Cortland or McIntosh), peeled, cored, and diced
1 ripe banana, peeled and sliced 1/2 inch thick
1 large navel orange, peeled, sectioned, and sections cut in half
1 kiwi, peeled and sliced 1/2 inch thick
1 1/2 cups apple cider
1 cinnamon stick
1 1/2 teaspoons whole cloves

1. Combine all of the fruit in a serving bowl.

2. Combine the cider, cinnamon stick, and cloves in a medium-size saucepan and boil rapidly over high heat for about 8 minutes, or until the sauce is reduced to 3/4 cup (measure it to be sure).

3. Strain the sauce over the fruit, and toss to coat. Cover, chill, and let marinate for at least 2 hours. Serve in decorative goblets. For optimal flavor it is best to serve this fruit salad cool, not cold.

informal menus

These are "in-between" menus that require a moderate amount of attention and forethought. They aren't as elaborate as the Elegant Menus, yet could be suitable for casual entertaining, and they aren't as fast as the Quick Menus, yet could oftentimes make a rather easy meal with a little planning. They are just what is needed when you want to prepare a multi-course meal that is distinctive yet not too demanding.

menu one

indonesian salad with spicy peanut dressing
indonesian curried vegetable stew with coconut milk
stuffed bananas with rum cream and cashews

This is a good menu for people who like spicy food and enjoy being introduced to a new cuisine. If you feel that bread should be served with soups and stews, then try serving warm pita bread. I like to have beer with this menu, or sometimes a rum and fruit drink.

The stuffed bananas are delicate and rich — a nice change from the more common uses of bananas in desserts.

indonesian salad with spicy peanut dressing

serves 4–6

2 small cucumbers, peeled and sliced
  1/4 inch thick
2 cups finely shredded cabbage
1 cup fresh bean sprouts (*not* canned)
3 radishes, thinly sliced
3 scallions, sliced into 1-inch lengths

dressing:
2/3 cup crunchy natural peanut butter
3 tablespoons milk
Juice of 1/2 lemon
1/2 teaspoon minced gingerroot
2 cloves garlic, minced
1 teaspoon honey
Dash cayenne pepper
Salt to taste
3–4 tablespoons water

1. Place all of the salad ingredients in a bowl and toss.

2. To make the dressing: In a medium-size bowl beat the peanut butter and milk together with a fork until well blended; it will be very thick.

3. Add all of the remaining ingredients for the dressing and mix well. Use the greater amount of water if the sauce is too thick. Taste to correct seasoning.

4. Divide the salad evenly among the serving plates, reserving some radish slices for garnish. Top each portion with a few spoonfuls of dressing and garnish with a slice of radish. Serve the remaining sauce at the table so more can be added if desired.

indonesian curried vegetable stew
with coconut milk

This is a meatless version of a delicious and exquisite-looking Indonesian stew. It is bright golden yellow with flecks of green and fiery red interlaced. The coconut milk gives this a satiny smoothness, and adds a rich, faintly sweet flavor.

serves 4–6

3 tablespoons oil
2 medium-size onions, finely chopped
1 small fresh red chili,
    seeded and minced,G or
      1/8 teaspoon cayenne pepper
4 cloves garlic, minced
2 teaspoons minced gingerroot
2 teaspoons ground coriander
1 teaspoon ground cumin
1 teaspoon turmeric
1/2 teaspoon ground black pepper
Grated rind of 1 lemon
1 1/2 cups (4 ounces) sliced mushrooms
3 cups Vegetable Stock, homemade (p. 267)
    or store-bought
2 1/2 cups coconut milk G
1 teaspoon salt
2 large potatoes, peeled and diced
1 1/2 cups fine egg noodles
    (or vermicelli broken into
    1-inch lengths)
2 cups small broccoli florets*
Juice of 1 lemon
Lemon wedges (1 per serving)

GSee Glossary of Ingredients about handling chilies and making coconut milk.
*Broccoli stalks can be used in Lemon-Glazed Broccoli Stalks Julienne (p. 30).

1. Set all of the ingredients in front of you before you begin cooking. In a medium-size saucepan heat the oil and add the onions and chili. Sauté for 5 minutes, or until the onions begin to get golden. Add the garlic and gingerroot, stir, then add all of the spices and the lemon rind. Cook for 3 minutes, stirring often.

2. Add the mushrooms and cook for 5 minutes, then add the vegetable stock, coconut milk, and salt.

3. Bring the contents to a boil and add the potatoes. Cook, uncovered, for about 10 minutes, stirring occasionally, or until the potatoes are almost tender.

4. Add the noodles, let the mixture return to a boil, then add the broccoli. Cook for about 5 minutes, stirring frequently, or until the noodles are tender but slightly firm to the bite. The broccoli should retain its bright green color.

5. Add the lemon juice and stir to blend. Serve in bowls with lemon wedges on the side.

note:
If you are preparing this stew in advance, add the broccoli in step 4 but do not cook it. Chill until ready to serve. Reheat over low heat and add a few tablespoons of water if it is too thick. Stir frequently.

stuffed bananas with rum cream and cashews

A relatively simple dish to prepare that is unusual and delicious. Banana sections are stuffed with rum cream and cashews, then topped with a light but richly fragrant rum raisin sauce.

serves 4–6

sauce:
1/4 cup dark rum
1 tablespoon honey
1 tablespoon raisins

2/3 cup cream cheese,
    softened (about 5 ounces)
3 tablespoons honey

2 tablespoons dark rum
1/2 cup finely chopped
    toasted cashews*
3 large ripe bananas
Juice of 1/2 lemon or 1 lime

*Raw cashews can be purchased in a health food store and toasted in a moderate (350-degree) oven for 10–15 minutes, or until lightly browned. Otherwise dry-roasted, unsalted cashews may be used.

1. Place the rum, honey, and raisins in a small saucepan. Bring this mixture to a boil and cook 1 minute. Remove from the heat and let sit at room temperature, or refrigerate, until cooled.

2. In a medium-size bowl beat the cream cheese and honey until blended and creamy. Beat in the rum, then mix in the cashews. Chill this mixture until it gets somewhat firm—for at least 30 minutes.

3. Peel the bananas and slice in half crosswise. Slice each piece in half lengthwise. Make a shallow 1/4-inch indentation, cutting out the seeds. Discard them.

4. Put the lemon or lime juice in a small bowl and dip each banana piece in, rubbing the juice all over the pieces to prevent them from turning brown.

5. Stuff each banana piece with an equal portion of the chilled rum cream. Place in a serving dish and spoon over the rum raisin sauce. Be sure to arrange some raisins on each stuffed banana.

6. Chill for at least 1 hour before serving, or up to 8 hours. Cover the dish with plastic or foil.

menu two

watercress and jerusalem artichoke salad
with sweet mustard dressing
baked mexican-style beans with sour cream and chilies
sautéed greens with garlic
sangría
chocolate-chip fudge brownies

This is a very flavorful, hearty menu, and it would be a good choice for an informal get-together that isn't a sit-down dinner. Everything can successfully be doubled or tripled, although in the case of the brownies I would make them in separate batches so that the batter will conform to the pan size.

If you'd like to serve some fruit along with the brownies, try a platter of orange slices, since orange and chocolate are a delicious combination.

watercress and jerusalem artichoke salad with sweet mustard dressing

serves 4

dressing:
2 tablespoons red wine vinegar
1 tablespoon Dijon-style mustard
1 teaspoon honey
1 teaspoon dried tarragon
1/3 cup olive oil
Salt to taste
Freshly ground pepper to taste

6 medium-size Jerusalem artichokes
1 bunch watercress
1 head Boston lettuce

1. To make the dressing: In a small bowl beat the vinegar, mustard, honey, and tarragon with a wire whisk until well blended. Gradually beat in the oil, then add the salt and pepper to taste.

watercress and jerusalem artichoke salad (continued)

2. Peel the Jerusalem artichokes with a vegetable peeler or a paring knife and slice thin. Add to the dressing to prevent discoloration. Toss well.

3. Wash the watercress and spin or pat dry with a towel. Remove the stems and discard (or freeze for use in Unyeasted Gruel Bread, p. 257). Place in a large salad bowl.

4. Wash the Boston lettuce very well by rinsing the leaves individually (they are usually very sandy). Spin or pat each leaf very dry, then tear into bite-size pieces and add to the watercress.

5. Just before serving pour on the dressing and artichokes and toss well. Serve immediately.

baked mexican-style beans with sour cream and chilies

serves 4

3 cups dried pinto beans (1 pound)
   or kidney beans
2 tablespoons olive oil
2 medium-size onions, diced
2 cloves garlic, minced
28-ounce can imported plum tomatoes,
   roughly chopped and well drained
1 tablespoon tomato paste

4-ounce can mild green chilies,
   drained and diced
1/4 teaspoon oregano
1/2 teaspoon salt
Freshly ground pepper to taste
1 cup sour cream
2 cups grated (8 ounces)
   Monterey jack cheese

1. Rinse the beans in a strainer or colander under cold running water and pick out any stones, etc. Soak them overnight in water to cover, or boil them for 2 minutes in a covered pot and let them sit, covered, for 1 hour. Drain very well.

2. In a large pot cover the beans with about 2 inches of water, and cook until they are tender, about 1 hour. Drain very well.

3. In a large skillet heat the oil over medium heat. Add the onions and garlic and sauté for 5 minutes. Add the drained tomatoes, tomato paste, chilies, oregano, salt, and pepper, and raise the heat to high. Cook, stirring frequently, just until the juice from the tomatoes has evaporated, about 5 minutes.

4. Add the beans to the skillet and toss. Remove the pan from the heat. *May be prepared to this point up*

to 8 hours in advance, refrigerated, and assembled just before cooking.

5. Preheat the oven to 375 degrees. Put half of the bean mixture in a large casserole, cover with half of the sour cream and half of the cheese, add the remaining bean mixture, and top with the remaining sour cream and cheese.

6. Bake for 20–25 minutes, or until hot and bubbly.

sautéed greens with garlic

serves 4

1 1/2 pounds (weight with stems) greens
(either spinach, kale, collards,
mustard greens, or escarole)
1 1/2 tablespoons butter
1 tablespoon olive oil
4 cloves garlic, minced
Freshly ground pepper to taste

1. Cut the stems off the greens and discard. Wash the greens very well by dunking them in a large pot of cold water several times. Pour out the water and repeat until the water is free of sand.

2. Coarsely chop the greens, then put them in a large skillet with just the water that clings to them. (For kale and collards add a few more tablespoons water.) Cover the pan and cook over medium heat until they wilt, about 5–7 minutes. They should retain their bright green color. (The kale or collards may take a little longer; taste to make sure they are tender.) Do not overcook.

3. Drain in a colander and press out all of the liquid with the back of a large spoon.

4. In the same skillet over medium heat melt the butter with the olive oil. Add the garlic and cook 2–3 minutes, or until it begins to turn golden. Be careful not to burn it.

5. Add the drained greens and mix well. Sauté for 5 minutes, or until hot and fragrant. Season with freshly ground pepper. Serve immediately, or you can reheat later if necessary.

sangría

serves about 6

    1 bottle (.75 liter) chilled dry red wine
    1/3 cup Triple Sec or Cointreau
    1 lime, thinly sliced
    1 orange, halved vertically
       and thinly sliced
    1 lemon, thinly sliced
    1 cup chilled seltzer

1. In a large pitcher or decorative punch bowl combine the wine, Triple Sec or Cointreau, and the sliced fruit. Chill for at least 1 hour.

2. Just before serving add the seltzer and some ice. Serve with some of the fruit slices in each glass.

---

chocolate-chip fudge brownies

The size of the pan will determine the texture of brownies. The smaller the pan the cakier the results. I prefer chewier brownies so I use a 9-by-13-inch pan. For best results make these the day before, and, by all means, *don't overcook them.*

makes 24 brownies

    4 ounces unsweetened chocolate
    3/4 cup (1 1/2 sticks) butter
    4 eggs
    2 cups sugar
    1 teaspoon vanilla extract
    1 cup unbleached white flour
    1 cup (6 ounces) semisweet
       chocolate chips

1. Preheat the oven to 350 degrees. (If you are using a glass pan, then turn to 325 degrees.) Butter and flour a 9-by-13-inch pan and set aside.

2. In a medium-size saucepan melt the unsweetened chocolate with the butter over medium heat. Set aside to cool until it is barely warm.

3. In a large bowl beat the eggs, sugar, and vanilla until light-colored and well blended. *By hand* stir in the chocolate mixture and blend. Add the flour and mix by hand until blended. Do not overbeat. (This must be done by hand or a funny crust will develop.)

4. Pour into the prepared pan. Sprinkle the chocolate chips evenly on the top, and carefully run a knife through the batter to immerse some of the chips.

5. Bake for 35 minutes, or until a knife inserted in the center comes out clean. Do not overcook. Cool on a rack completely (at least 3 hours) before cutting.

Store in a covered tin or individually wrapped in foil or plastic wrap. To freeze, place individually wrapped brownies in a plastic bag and freeze up to 1 month.

menu three

fresh pea salad rémoulade
stir-fried asparagus, tofu, and red pepper
perfect brown rice (p. 266)
rhubarb tart

When spring is well on its way and fresh peas, asparagus, and rhubarb are available, this menu is a good choice so that one can enjoy these delicacies while they are at their best. If fresh peas aren't available, try Salad with Sesame Ginger Dressing (p. 36) or Avocado and Bathed Bread Vinaigrette (p. 10) for a first course.

fresh pea salad rémoulade

I love to eat fresh peas raw; they are so sweet and delicate, and have a delightful crunchiness. The pungency of this dressing provides a nice contrast, making this salad very special.

serves 4

1/3 cup mayonnaise, homemade (p. 269)
   or store-bought
1 teaspoon Dijon-style mustard
2 tablespoons minced red onion
1 teaspoon capers
1/2 teaspoon fresh tarragon, or
   1/4 teaspoon dried tarragon, crumbled
1 tablespoon minced fresh parsley
Freshly ground pepper to taste
1 cup freshly shelled raw peas
   (1 pound whole peas)
1/2 head green or red leaf lettuce
1 1/2 tablespoons lemon juice
1/3 cup olive oil
Salt to taste

1. In a medium-size bowl combine the mayonnaise and mustard and beat until smooth. Add the onion, capers, tarragon, parsley, and freshly ground pepper. Stir to mix.

2. Add the peas, stir, and set aside.

3. Thoroughly wash the lettuce to rid it of any sand. Spin or pat very dry with paper towels or a kitchen towel. Tear the leaves into small pieces and place in a large bowl.

4. In a small bowl combine the lemon juice, olive oil, and salt and pepper to taste. Mix well. Pour onto the lettuce leaves and toss until well coated.

5. Place equal portions of the lettuce on 4 small serving plates. Top each portion with a mound of the pea mixture. Garnish with minced parsley. Serve immediately.

stir-fried asparagus, tofu, and red pepper

A quick, attractive dish that is a great way to celebrate spring's first asparagus (or you could substitute broccoli, if you like). To serve with rice, prepare 1 1/2 cups (raw) Perfect Brown Rice (p. 266) before you begin, and keep it warm while you are preparing this.

serves 4

1/4 cup peanut oil
1 pound firm tofu, cut into 1-inch cubes
    and patted very dry
2 teaspoons minced gingerroot
1 pound asparagus (preferably thin)
1 tablespoon water
1 large red bell pepper, cored and cut
    into 1-inch squares
8 ounces sliced water chestnuts, rinsed
    and well drained

sauce:
1/4 cup tamari soy sauce
1/4 cup Chinese rice wine or dry sherry
2 teaspoons cornstarch
1 teaspoon Oriental sesame oil G
A few drops hot spicy oil G (or Tabasco)

1. Have all of the ingredients prepared and laid out in front of you. Cut off only the very tough bottoms of the asparagus, and with a sharp paring knife peel the bottom half of each one. Cut the asparagus on the diagonal into 2-inch lengths. In a small bowl or cup combine the soy sauce, rice wine, and cornstarch, and set aside.

2. Heat a wok or large skillet over high heat until hot. Add the peanut oil, and when it is hot but not smoking add the tofu. Stir-fry until golden all over, about 5–8 minutes. Remove from the pan to a platter and set aside.

3. Reduce the heat to medium high and add the gingerroot. Cook for 15 seconds. Add the asparagus and toss, then add 1 tablespoon of water. Cover the pan and cook for 2 minutes, or until the asparagus is almost tender (this will depend on the thickness of the stalks).

4. Remove the cover and add the red pepper and water chestnuts. Stir-fry uncovered for 3 minutes.

5. Return the tofu to the pan and toss.

6. Quickly stir the soy sauce mixture and add. Toss and cook 1 minute.

7. Turn off the heat and sprinkle on the sesame oil and hot spicy oil. Serve immediately over rice.

rhubarb tart

for a 10½-inch tart dish

1 recipe Pâte Sucrée (p. 276)
5 cups rhubarb in ½-inch dice
  (1¼–1½ pounds)
½ cup unsweetened applesauce
  (preferably homemade or Mott's)
⅓ cup unbleached white flour
1 cup honey
½ teaspoon ground cardamom
Sweetened whipped cream (optional)

1. Make the pâte sucrée following the directions only through step 5; do not prebake. (You will not need the extra egg white.) Chill for at least 20 minutes or up to 2 days. Cover well with foil or plastic wrap if you are going to chill for longer than 20 minutes.

2. To make the filling: Combine all of the remaining ingredients in a large bowl, and toss to blend well.

3. Preheat the oven to 400 degrees. Pour the filling into the prepared crust and bake for 5 minutes. Reduce the heat to 375 degrees and bake an additional 35–40 minutes, or until the crust is golden. Cool to room temperature before serving. Serve plain or with whipped cream.

menu four

tamale pie
apple crisp

Tamale Pie is a wonderfully nutritious dish that is easy to make and very substantial. The beans, cheese, and cornmeal provide a good amount of protein, and cooked with the peppers, corn, and tomatoes it makes a well-balanced meal in one dish. You might want to serve a salad beforehand; in that case try Arugula and Boston Lettuce Salad (p. 84), Mixed Green Salad (p. 21), or Spinach Salad with Creamy Dill Dressing (p. 62).

If you've made the Apple Crisp in advance, you can warm it up once the Tamale Pie has been removed and the oven turned off. It won't take long for it to heat through, so the oven need not be kept on.

tamale pie

There's something heartwarming about serving a pie for dinner. Tamale Pie is a delicious low-fat, high- protein pie that is made with a cornmeal crust. It is especially quick to make if you use canned beans.

serves 4–6

3 tablespoons oil
2 medium-size onions, diced
1 large green pepper, diced (1/2-inch dice)
1 teaspoon chili powder
1/2 teaspoon ground cumin
16-ounce can imported plum tomatoes,
    chopped and well drained (1 cup pulp)
16-ounce can (2 cups) kidney beans,
    drained, rinsed, and drained again
1 cup corn, fresh or frozen

1/2 teaspoon salt
Liberal seasoning freshly ground pepper

crust:
2 1/2 cups cold water
1 1/2 cups cornmeal
1/2 teaspoon chili powder
1/2 teaspoon salt
1 cup (4 ounces) grated Monterey jack cheese
1 tablespoon butter, cut into bits

1. In a large skillet heat the oil over medium heat. Add the onions and green pepper, and cook until tender yet still crunchy, about 10 minutes.

2. Add the chili powder, cumin, tomatoes, and beans, and toss well. Cook for 5 minutes, or until the mixture is heated through and begins to get dry.

3. Add the corn, salt, and pepper and cook 1 minute more. Remove from the heat. *May be prepared to this point and chilled up to 24 hours in advance. Bring to room temperature before proceeding with the next step.*

4. To make the crust: Butter a pie plate. Preheat the oven to 350 degrees. Place the water, cornmeal, chili powder, and salt in a medium-size heavy-bottomed saucepan. Bring to a boil over medium heat and whisk frequently with a wire whisk until smooth and thick. (As it begins to thicken whisk constantly.) When the mixture begins to tear away from the sides of the pan it is ready, about 5 minutes.

5. Immediately spread two-thirds of the cornmeal on the bottom and sides of the pie plate. Smooth over with a rubber spatula. Top with the bean mixture and smooth over the top. Evenly sprinkle on the cheese. Top with the remaining cornmeal by dropping on small spoonfuls, and use your fingers to spread it out. Top with the butter.

6. Bake for 45 minutes, or until lightly golden. Serve immediately.

note:
If you want to cook the beans from scratch, soak 1 cup of dried kidney beans overnight, or boil them for 2 minutes in a large pot of water and let sit covered for 1 hour. Drain and add fresh water to cover plus 2 inches. Boil until tender, about 1–1 1/2 hours. Drain again.

apple crisp

This classic American dessert is a favorite of mine, but it must be well spiced and have a rich, crunchy topping, as it does here. I have found that almost any variety of apple will do (except Red Delicious — they're too mealy); if the apple is crisp and fresh and delicious as an eating apple, then it will be good for baking.

serves 6

> 8 medium-size apples, peeled,
>   cored, and thinly sliced
> 1/4 cup water
> 2 tablespoons firmly packed
>   light brown sugar
> 1/2 teaspoon cinnamon
>
> topping:
> 1/2 cup whole wheat pastry flour,
>   or 1/4 cup unbleached white flour
>   and 1/4 cup whole wheat flour
> 1/2 cup firmly packed light brown sugar
> 1 teaspoon cinnamon
> 1/4 teaspoon salt
> 6 tablespoons butter

1. Preheat the oven to 350 degrees. Arrange the apple slices in an 8-by-8-inch baking pan or other shallow ovenproof dish of comparable size. Pour the water over them, then sprinkle on the brown sugar and cinnamon and toss gently.

2. To make the topping: Combine the flour, sugar, cinnamon, and salt in a small mixing bowl, and mix well.

3. Cut the butter into the mixture with a pastry cutter or your fingertips until it resembles coarse meal. Sprinkle evenly over the apples.

4. Bake for 30–40 minutes, or until the apples are tender and the topping is lightly browned. The topping will get crisp as it cools. Cool on a wire rack and serve warm or at room temperature. It is perfectly delicious served plain, and also exceptionally good topped with whipped cream or vanilla ice cream.

menu five

simple salad with lemon soy dressing
szechuan braised bean curd and vegetables
perfect brown rice (p. 266)
(fresh pineapple)

Sweet, succulent pineapple makes a great dessert for a hot, spicy meal. To test a pineapple's ripeness you should first smell it—it should have a noticeable sweet aroma, the eyes on the bottom third of it should have turned yellow, and you should be able to easily pull out one of the leaves in the middle of its crown. The larger the pineapple the greater the proportion of flesh, so select the biggest one available.

simple salad with lemon soy dressing

This is a light and simple salad with an aromatic, piquant dressing, tossed at the last minute with a sprinkling of Parmesan cheese and garnished with red onion rings.

serves 4

1 small head romaine lettuce,
    or 1/2 large head
Lemon Soy Dressing (next recipe)

1/4 cup grated Parmesan cheese
1 small red onion, sliced

1. Rinse the leaves of the romaine lettuce under cold water and spin dry or pat dry with a towel. Tear them into small pieces and place in a large bowl.

2. Stir the dressing until well mixed and pour on the salad. Toss until well coated. Add the Parmesan cheese and gently toss again.

3. Separate the rings of the red onion slices and garnish the salad with these rings. Serve immediately.

lemon soy dressing

A light and flavorful salad dressing that is a welcome change from the usual vinegar-based dressings.

makes 2/3 cup

2 cloves garlic, minced
2 tablespoons lemon juice
(about 1/2 lemon)
1 teaspoon tamari soy sauce
1/2 cup olive oil or vegetable oil
Dash salt
Freshly ground pepper

1. Combine the garlic, lemon juice, soy sauce, oil, salt, and pepper in a jar with a tight-fitting lid. Shake vigorously.

2. Just before serving, shake the dressing well again and add to the salad. Toss well and serve immediately.

---

szechuan braised bean curd and vegetables

This is one of my favorite Chinese dishes. The bean curd and eggplant absorb the hot, spicy sauce superbly, and create a rich, haunting flavor. It is very easy to prepare, and all of the ingredients should be set out in front of you close to the stove at the time of cooking.

serves 4

Oil
1 pound firm bean curd (tofu), cut into
strips 1/2 inch by 2 inches and patted
very dry
1 small eggplant (3/4 pound), peeled and
cut into strips 1/2 inch by 2 inches
3 cups (8 ounces) sliced mushrooms

2 cups (8 ounces) diced green beans,
2-inch lengths
1/4 cup water, plus 3 tablespoons
1 tablespoon chili paste with garlicG
3 tablespoons tamari soy sauce
4 1/2 tablespoons Chinese rice wine
or dry sherry

1. Heat about 3 tablespoons of the oil over medium-high heat in a wok or large skillet. When the oil is hot but not smoking, add half of the bean curd and stir-fry until lightly golden. Remove to a platter and add a little more oil to the pan if it is dry. Repeat with the remaining bean curd.

2. If there is no oil left in the pan add a little more. Raise the heat to high. When the oil is hot add the eggplant. Stir-fry for 4 minutes. It will probably absorb the oil but do not add any more; just keep tossing.

3. Add the mushrooms and green beans, and stir-fry for 3 minutes. At this point if the mixture is very dry you can add a tiny bit of oil.

4. Add the ¼ cup of water, cover the wok or skillet, and cook for 5 minutes, or until the water is absorbed and the beans and eggplant are tender.

5. Add the bean curd and toss.

6. In a small bowl blend together the chili paste, soy sauce, rice wine, and 3 tablespoons of water.

7. Pour over the bean curd mixture and toss until well coated. Stir-fry 3 minutes more, or until the sauce is slightly thickened. Serve immediately on rice.

menu six

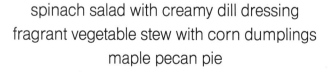

spinach salad with creamy dill dressing
fragrant vegetable stew with corn dumplings
maple pecan pie

I would serve this menu during any season except the summer, which would be too hot for a hearty stew. The salad and the stew are full of vegetables and are not rich at all, and so they go well with the sumptuous and filling pecan pie.

spinach salad with creamy dill dressing

serves 6

12 ounces fresh spinach, washed,
    stems removed, and patted
    or spun dry
1/2 medium-size red onion, thinly sliced
6 ounces mushrooms, sliced
    (2 cups sliced)
1 hard-boiled egg, minced
Creamy Dill Dressing (p. 268)

1. Tear the spinach into bite-size pieces and place in a large bowl.

2. Separate the onion into rings and slice in half any that are too large. Add to the spinach.

3. Add the mushrooms and minced hard-boiled egg, and toss.

4. Just before serving pour on the salad dressing and toss, or serve it separately in a sauceboat.

fragrant vegetable stew with corn dumplings

This is one of my most treasured recipes, and one that my stepdaughter asks me to make for her when she wants a special treat. Buttery corn dumplings top clove-scented vegetables to make this a wonderfully fragrant and colorful stew.

serves 6 as a main course

1 1/2 cups dried baby lima beans
6 tablespoons butter
3 tablespoons oil
3 medium-size onions, diced
3 cloves garlic, minced
2 bay leaves
4 cloves
1/4 teaspoon cayenne pepper
10 cups Vegetable Stock,
    homemade (p. 267) or store-bought

1 teaspoon salt
28-ounce can imported plum tomatoes,
    roughly chopped, with their juice
3/4 cup minced fresh parsley
3 medium-size parsnips
2 medium-size carrots
2 medium-size potatoes
2 cups corn, fresh or frozen
    (from 10-ounce package frozen corn)
Freshly ground pepper to taste

dumplings:

3/4 cup unbleached white flour
1/4 cup whole wheat flour
2 tablespoons cornmeal
2 teaspoons baking powder
1/2 teaspoon salt
1 teaspoon sugar
1 tablespoon chilled butter
1/2 cup corn, thawed if frozen
2/3 cup cold milk

1. Cover the lima beans with plenty of water and soak overnight, or boil, covered, for 2 minutes, and soak for 1 hour. Drain very well.

2. Melt 3 tablespoons of the butter with the oil in a large pot and sauté the onions and garlic for 5 minutes. Add the bay leaves, cloves, and cayenne pepper, and sauté for 1 more minute.

3. Add the vegetable stock, salt, tomatoes, drained lima beans, and 1/2 cup of the parsley, and bring to a boil. Reduce to a simmer, stir occasionally, and cook for 45 minutes.

4. Meanwhile peel the parsnips and carrots and thinly slice them. Dice the potatoes, unpeeled if you like, and add these vegetables to the stew. Cook 45 minutes more.

5. Meanwhile prepare the dumplings. Combine the flours, cornmeal, baking powder, salt, and sugar in a medium-size bowl, and mix well. Cut in the butter until small crumbs are formed, then stir in the 1/2 cup corn and milk just until evenly moistened. Do not overmix. Cover and chill until ready to use. (The chilled batter will keep up to 24 hours.)

6. Add the 2 cups corn, remaining 3 tablespoons of butter, and remaining 1/4 cup of parsley to the stew, season to taste with freshly ground pepper, and cook 10 minutes more. *May be prepared up to 24 hours in advance to this point, covered, and chilled. Reheat to boiling before proceeding with the next step.*

7. Keeping the soup at a simmer, drop the dumpling mixture in by tablespoonfuls and cover the pot. Cook for 15–20 minutes, or until a toothpick inserted in the center of a dumpling comes out clean. Serve the stew with one dumpling to each bowl.

maple pecan pie

Most pecan pies are cloying and leave one feeling a bit *too* satisfied at the end of a meal. I believe that you should leave the table with the feeling that you could enjoy one more bite, not that you had one too many.

This recipe is not overly sweet, although a little does go a long way. I prefer it with *un*sweetened whipped cream for an interesting contrast in flavor.

maple pecan pie (continued)

serves 8

1 recipe Pâte Brisée (p. 274) made with sugar
4 eggs
1 1/4 cups firmly packed
    light brown sugar

1 cup pure maple syrup
2 tablespoons melted butter
1 1/2 cups whole pecans
Unsweetened whipped cream (optional)

1. Line a pie plate with the crust and chill for 30 minutes. Do not prebake it. Preheat the oven to 425 degrees.

2. Beat the eggs well with a wire whisk in a medium-size bowl, then beat in the brown sugar, maple syrup, and melted butter. Stir in the pecans.

3. Pour this mixture into the pie shell and bake at 425 degrees for 10 minutes, then reduce the heat to 325 degrees and bake an additional 35–40 minutes, or until a knife inserted in the center of the pie comes out clean. Serve warm or at room temperature, with unsweetened whipped cream, if desired.

menu seven

mixed green salad (p. 21)
neapolitan pizza
carrot cake with cream cheese icing

Pizza, although Italian in origin, has practically been adopted by Americans as our national dish. There is hardly a town or city in the U.S. that doesn't have a "pizza house." Yet each time I make a homemade pizza from scratch everyone responds with great enthusiasm for this special treat. It's not only the fact that people appreciate the time and effort involved (although it really isn't that time-consuming), but there is a fresh *flavor* in homemade pizza that is not duplicated in restaurants.

I always serve a salad beforehand because it offsets the starchiness of the pizza. Carrot Cake is another very popular treat in this country, and although it is sometimes too heavy to end a meal with, it enhances this one splendidly. Try this menu when children are going to be served, and you'll be pleasing even the most finicky eater.

neapolitan pizza

This is a memorable pizza with a thin, crisp crust. If you use black or dark pans your crust will be especially crisp, although lighter pans work well also.

makes one 17-inch rectangular pizza (serves 4)

1 cup warm water
1 package dry active yeast
3 tablespoons olive oil
2/3 cup whole wheat flour
1 3/4 cups unbleached white flour
1/2 teaspoon salt
1 teaspoon cornmeal
1 1/4 cups Marinara Sauce (p. 273)
1 1/2 cups (6 ounces) grated
   mozzarella cheese
1 1/2 cups (6 ounces) grated
   Muenster cheese
4 cups (12 ounces) sliced mushrooms,
   sautéed (optional)

1. Pour the warm water into a large bowl and sprinkle in the yeast. Stir to mix and let sit for 5 minutes.

2. Stir in the oil, then add the flours and salt. Beat with a wooden spoon until well mixed.

3. Turn the dough onto a lightly floured board or work surface and knead for 10 minutes (no less!). You will have to keep lightly flouring the work surface to prevent the dough from sticking.

I prefer a combination of mozzarella and Muenster cheese for heightened flavor.

4. Put the dough in a lightly oiled bowl, then invert the dough so the oiled surface is on top. Cover the bowl with a newspaper and let rise in a warm place (no hotter than 85 degrees) for 1 1/2 hours, or until double in bulk. (You can place the bowl in the oven if there is a pilot light, or lightly heat the oven for a few seconds, turn off the heat, then let it sit in the barely warm oven.)

5. Punch down the dough and knead a few times. Lightly flour your work surface, and with a rolling pin roll the dough into a rectangle large enough to fit your jelly roll pan. Sprinkle the cornmeal on the pan and line with the dough. It is not necessary to form an edge.

6. Preheat the oven to 500 degrees.

7. Spread a layer of Marinara Sauce over the dough. Cover the pizza with a mixture of the two cheeses. Top with the sliced mushrooms, if you wish.

8. Bake for 15–17 minutes, or until the crust is golden underneath and the cheese lightly browned. (To test the crust insert a knife or spatula under the crust and lift carefully to peek.) Cut into squares and serve immediately.

carrot cake with cream cheese icing

So many people have their own versions of carrot cake. This is the best I've tasted; it is very moist and has the right touch of spiciness.

2 cups unbleached white flour
2 teaspoons baking soda
2 teaspoons cinnamon
1 teaspoon salt
2 cups sugar
1½ cups oil
3 eggs
3 cups grated carrot (about 7 medium-
   size carrots)
8-ounce can crushed pineapple,
   undrained
1 cup chopped walnuts or pecans

icing:
½ cup (1 stick) butter, softened
1 teaspoon vanilla extract
8 ounces cream cheese,
   at room temperature
2½ cups confectioners'
   (powdered) sugar
1 cup ground walnuts or pecans for
   garnish (optional)

1. Preheat the oven to 350 degrees. Oil and flour a 9½-inch tube pan and set aside.

2. In a medium-size bowl combine the flour, baking soda, cinnamon, and salt.

3. In a large bowl beat together the sugar, oil, and eggs until well blended. Add the carrot, pineapple, and walnuts.

4. Beat in the dry ingredients until well blended. Pour into the prepared pan and bake for 70 minutes, or until a knife inserted in the cake comes out clean.

5. Cool the cake on a wire rack for 10 minutes, then remove the cake from the pan by inverting it onto a plate. Invert it again onto another plate and cool completely.

6. To make the icing: With an electric beater cream together the butter, vanilla, and cream cheese until well blended. Slowly add the confectioners' sugar and beat until smooth.

7. Carefully place strips of wax paper partially underneath the bottom rim of the cake to keep the plate clean while icing the cake. Spread the icing all over the cake. Decorate the sides with ground nuts, if desired, by pressing them all around the cake. Remove the wax paper strips.

menu eight

baked eggplant stuffed with curried vegetables
perfect brown rice (p. 266)
(plain yogurt)
strawberries and wine

In addition to the yogurt that is in the eggplant, I like to serve a side dish of plain yogurt as an accompaniment to balance the spiciness of the eggplant. This is a very satisfying low-fat menu. If you want to serve it during a season in which fresh strawberries aren't available, or are too costly, you could substitute Marinated Oranges in Grand Marnier Sauce (p. 114) or Poached Pears in Red Wine with Raisins (p. 78).

baked eggplant stuffed with curried vegetables

Eggplant has a very prominent place in Indian vegetarian cooking for its resemblance to meat and because it absorbs spices so well. Although it is not a particularly nutritious vegetable, it can serve as the basis for a very substantial dish. This stuffed eggplant makes a delicious and attractive main course, and it is low in calories. Choose firm, glossy eggplants, and check to see that they are free of bruises.

baked eggplant stuffed with curried vegetables (continued)

serves 4

    2 small eggplants
      (about 1/2 pound each)
    3 tablespoons oil
    2 medium-size onions, diced
    3 cloves garlic, minced
    1 teaspoon minced gingerroot
    1 tablespoon ground coriander
    1 teaspoon turmeric

1 teaspoon ground cumin
Pinch cumin seeds
1/4 teaspoon cayenne pepper
2 cups (6 ounces) quartered
    mushrooms
2 medium-size tomatoes, seeded and
    chopped (fresh or canned)
1 cup peas, fresh or frozen
1/2 teaspoon salt
1 cup yogurt (preferably low-fat)

1. Wash the eggplants, cut off their stems, and slice them in half lengthwise. Scoop out the pulp with a spoon, leaving a wall of eggplant about 1/4 inch thick all around. Roughly chop the pulp and set aside.

2. Preheat the oven to 400 degrees. Bake the eggplant shells face down on a greased baking sheet for 15–20 minutes, or until almost tender. Remove and reduce the heat to 350 degrees.

3. Meanwhile prepare the filling. Heat the oil in a large skillet over medium heat until it is hot but not smoking. Add the onions, garlic, and gingerroot, and sauté for 2 minutes. Then add the remainder of the spices and sauté 2 minutes more, stirring often.

4. Add the mushrooms and sauté for 2 minutes, then add the tomatoes and cook 2 minutes more. Add the eggplant pulp and fresh peas if you are using them and cook for 5 minutes, or until the eggplant is almost, but not quite, tender. If you are using frozen peas add them now and cook until the peas are heated through, about 2 more minutes.

5. Turn off the heat under the skillet, add the salt and yogurt, and stir to mix. Fill the eggplant shells with this mixture, then place them in a lightly greased shallow baking dish (a 12-by-2-by-7-inch dish works well). *May be prepared to this point up to 8 hours in advance, covered, and chilled.* Bake for 30 minutes, or until brown on top and piping hot.

strawberries and wine

This is a simple, low-calorie, and delicious dessert.

serves 4

    1/2 tablespoon honey
    1/4 cup dry red wine
    2 pints strawberries

1. Combine the honey and wine in a medium-size bowl.

2. Wash the strawberries and pat dry. Remove their hulls, slice each strawberry in half—cut the very large ones into quarters—and toss in the bowl with the honey and wine. Cover and chill for at least 1 hour before serving. Serve in large wine glasses or decorative goblets.

---

menu nine

salsa picante with hot pita triangles
mexican-style stuffed summer squash
sangría (p. 52)
fresh fruit with yogurt lime sauce

I like to serve this meal during the summer, when squash and tomatoes are inviting and many fresh fruits are at their prime. The squash are a meal in themselves; however, if you'd like something alongside them, try Sautéed Greens with Garlic (p. 51) for a pleasing contrast in color and texture.

salsa picante

Here is a low-calorie, uncooked, thick Mexican sauce that also works well as a dip. It is quick to prepare and will keep, chilled, for one week. I like to serve it with hot whole-wheat pita bread triangles for an appetizer. The best season to prepare this dip is in the summer when fresh tomatoes are at their peak, but good-quality canned tomatoes can also be used.

3 medium-size tomatoes,
    cored and minced by hand
1 very small onion, minced
2 cloves garlic, minced
1 teaspoon seeded,
    minced jalapeño pepper G
    (or more to taste)
1 teaspoon vinegar
1/4 teaspoon ground cumin
Salt to taste

G See Glossary of Ingredients about handling chilies.

1. Mix all of the ingredients together in a medium-size bowl. Cover and chill until needed. Bring to room temperature before serving.

2. Put in a serving dish and serve with hot pita bread triangles or corn chips, or use as a sauce with Mexican food.

mexican-style stuffed summer squash

By the end of each summer many people are hard-pressed to find new ways to prepare the seemingly endless gifts of squash that arrive on their doorsteps from overenthusiastic gardening neighbors. I relish the Mexican flavors of beans, chilies, and sour cream, and think they work sensationally as a stuffing for squash. This dish can be prepared up to 48 hours in advance so it is a good choice for entertaining.

serves 4

1 1/4 cups dried kidney beans
   (2 1/2 cups cooked)*
4 medium-size yellow summer squash
   (8 inches)
4 tablespoons butter
Salt to taste
Freshly ground pepper to taste
2 medium-size onions, diced
2 teaspoons ground cumin
1 teaspoon oregano
1 small jalapeño pepper, seeded and minced G

4-ounce can mild green chilies,
   drained and chopped
1/2 cup sour cream
2 cups (8 ounces) cubed Monterey jack
   cheese (1/2-inch cubes)
Minced fresh parsley for garnish

* If you use canned cooked beans, be sure to rinse them under cold water in a strainer and drain them well. Leftover beans can be marinated in olive oil, vinegar, and herbs.
G See Glossary of Ingredients about handling chilies.

1. Rinse the beans very well and soak them overnight with water to cover. (Alternatively, put them in a saucepan with water to cover and boil 2 minutes. Let sit covered for 1 hour.) Drain very well. Add fresh water to cover and cook the beans until tender, about 1–1 1/2 hours. Drain again.

2. Slice the ends off the summer squash and discard. Cut the squash in half lengthwise, and with a teaspoon or melon baller cut out the inside of the squash, leaving a thin wall intact. Finely chop the squash centers and set aside.

3. In a large skillet place enough squash halves to fit comfortably and add 1/2 inch of water. Cover the pan and steam the squash just until tender, about 5 minutes. Repeat with the remaining squash. Drain each one well and place in a shallow buttered baking dish (or two). Cut 2 tablespoons of the butter into bits and place in the hot squash halves. Season with salt and pepper.

4. Drain the water out of the skillet. Over medium heat melt the remaining 2 tablespoons of butter. Add the onions and sauté for 5 minutes. Add the cumin, oregano, and jalapeño pepper, and cook 1 minute. Add the chopped squash centers and cook 5 minutes more, stirring often.

5. Add the cooked beans, canned green chilies, salt and pepper to taste, and cook until the squash is tender. Remove from the heat and let cool 10 minutes. Stir in the sour cream and cheese.

6. Preheat the oven to 350 degrees. Stuff each squash shell with the filling. Press it in gently. *May be prepared to this point up to 48 hours in advance, covered, and refrigerated. Bring to room temperature before baking.*

7. Bake for 20–30 minutes, or until piping hot and bubbly. Garnish with minced parsley before serving.

fresh fruit with yogurt lime sauce

A quick, light dish that can be prepared in any season. Pick the best fruit that you can get and strive for an attractive color combination. If you cannot get straw-berries for the sauce, then try mashed banana, although the color will not be as striking.

serves 6

sauce:
4 strawberries, hulled
2 tablespoons honey
Juice of 1 lime
1½ cups yogurt (preferably low-fat)

Mint sprigs for garnish

fruit: a combination of 3 or more
of the following:

blueberries	sliced kiwi
diced melon	strawberries
diced mango	finely diced apple
sliced banana	pineapple chunks
diced papaya	diced pears
orange sections	

1. In a small bowl mash the 4 strawberries with the honey and lime juice to form a paste. Stir in the yogurt, and cover and chill for at least 2 hours or up to 48 hours before serving.

2. Put a mixture of fruit in each serving dish and spoon on some sauce, or arrange an attractive fruit platter using hollowed-out melon halves or pineapple halves and serve the sauce in a sauceboat. Garnish with mint sprigs.

menu ten

cheese and crackers
stir-fried noodles and vegetables
with sesame seeds
susanne's spice cake

For a nice change try serving a mild Chinese tea with the main course. Lichee tea, oolong tea, and many of the Chinese green teas make fragrant and sooth-ing drinks (they are best served without milk or sugar), and they are noticeably lighter than most black teas.

cheese and crackers

It might seem superfluous to write about such a simple thing as cheese and crackers, but in fact the final presentation can range from a dull, predictable platter, with packaged cheese and insipid national-brand crackers, to an aromatic, stimulating assortment of well-chosen items, depending on one's imagination and knowledge.

When I am going to use cheese in cooking—for example, in a cheese sauce, or melted in a sandwich, or in a stuffing—I sometimes will use packaged super-market cheese and I get satisfactory results. But, if the cheese is going to be the showpiece of an appetizer platter, then I purchase it at a cheese shop and ask to sample it beforehand. If you want to have an assortment of cheeses, it's nice to contrast firm cheese (such as an aged sharp Cheddar or a wedge of Parmesan) with soft, creamy cheese (such as Brie, Camembert, or Boursin) and pungent cheese (such as Gorgonzola or jalapeño pepper cheese).

Because cheese is so rich and high in fat, I like to serve it before a low-fat meal, that is, one that has little or no dairy products in it. Always serve cheese at room temperature, and try offsetting it with a little fruit, such as seedless grapes, or sliced pear or apple. Wine and sherry, remember, are natural companions to cheese.

Now, regarding the crackers. I can rarely find good crackers in supermarkets; they usually carry only the national brands and they are predictably characterless, overly salted, and laden with preservatives. I have found that health food stores usually carry a wonderful variety of very flavorful, interesting crackers—oftentimes far better than most cheese stores carry—and they are additive-free. If you haven't discovered this already, make a trip expressly for this purpose and try a few kinds; I'm sure you'll agree.

stir-fried noodles and vegetables
with sesame seeds

Don't overcook the vegetables for this dish: the onions and broccoli should be crunchy. As with any stir-fried noodle dish you must use *cold* cooked noodles to ensure best results. Be sure to have all of the ingredients in front of you before you proceed.

serves 3

2 cups broccoli florets*
1/4 cup oil (preferably peanut oil)
2 slices gingerroot (about 1 inch wide
    and 1/4 inch thick)
1/2 pound firm tofu,
    cut into 1/2-inch cubes
    and patted dry
2 large onions, quartered vertically
    and separated
3 cloves garlic, minced

1/2 pound (weight before cooked)
    cold cooked noodles such as
    linguine, spaghetti, or lo mein
    (6 cups cooked)
2 tablespoons tamari soy sauce
1 tablespoon sesame seeds
1 teaspoon Oriental sesame oil G

*The remaining broccoli stalks can be used in Lemon-Glazed Broccoli Stalks Julienne (p. 30).

1. In a covered wok or large skillet precook the broccoli over medium heat with 1/4 cup water. Cook it until tender yet still bright green, about 3 minutes. Remove the broccoli and set aside. Drain all of the water out of the pan and wipe it dry.

2. Heat the wok or skillet over medium heat. Add the oil, and when hot add the gingerroot slices. Cook for 5 minutes or until golden. Remove and discard them.

3. Add the tofu to the hot oil and stir-fry until golden, about 5 minutes.

4. Add the onions and garlic and stir-fry for 5 minutes, or until the onions begin to get tender yet are still crunchy.

5. Add the broccoli and toss. Cook 1 minute.

6. Add the cold noodles and toss well. Add the soy sauce and stir-fry for 2 more minutes, or until the noodles are hot.

7. Sprinkle on the sesame seeds and sesame oil. Toss to coat and serve immediately.

note:
If you don't have leftover pasta and must cook it especially for this dish, then drain it in a colander and run cold water over it until cold. Drain again and pat dry.

susanne's spice cake

My eight-year-old stepdaughter, Susanne, created this delicious tea cake, much to my astonishment. One night when I came home late I found a small cake on the kitchen counter. My husband informed me that Susanne had shut herself in the kitchen and mixed together flour, spices, sugar, etc., and baked it in the oven as a surprise for me. The next morning we tasted it and decided it would make a great cake as long as we eliminated the *teaspoon* of cayenne pepper and the black peppercorns she had put into it. (She kept a log of the ingredients she used, just as I do.) So she made it again with a minimum of help from me, and we found it to be so delicious that the three of us ate the whole thing in one sitting! (Incidentally, she also informed me that if I used it in this book she wanted some of the profits!)

makes one 8-by-8-inch cake

2 cups unbleached white flour
1 1/2 teaspoons cinnamon
1/2 teaspoon ground cardamom
1/2 teaspoon ground cloves
1/4 teaspoon allspice
2 teaspoons baking powder
1/2 teaspoon salt
4 tablespoons butter

1/4 cup honey
1 egg
1 cup sugar
1 teaspoon vanilla extract
1 cup milk
Powdered (confectioners') sugar
    for decoration

1. Preheat the oven to 350 degrees. Butter an 8-by-8-inch pan.

2. In a medium-size bowl combine the first seven ingredients and mix well.

3. Melt the butter with the honey in a small saucepan. Set aside.

4. In a large bowl beat the egg with the sugar and vanilla with an electric beater. Add the melted butter and honey mixture and beat just until combined. Add the dry ingredients alternately with the milk and beat until well blended.

5. Scrape the batter into the prepared pan and bake for 25–30 minutes, or until a knife inserted in the center comes out clean.

6. Let sit for 10 minutes, then invert onto a plate or platter. Invert again and cool completely. Decorate with powdered sugar sprinkled through a sieve.

menu eleven

crudités with yogurt herb dip
vegetarian chili
cornbread (p. 259)
poached pears in red wine with raisins

Chili and cornbread are a very compatible match, but because they are heavy and filling, I like to serve a light dessert and a light appetizer with them. For a beverage you might want to serve Sangría (p. 52).

---

yogurt herb dip

makes 1 1/2 cups

1 1/2 cups yogurt (preferably low-fat)
1 clove garlic, minced
2 teaspoons minced fresh dill
    (or 1 teaspoon dried dill weed)
1/4 teaspoon oregano
1/4 teaspoon basil
Salt to taste
Freshly ground pepper to taste

1. Mix all of the ingredients in a medium-size serving bowl and chill, covered, for 2 hours or up to 24 hours.

2. Serve with crudités of your choice, such as: red peppers, green peppers, carrots, cauliflower, jícama, blanched broccoli, zucchini, endive, and celery.

vegetarian chili

This recipe can be easily doubled or tripled and, therefore, is a good choice for serving at a large informal gathering. The bulghur adds a meaty flavor and texture so be sure to include it. Try serving it with Cornbread (p. 259) for a delicious combination.

serves 4 as a main course

2 cups dried kidney beans
(about 4 cups cooked)*
1/3 cup oil
2 large onions, diced
6 cloves garlic, minced
1 tablespoon chili powder
1 tablespoon ground cumin
1 teaspoon oregano
1/8 teaspoon cayenne pepper
2 bay leaves
1/2 cup bulghur G

28-ounce can imported plum tomatoes
with their juice
1 tablespoon tamari soy sauce
3 cups water
1 teaspoon salt
Liberal seasoning freshly ground pepper
2 tablespoons butter
1/2 cup finely chopped red onion

*If you choose to use canned cooked beans, then be sure to rinse them off in a sieve before proceeding with step 3.

1. Rinse off the kidney beans in sieve and remove any stones, etc. Soak overnight in water to cover. (Alternatively, put the beans in a pot, cover with water, bring to a boil, and cook for 2 minutes. Cover the pot and let sit for 1 hour.)

2. Drain the water off the beans, add fresh water to cover by about 2 inches, and cook the beans until tender—not mushy—about 1 1/2 hours. Keep the pot partially covered. Drain again.

3. In a large (6-quart) pot heat the oil. Put in the onions and garlic and sauté for 10 minutes.

4. Add the chili powder, cumin, oregano, cayenne pepper, bay leaves, and bulghur, and cook for 2 minutes (no less), stirring frequently.

5. Roughly chop the tomatoes and add them with their juice. Add the cooked kidney beans, soy sauce, water, salt, and pepper. Cook over low heat for 30 minutes, or until the chili is thick and fragrant. Stir occasionally. Just before serving add the butter and stir until melted. Taste to adjust the seasoning. If you like it spicier add a few dashes of cayenne pepper. Serve with chopped onion on each portion.

poached pears in red wine with raisins

This is a very pretty dessert. Dark red spicy wine colors the pears and makes them deep maroon on the outside while they remain white within. They are especially light and flavorful and are wonderful served after a rich meal.

serves 4

4 ripe but slightly firm pears
   (preferably Bosc, Comice, or Anjou)
1½ cups dry red wine
2 tablespoons lemon juice

⅓ cup honey
Pinch ground cloves
1 cinnamon stick
½ cup seedless raisins

1. Peel the pears and slice in half vertically. Remove the cores, then make a shallow incision in the necks to remove the strings.

2. In a large stainless-steel or enamel skillet or 6-quart stockpot combine the wine, lemon juice, honey, cloves, cinnamon stick, and raisins. Bring to a boil.

3. Add the pears and spoon some liquid on them. Reduce the heat to a simmer and partially cover the pan. Cook the pears for 15–20 minutes, or until they are tender when carefully pierced with the tip of a knife. Do not overcook them. Turn the pears occasionally to baste them.

4. When the pears are done, remove them to a serving dish or individual decorative goblets, cavity side up. Allow 2 halves per serving.

5. Boil the remaining liquid over high heat until reduced by one-third. Spoon some raisins into each cavity and pour the sauce over the pears. Serve warm, at room temperature, or chilled. *May be prepared up to 8 hours in advance.*

menu twelve

asparagus vinaigrette
baked eggplant, chickpeas, and tomatoes
(hot french bread)
apricot orange mousse (p. 9)

I like to serve crusty bread with the eggplant casserole so that it can be used to mop up all the delicious juices, and I think a light, dry red wine is an ideal match with these flavors.

asparagus vinaigrette

I have tried all methods of preparing asparagus to ensure even cooking—dicing the stalks, tying them together with a string and cooking them upright, cutting a cross in the stalks to encourage quicker cooking, etc., and none of them has ever been satisfactory to me; the bottom half of the asparagus still remains slightly tough. The one foolproof method to ensure tender, evenly cooked asparagus is to peel the bottom half of each one with a paring knife—not a vegetable peeler. Although you do lose some nutrients by peeling away that top layer, you gain by being able to use almost the whole asparagus.

asparagus vinaigrette (continued)

serves 4

1 pound asparagus

vinaigrette:
1/3 cup olive oil
1 1/2 tablespoons red wine vinegar
2 cloves garlic, minced
1/2 teaspoon Dijon-style mustard
1/4 teaspoon salt
Liberal seasoning freshly ground pepper

1 hard-boiled egg yolk, minced

1. Cut off only the very tough bottoms on the aspara-gus, and with a sharp paring knife carefully peel the bottom half of each one. Bring about 1 inch of water to a boil in a large skillet, lay the asparagus in the water, and cover the pan. Cook for about 10 minutes, or until tender but not mushy. (They will continue to cook a little more while cooling.) Drain very well and arrange on a large serving platter or on individual serving dishes.

2. To make the vinaigrette combine all of the re-maining ingredients except the egg yolk in a jar with a tight-fitting lid and shake vigorously. Pour over the asparagus and refrigerate them, uncovered, until chilled.

3. When ready to serve, roll the asparagus around in the dressing to coat them, then sprinkle the egg yolk over them in a horizontal strip. Serve cool or at room temperature—not cold.

baked eggplant, chickpeas, and tomatoes

A myth has developed that says that eggplant must be salted before it is cooked in order to remove its bitterness and/or cut down on its absorption of oil during cooking. I have cooked eggplant in myriad ways and have experimented with both the salted and unsalted methods; I hereupon declare that it makes no difference. I no longer salt eggplant and I have never had a bitter one, nor has the eggplant absorbed any more or less oil as a result.

serves 4

1 large eggplant (about 1 1/2 pounds)
5 tablespoons oil
2 medium-size onions, diced
4 cloves garlic, minced
16-ounce can imported plum tomatoes,
    roughly chopped and well drained

2 cups cooked chickpeas
    (from 16-ounce can or see Note)
Salt to taste
Liberal seasoning freshly ground pepper
1/3 cup minced fresh parsley

1. Preheat the oven to 350 degrees. Peel the eggplant and slice it lengthwise into 1/2-inch thicknesses. Cut these slices into 1/2-inch strips then cubes.

2. Heat 2 tablespoons of the oil in a large skillet over medium heat. When the oil is very hot but not yet smoking add enough eggplant just to make one layer. (You will probably have to do 2 batches, so as not to overcrowd the eggplant.) Fry the eggplant, tossing regularly, until it is browned and tender, though not mushy.

3. Remove the cubes to a platter, put 2 more tablespoons of the oil in the skillet, and when very hot fry the next batch of eggplant in the same manner. Remove to the platter.

4. Put 1 more tablespoon of oil in the skillet and sauté the onions and garlic until the onions are tender, not mushy, about 5 minutes.

5. Add the drained tomatoes and cook for 5 minutes. Add the chickpeas and eggplant and toss well. Season with salt and pepper, and cook 5 more minutes. Spoon into a medium-size baking dish and stir in the parsley. *May be prepared and chilled up to 24 hours in advance. Bring to room temperature before baking.*

6. Bake for 20 minutes, or until hot and bubbly. Serve immediately.

note:
If you want to use dried chickpeas, then soak approximately 1 cup of beans overnight in water to cover, or put them in a pot, cover with water, and boil for 2 minutes. Cover and let soak 1 hour. In either case drain and add fresh water to cover plus 2 inches. Cook until tender, about 1 1/2 hours. Drain again. If you use canned chickpeas, then drain, rinse with cold water, and drain again.

menu thirteen

mixed green salad (p. 21)
braised tofu and vegetables with white wine and tarragon
perfect brown rice with peas (p. 266)
sweet potato pie

Here is a rather low-fat menu, one that will allow you to put a spoonful of whipped cream on the Sweet Potato Pie without feeling you've overindulged. If you'd like to divide your cooking time, you can make the pie one day in advance with no noticeable loss in flavor or texture.

braised tofu and vegetables
with white wine and tarragon

Tofu gets much firmer when reheated so it is best to cook this dish just before serving. If you want to get a head start earlier in the day, you can prepare all of the ingredients beforehand, and set them in front of you at the time of cooking.

serves 4

¼ cup oil
1 pound firm tofu, cut into 1-inch cubes
    and patted very dry
2 medium-size onions, minced
2 cloves garlic, minced
3 cups (8 ounces) sliced mushrooms
1½ cups minced peeled tomatoes,
    well drained (from 28-ounce can)
2 teaspoons fresh tarragon,
    or 1 teaspoon dried tarragon,
    crumbled

sauce:
⅓ cup dry white wine
1 teaspoon tamari soy sauce
1½ teaspoons tomato paste
¼ cup Vegetable Stock,
    homemade (p. 267) or store-bought
Dash cayenne pepper
½ teaspoon salt
Liberal seasoning freshly ground pepper

1. In a large skillet heat the oil over medium-high heat until it is hot but not smoking. Add the tofu and stir-fry until it is golden. Remove from the pan and set aside.

2. If the skillet is dry pour in a little more oil. Add the onions and garlic and sauté for 2 minutes. Add the mushrooms and sauté, tossing frequently, for 10 more minutes, or until they are brown and tender.

3. Add the drained, chopped tomatoes and tarragon, and toss. Add the reserved tofu and toss again.

4. Mix together the sauce ingredients in a small bowl, and pour over the tofu mixture. Reduce the heat to a simmer and cook slowly, tossing occasionally, for 10 minutes, or until the sauce has thickened. Serve immediately.

sweet potato pie

I prefer to make this nutritious pie with what we call "yams" (though they technically aren't true yams but a variety of sweet potato) for their bright color, although sweet potatoes work well also. You could even substitute pumpkin or butternut squash with successful results, but yams or sweet potatoes are by far the most nutritious choice.

1 recipe Pâte Brisée with Whole Wheat
   Flour (p. 275) with 1 1/2 teaspoons
   vanilla extract
3 medium-size yams or sweet potatoes
   (1 pound)
2 eggs
2/3 cup honey

1 2/3 cups milk
1 1/2 teaspoons cinnamon
1 teaspoon ground ginger
1/2 teaspoon ground cloves

Sweetened whipped cream (optional)

1. Prepare the Pâte Brisée as directed but mix 1 1/2 teaspoons vanilla with the 3 tablespoons of ice water before adding it. Chill for 30 minutes. Do not pre-bake it.

2. Boil the yams until tender. Drain very well. Peel them, then press them into a measuring cup until they measure 1 1/2 cups. If there are any potatoes left over try Sweet Potato Biscuits (p. 260) or Sweet Potato Home Fries (p. 230).

3. Preheat the oven to 400 degrees. Combine the measured yams and all of the remaining ingredients in the blender or food processor, and blend until smooth.

4. Pour into the chilled pie shell. Bake at 400 degrees for 10 minutes, then reduce the heat to 350 degrees and bake for 30–35 additional minutes, or until the center of the pie has set. (Test by shaking it slightly; it shouldn't wobble.)

5. Cool thoroughly before serving. (This is one pie that I prefer slightly chilled.) Serve plain or with sweetened whipped cream.

menu fourteen

arugula and boston lettuce salad
baked macaroni and cheese with cauliflower
and jalapeño peppers
poached pears in red wine with raisins (p. 78)

Here is a pleasingly different version of macaroni and cheese that is rich and satisfying. A light salad and light dessert are all that are needed to round out the meal.

---

arugula and boston lettuce salad

The incomparable flavor of arugula can easily be overpowered by a strong salad dressing. The best way to accentuate its wonderful flavor is to use only a light dressing of lemon juice and olive oil with a sprinkling of Parmesan cheese.

serves 4

1 head Boston lettuce
1 bunch arugula
1/4 cup olive oil
1 1/2 tablespoons lemon juice
1 tablespoon grated Parmesan cheese
Salt to taste
Freshly ground pepper to taste

1. Wash both the lettuce and the arugula by dunking them in a large pot of cold water. Discard the water and repeat until the water is clean. Separate the lettuce leaves and tear off the stems of the arugula. Pat or spin both greens until very dry.

2. Tear the lettuce into bite-size pieces and each arugula leaf in half, and place the greens in a large salad bowl.

3. Sprinkle on the olive oil. Toss to coat. Sprinkle on the lemon juice and toss well. Sprinkle on the Parmesan cheese and toss again. Season with a little salt and freshly ground pepper and serve immediately.

note:
The size of a lettuce head and a bunch of arugula will vary so use your judgment as to whether or not you need more or less dressing.

baked macaroni and cheese
with cauliflower and jalapeño peppers

serves 4

1 cup macaroni, cooked and drained
   (2 cups cooked)
1 small to medium cauliflower,
   cut into bite-size florets and
   steamed until tender
4 tablespoons butter
4 tablespoons unbleached white flour
2 1/3 cups milk

2 cups (8 ounces) grated sharp Cheddar
   cheese, preferably Wisconsin Cheddar
1 cup (4 ounces) grated Monterey jack and
   jalapeño pepper cheese (see Note)
1/2 teaspoon salt
Freshly ground pepper to taste
2 tablespoons bread crumbs
   (preferably whole wheat, p. 278)

1. Preheat the oven to 350 degrees. Make sure the macaroni is well drained. If you want to cook it in advance, then toss it with a little oil to prevent sticking. Make sure the cauliflower is well drained.

2. Melt the butter in a medium-size saucepan over medium heat. Whisk in the flour and cook this roux for 2 minutes, whisking constantly.

3. Whisk in the milk and cook, whisking often, until it thickens and begins to boil, about 7 minutes. Remove from the heat and stir in the cheeses, salt, and pepper. *May be prepared up to 24 hours in advance to this point. Chill the macaroni, cauliflower, and sauce separately. When ready to cook, heat the sauce and proceed with the next step.*

4. Put the macaroni and cauliflower in a 10-by-10-inch baking dish (or something comparable) and pour on the sauce. Toss gently to mix. Sprinkle on the bread crumbs.

5. Bake for 20–25 minutes, or until browned and bubbly.

note:
If you cannot get jalapeño pepper cheese then you can use all Cheddar cheese and add 1 jalapeño pepper, seeded and minced. (See Glossary of Ingredients about handling chilies.)

menu fifteen

watercress and jerusalem artichoke salad
with sweet mustard dressing (p. 49)
celery root au gratin
kasha pilaf
honey bread pudding with apricot sauce

This is a good winter menu for people who love to try new vegetables and enjoy unusual flavors. If you cannot get kasha or are not fond of it, then Bulghur Pilaf (p. 25) would be a good substitute.

---

celery root au gratin

Celery root, also called celeriac, knob celery, and celeri rave, has a deliciously mild celery flavor, hence its name. It is virtually unknown in this country, which is unfortunate because its ugly, gnarled, dark exterior hides a creamy white interior, delicate in both texture and flavor. It must be cooked in a blanc—a mixture of water, flour, and lemon—to prevent discoloration. Choose celery roots that are small or medium-size because very large ones tend to be fibrous in the center.

serves 4

1 lemon
2 pounds celery root
   (about 4 medium-size roots)
1/4 cup unbleached white flour
1 tablespoon oil

sauce:
5 tablespoons butter
3 tablespoons unbleached white flour

2 cups milk
Dash nutmeg
Dash cayenne pepper
1/2 teaspoon salt
1 1/2 cups (6 ounces) grated Cheddar
   or Gruyère cheese
1/4 cup bread crumbs
   (preferably whole wheat, p. 278)

1. Put 4 cups of water in a large bowl, then cut the lemon in half and mix the juice from *one* of the halves into the water. (This acidulated water will prevent discoloration of the celery root.) Cut the ends off one of the celery roots, then peel it with a vegetable peeler and trim off any dark spots. Cut the root in half, slice each half into slices ¼ inch thick, then immediately drop them into the acidulated water. Repeat with the remaining celery roots.

2. Put the ¼ cup of flour in a medium-size saucepan, then whisk in 4 cups of water, the tablespoon of oil, and the juice from the remaining half of the lemon. Bring to a boil and cook for 2 minutes, whisking occasionally.

3. Drain the celery root and add to the blanc, then cook, uncovered, over medium heat for 15 minutes, or until the celery root is tender, not crunchy. Drain very well.

4. Meanwhile make the cream sauce. Melt 4 tablespoons of the butter in a medium-size saucepan over medium heat, then whisk in the flour and cook this roux for 2 minutes, whisking constantly. Add the milk, nutmeg, cayenne pepper, and salt, and whisk often until the sauce has thickened and begun to boil. Remove from the heat and gently stir in the drained celery root.

5. Spread half of the mixture in a medium-size shallow baking dish and top with half of the cheese, then add the remaining celery root and top with the remaining cheese. Sprinkle on the bread crumbs and dot with the remaining tablespoon of butter. *May be prepared to this point up to 8 hours in advance, covered, and chilled. Bring to room temperature before baking.*

6. Preheat the oven to 375 degrees. Bake for 20 minutes, or until hot and bubbly and crispy on top.

kasha pilaf

serves 4

1 tablespoon butter
8 ounces mushrooms,
    quartered (3 cups)
1 medium-size onion, minced
1 1/4 cups kasha[G] (medium granulation)

1 egg
2 1/4 cups hot Vegetable Stock,
    homemade (p. 267) or store-bought
1/4 teaspoon salt

1. Melt the butter in a small skillet over medium heat. Add the mushrooms and onion, and cook until the mushrooms are brown and tender, about 10 minutes.

2. Mix the kasha and egg together in a medium-size saucepan, and stir briskly over low heat until all of the kasha is coated with the egg. Turn the heat to medium and "toast" the kasha by stirring constantly until the grains are dry and separate, about 3 minutes.

3. Add the mushrooms and onion and toss. Add the vegetable stock and salt, and cover the pan. Simmer for 10 minutes, or until *all* of the liquid is absorbed. Fluff with a fork before serving.

---

honey bread pudding with apricot sauce

A highly nutritious, quick, and deliciously moist bread pudding. I like this served warm, contrasting with the cool sauce.

serves 4–6

3 cups cubed whole wheat bread, crusts
    removed (about 7 slices)
2 1/2 cups hot milk
2 eggs

1/2 cup honey
1 teaspoon vanilla extract
1/2 teaspoon cinnamon
1/2 cup chopped dates, or 1/2 cup raisins

sauce:
3 tablespoons apricot preserves
2/3 cup yogurt
    (preferably low-fat)

1. Preheat the oven to 350 degrees. Put the bread in a medium-size (2-quart) baking dish, and pour the hot milk over it. Let soak for 15 minutes.

2. Beat the eggs well in a medium-size bowl. Add the honey, vanilla, and cinnamon, and beat until well mixed. Pour over the soaking bread, then add the dates or raisins and gently incorporate.

3. Place this dish in a larger baking dish and fill the outside dish with enough hot water to reach halfway up the sides of the bread pudding dish. Bake for 55–60 minutes, or until a knife inserted in the center comes out *almost* clean.

4. Meanwhile make the sauce: Stir the preserves into the yogurt and chill for 1 hour.

5. When the pudding is done, remove the dish from the hot water and cool on a wire rack. Serve warm with the apricot sauce over each serving.

note:
To reheat the pudding the next day, sprinkle a few tablespoons of milk on the pudding and place the dish in a 350-degree oven that has just been turned off. Heat 10–15 minutes, or until warm throughout.

menu sixteen

pesto on toasted french bread
tofu fra diavolo with spinach fettuccine
fresh fruit (p. 279) or
chocolate-chip walnut squares (p. 130)

You could substitute any type of long pasta (such as regular fettuccine, linguine, or spaghetti) for the spinach fettuccine and get very good results, or if you don't fancy spicy food you could eliminate the hot pepper flakes to make a mild sauce. In both cases the garlicky Pesto on Toasted French Bread will be an excellent appetizer to serve with this meal.

pesto on toasted french bread

Pesto is usually served as a sauce on pasta and sometimes is used to enhance vegetables. But by far the most luscious way to enjoy pesto that I know of is to spread it on slices of toasted French bread, and serve them as an appetizer along with a glass of full-bodied dry red wine.

makes 12

12 slices French bread (1/2 inch thick)
1/2 cup Pesto (p. 270) or Winter Pesto (p. 271)

1. Toast the French bread under the broiler on a cookie sheet until lightly golden on both sides.

2. Spread about 2 teaspoons of pesto on each slice. Serve within 20 minutes.

note:
If you want to take this on a picnic, then pack the pesto in a container and place the warm toasted French bread in a plastic bag. Spread when you get there.

tofu fra diavolo with spinach fettuccine

Chunks of tofu are cooked in a tomato sauce with hot peppers, then spooned onto a bed of spinach fettuccine. I find that no grated cheese is needed, but you can add it if you like.

serves 4

1 pound spinach fettuccine
2 tablespoons olive oil
1 pound firm tofu, cubed
   (3/4-inch cubes) and patted dry
4 cloves garlic, minced
2 medium-size onions, finely diced

1/2 teaspoon dried red pepper flakes
2 1/2 cups tomato purée
1/2 teaspoon salt
Freshly ground pepper to taste
Minced parsley for garnish

1. Bring a large (6-quart) pot of water to a boil. Add the fettuccine and cook until al dente — tender yet still slightly firm to the bite, about 10 minutes.

2. Meanwhile heat the olive oil in a large skillet over medium-high heat until it is hot but not smoking. Add the tofu and cook until golden, tossing continuously. Remove to a platter and set aside.

3. If all of the oil has disappeared, then add just a little to cover the bottom of the pan. Lower the heat to medium and add the garlic, onions, and red pepper flakes. Sauté, tossing often, until the onions are tender, about 5 minutes.

4. Return the tofu to the pan and toss. Add the tomato purée, salt, and pepper. Simmer the mixture for about 8 minutes, or until the sauce is hot and thickened.

5. When the fettuccine is cooked, drain it very well in a colander and divide it evenly among the serving plates. Spoon the tofu and sauce on top of each serving. Garnish with the minced parsley.

menu seventeen

mixed green salad (p. 21)
chalupas
apple crisp (p. 58)

I like to serve this menu to company when I want something distinctive yet casual. All of the dishes are easy and quick to assemble, and most of the work can be done in advance. If you make the Apple Crisp ahead of time, you can turn the oven off after cooking the Chalupas and place the Apple Crisp inside it to heat through. You don't need to keep the oven on.

chalupas

Here is a sensational Mexican delicacy of crisp wheat tortillas covered with jalapeño peppers, melted cheese, and avocado purée. They can be served as a main course as one would serve pizza or tostadas, or they can be made cocktail-size and served as an appetizer. No drink suits them as well as ice-cold beer.

serves 4 as a main course

3 ripe medium-size avocados
    (preferably black pebbled-skin variety)
Juice of 1/2 lemon
3 tablespoons sour cream
    (or 1 1/2 tablespoons yogurt and
    1 1/2 tablespoons mayonnaise)
Salt to taste
Freshly ground pepper to taste

8 Wheat Tortillas (p. 277),
    or store-bought wheat (flour) tortillas
3 tablespoons oil
4–5 seeded and minced jalapeño
    peppers (pickled, canned, or fresh)[G]
3 1/2 cups grated Monterey jack cheese
    (about 14 ounces)

[G] See Glossary of Ingredients about handling chilies.

1. Slice the avocados in half vertically and discard the pits. To remove the skin, insert the handle of a spoon between the flesh and the skin and move it all around the avocado until the flesh is released from the skin. Put the flesh in a medium-size bowl and mash it thoroughly with the lemon juice, sour cream, salt, and pepper. Cover and chill until ready to use — no longer than 3 hours in advance.

2. Preheat the broiler. Brush both sides of the tortillas with the oil and lay them on a cookie sheet; this will have to be done in batches. Broil on both sides until golden. Keep the broiler on. *The tortillas may be prepared up to 2 days in advance. When cool wrap in plastic and keep at room temperature.*

3. Place as many tortillas on the baking sheet as will fit, and top with some of the minced jalapeño peppers. Cover with some of the grated cheese, then broil until the cheese is thoroughly melted. Repeat with the remaining tortillas.

4. Top each chalupa with some avocado purée in the shape of an X (or you can spoon the purée into a pastry bag and pipe it on with a star tube). Serve immediately.

note:
Instead of making the 8-inch tortillas, you can make them 2–4 inches for cocktail-size chalupas, or cut store-bought tortillas into small triangles.

menu eighteen

mixed vegetable slaw
baked lima beans basque-style
chilled zabaglione with honey

Here is a colorful selection of dishes that make up a good fall or winter menu. The Zabaglione is rich but also light, and is a delightful finale to this hearty meal.

---

mixed vegetable slaw

Here is a delicious grated raw vegetable salad made primarily with cabbage and winter squash (I prefer butternut). This salad has a crunchy texture, sweet flavor, and brilliant color, and I think it is far superior to traditional cole slaw.

serves 6–8

3 cups grated butternut (or Hubbard) squash (about 1 pound)
3 cups finely shredded cabbage
1 medium-large carrot, grated
1 medium-size green pepper, finely shredded by hand (not on a grater)
1 cup raisins

dressing:
1 cup mayonnaise
(preferably homemade, p. 269)

2/3 cup yogurt
(preferably low-fat)
2 teaspoons sugar
2 teaspoons Raspberry Vinegar
(p. 273), or red wine vinegar
1/2 teaspoon salt
Freshly ground pepper to taste

3 half-inch-wide green pepper strips
(optional garnish)

mixed vegetable slaw (continued)

1. Mix the squash, cabbage, carrot, green pepper, and raisins together in a large bowl.

2. Mix the ingredients for the dressing (not the green pepper strips) in a small bowl and pour onto the vegetable mixture. Toss to coat well, cover, and chill for at least 1 hour before serving.

note:
If you are going to present the bowl before serving, then you can garnish it with the green pepper strips. Cut each strip diagonally in half, and arrange them in a circular pattern (curled end on the outside) to resemble a flower.

baked lima beans basque-style

This dish is quick if you cook the lima beans beforehand. They need little attention, just a quick soaking for 1 hour then they are boiled for 1 hour. You can do this step the night or morning before if you will be pressed for time.

serves 4

1 pound dried baby lima beans
1/4 cup olive oil
4 onions, diced
4 cloves garlic, minced
16-ounce can imported plum tomatoes,
    roughly chopped, with their juice
    (2 cups)
1 tablespoon tomato paste
1/4 cup Vegetable Stock,
    homemade (p. 267) or store-bought
2 green peppers, cored and finely diced
    (1/2-inch dice, no larger)

1 red bell pepper, cored and finely diced
2 teaspoons paprika
1 bay leaf
1/2 teaspoon basil
1/4 teaspoon oregano
Liberal seasoning freshly ground pepper
1/2 teaspoon salt
A few dashes Tabasco or
    cayenne pepper
1/2 cup bread crumbs
    (preferably whole wheat, p. 278)
2 tablespoons butter

1. Put the lima beans in a medium-size saucepan and cover with water by 2 inches. Bring to a boil for 2 minutes, covered, then remove from the heat. Keep covered and let soak for 1 hour. Drain very well.

2. Return the beans to the pot and again add enough water to cover by about 2 inches. Boil, uncovered, for 1 hour, or until the beans are tender when tasted. Stir occasionally. Drain very well. *May be prepared*

to this point up to 24 hours in advance, covered, and chilled.

3. Preheat the oven to 350 degrees. Heat the oil in a large skillet over medium heat and add the onions and garlic. Sauté for 10 minutes, stirring often.

4. Add the tomatoes with their juice and toss. Mix the tomato paste and vegetable stock together and add. Add the peppers, paprika, bay leaf, basil, oreg-

ano, pepper, salt, Tabasco, and the lima beans. Toss well and bring to a boil.

5. Put everything in a large baking dish (about 10 by 10 inches) and smooth over the top. Sprinkle on the bread crumbs and dot with butter. *May be prepared to this point up to 8 hours in advance. Cover and chill. Bring to room temperature before baking.*

6. Bake for 45 minutes, or until the peppers are tender and the sauce has thickened.

chilled zabaglione with honey

Zabaglione is a type of custard flavored with Marsala wine and it must be cooked in a double boiler. Traditionally it is served hot, but I much prefer this

cold version, in which the strawberries provide a nice contrast in flavor, texture, and color.

serves 4

4 egg yolks
2 1/2 tablespoons honey

5 tablespoons dry Marsala wine
6–8 fresh strawberries, thinly sliced

1. In the bottom of a double boiler put enough water to barely touch the pan that fits into it. Bring the water to a simmer. Set a mixing bowl close by so you can immediately scrape the zabaglione into it when it is ready.

2. Meanwhile, off the heat, beat the egg yolks and honey in the top part of the double boiler with a wire whisk until they are pale yellow and smooth.

3. Place this pot over the simmering water, add the Marsala, and whisk continuously until the mixture begins to form soft mounds and swells, about 5 minutes. Stop at this point or else you will get scrambled eggs. Immediately scrape the mixture into the mixing bowl.

4. Cover and chill for at least 1 hour or up to 24 hours before serving. Spoon into decorative glasses or small dishes and partially immerse some strawberry slices in each.

menu nineteen

curried rice, tofu, and vegetables
banana raita
cowboy cookies

Here is a very nutritious menu with ample protein from the tofu, brown rice, and yogurt. In the curried rice dish you can improvise and include any number of other vegetables, such as broccoli, cauliflower, carrots, green pepper, zucchini, artichokes, or cabbage. Add them during step 2, and if the vegetables are a hard variety like carrots, broccoli, cauliflower, or artichokes, you should precook them. If you'd like something to accompany the cookies for dessert, try applesauce, either homemade or a good quality, unsweetened commercial one.

curried rice, tofu, and vegetables

This is a dish I like to take to a potluck supper. It is bright-colored, easy to prepare, and will hold its heat if you put it in a hot covered baking dish, wrap the dish in newspaper, and place it in a plastic bag. As with any stir-fried rice dish, you must use *cold* cooked rice to get fluffy results. If you need to cool the rice quickly, spread it on a platter and put it in the freezer until it gets cold.

serves 4–6

1/4 cup oil
1 pound firm tofu, cut into 3/4-inch cubes
 and patted very dry
3 tablespoons butter
1 red bell pepper, cored and diced
 (1/2-inch dice)
4 cups (12 ounces) sliced mushrooms
1 1/2 teaspoons turmeric
2 teaspoons ground cumin

1 1/2 teaspoons ground coriander
1/4 teaspoon cayenne pepper
1/4 teaspoon salt
4–5 cups cold, cooked brown rice,
 made from 1 1/2 cups brown rice
 and 2 1/2 cups water (p. 266)
1 1/2 cups frozen peas, thawed,
 or fresh peas lightly cooked
2 tablespoons tamari soy sauce

1. Heat the oil in a large skillet over medium-high heat until it is hot but not smoking. Add the tofu and fry until it is golden, tossing often. Set aside on a platter and cover with foil to keep warm.

2. Put 2 tablespoons of the butter in the skillet and when melted add the red pepper and mushrooms. Sauté for 10 minutes, or until the peppers are tender and the mushrooms are brown.

3. Add all of the spices and the salt, toss to blend well, and cook for 1 minute.

4. Reduce the heat to medium and add the cold rice, peas, and tofu. (If your peas are frozen, you can quickly thaw them by putting them in a strainer and running hot water over them. Drain very well.) Toss until well mixed, then add the soy sauce and toss again. Cook, tossing often, for 5–10 minutes, or until the mixture is piping hot.

5. Just before serving cut the remaining tablespoon of butter into bits and add. Toss again and serve.

note:
If you want to prepare this dish in advance, don't add the peas until you are ready to reheat it; this will ensure that the peas retain their bright green color. You should be aware that the texture of tofu becomes firmer and drier upon reheating, and so there is an advantage to making this dish just before you are ready to serve it.

banana raita

serves 4–6

2 large ripe bananas
1/2 teaspoon ground coriander
Dash cayenne pepper
1/4 teaspoon salt
1 cup yogurt (preferably low-fat)

1. Peel one of the bananas and put it into a medium-size bowl. Mash it thoroughly with a fork until it is a purée. Stir in the spices and salt; then stir in the yogurt until well blended.

2. Peel the other banana and slice in half lengthwise. Slice each half into 1/4-inch-thick slices and add to the yogurt mixture. Toss to blend.

3. Spoon the raita into a serving dish and garnish with a sprinkling of cayenne pepper. Cover and chill at least 1 hour before serving.

cowboy cookies
(chocolate-chip oatmeal cookies)

These are the prized cookies of my childhood. My mother, Rita, would make large batches of these crisp, buttery cookies, and it was a challenge for all of us to control ourselves and not overindulge. Even now when I visit her this is the one dessert I look forward to. The brown sugar–oatmeal flavor is very pronounced, which makes these, in my estimation, the ultimate chocolate-chip cookies. (Incidentally, I never have been able to discover the origin of the name Cowboy Cookies.)

makes about 4 dozen

1 cup unbleached white flour
1/2 cup whole wheat flour
1/4 teaspoon baking soda
1/2 teaspoon baking powder
1/4 teaspoon salt
3/4 cup (1 1/2 sticks) butter, softened
3/4 cup sugar
3/4 cup firmly packed light brown sugar
2 eggs
1 teaspoon vanilla extract
2 cups rolled oats (non-instant oatmeal)
1 cup chopped walnuts
1 cup (6 ounces) semisweet chocolate chips

1. Preheat the oven to 350 degrees. Butter a cookie sheet.

2. Combine the flours, baking soda, baking powder, and salt in a medium-size bowl.

3. Cream together the butter, sugars, eggs, and vanilla in a large bowl until fluffy. Add the flour mixture and mix well.

4. Beat in the oats, nuts, and chocolate chips. (You might have to do this step by hand.) The dough will be crumbly.

5. Drop by teaspoonfuls 2 inches apart on the prepared cookie sheet. Bake for 12–15 minutes, or until golden brown. Be careful not to burn them. Thoroughly cool on a wire rack before storing in a tin.

note:
This recipe can be easily doubled, and these cookies freeze very well. Just be sure to keep them well stored in an airtight tin.

menu twenty

marinated shell bean and zucchini salad
polenta and pesto soufflé
sautéed grated beets and beet greens
fresh fruit (p. 279) or
pear and apricot crisp (p. 41)

The Marinated Shell Bean and Zucchini Salad is very substantial, and, therefore, is a good choice to serve with a soufflé. This is an ideal late summer or early fall menu because that's when fresh shell beans and beets are both at their prime.

---

marinated shell bean and zucchini salad

Shell beans, also called cranberry beans, are fresh beans that grow in red-and-white-flecked pods. Available throughout the summer and oftentimes throughout the fall, they are very substantial and have a wonderful nutty flavor. They are also a quick source of protein and iron because they don't require the lengthy soaking and cooking time of dried beans.

serves 4

2 pounds shell beans
   (3 cups beans shelled)
1 1/2 cups Vegetable Stock,
   homemade (p. 267) or store-bought
2 small zucchini, quartered lengthwise
   and *thinly* sliced
1 medium-size red onion, diced
1 cup chopped fresh parsley

marinade:
1 teaspoon Dijon-style mustard
1/4 cup red wine vinegar
1 cup olive oil
2 cloves garlic, minced
1/2 teaspoon oregano
1/2 teaspoon salt
Freshly ground pepper to taste

marinated shell bean and zucchini salad (continued)

1. Shell the beans and put them in a large skillet with the vegetable stock. Cover the pan and bring to a boil. Reduce the heat to a simmer, and cook the beans for 20 minutes, or until tender. Drain them very well and put them in a large serving bowl.

2. Add the sliced zucchini, onion, and parsley, and toss well.

3. Combine all of the marinade ingredients in a jar with a tight-fitting lid and shake vigorously. Pour over the bean mixture and toss well. Cover and chill the salad for at least 1 hour before serving. Serve cool or at room temperature, not cold. It looks particularly attractive served on a few large lettuce leaves.

---

polenta and pesto soufflé

I am not fond of extra light soufflés, which are airy and insubstantial. This one has a lot of character, and it is not difficult to prepare. Just follow the instructions carefully and you'll have glowing results.

serves 4

2½ cups milk
½ cup cornmeal
4 tablespoons butter, cut into small pieces
1 clove garlic, minced
1 tablespoon minced fresh basil,
    or 1 teaspoon dried basil
½ cup grated Parmesan cheese

½ teaspoon salt
3 egg whites, at room temperature
½ teaspoon cream of tartar
    (optional)
3 egg yolks
1 cup (4 ounces) diced
    mozzarella cheese (small dice)

1. Preheat the oven to 375 degrees. Bring the milk to a boil in a medium-size saucepan over medium heat. Gradually sprinkle in the cornmeal, whisking continuously, until it is blended. Continue to whisk until it becomes thick and smooth, about 5 minutes. (It should be the consistency of soft ice cream.) Remove the pan from the heat and stir in the butter, garlic, basil, Parmesan cheese, and salt. Scrape into a large bowl.

2. Beat the egg whites and cream of tartar (if you are using it) in a large bowl until they hold stiff peaks but are not dry. (They will whip better if they are tepid.)

3. Stir the egg yolks and mozzarella cheese into the polenta until blended. Stir in one-quarter of the egg whites to lighten the mixture, then fold in the remaining egg whites with a rubber spatula until evenly blended. Do not overmix or the egg whites will become deflated.

4. Butter a 6-cup soufflé dish or other 6-cup deep baking dish and scrape the soufflé mixture into it. *May be prepared in advance to this point, set aside in a warm draft-free place, and baked up to 30 minutes later.*

5. Bake in the center of the oven for 30 minutes, or until the center looks firm, not wobbly. Serve immediately.

sautéed grated beets and beet greens

My favorite way to eat beets — quick, beautiful, and so fresh tasting.

serves 4

> 1 bunch beets with their greens
>   (about 4 medium-size beets)
> 2 tablespoons butter
> 1 teaspoon sugar
> Extra butter

1. Cut the greens off the beets and set aside. Peel the beets with a vegetable peeler, then grate them on the coarse side of a grater, or shred them in a food processor.

2. Carefully wash the beet leaves and dry them. De-rib them in the following way: Fold each leaf in half (right sides together) and pull upward on the stem and rib until it peels off. Shred the beet greens by gathering them in bunches and cutting them into strips.

3. Melt the butter in a large skillet over medium heat. Add the beet greens and sauté for 1 minute.

4. Add the grated beets and toss. Cook, tossing often, until the beets are tender, about 5–7 minutes. Sprinkle the sugar on the beets, toss again, and cook 1 minute more. Serve immediately, with a pat of butter on each serving.

menu twenty-one

garden salad with creamy garlic tofu dressing
baked chickpeas provençale
almond butter cookies

Chickpeas, like most beans, are an excellent source of protein and iron. When cooked in combination with other vegetables—in this case potatoes, cabbage, and tomatoes—you get a dish that is nutritionally complete. All that is needed is a salad for contrast, and a light dessert such as these Almond Butter

Cookies, which can be served alone or with a simple platter of sliced fresh fruit. Try serving this menu on a cold fall or winter evening when you want something hearty, and can enjoy the fragrant aroma of garlic and herbs permeating your house.

---

garden salad with creamy garlic tofu dressing

serves 4–6

    1 medium-size head romaine lettuce,
        thoroughly washed and patted or
        spun dry
    1 medium-size carrot, grated
    1 small cucumber, peeled and sliced
    2 scallions, sliced into 1-inch lengths
        (including green part)
    2 ounces alfalfa sprouts
    1/4 cup sunflower seeds
    Creamy Garlic Tofu Dressing (p. 7)

1. Tear the lettuce into bite-size pieces and put into a large bowl together with the carrot, cucumber, and scallions. Toss thoroughly.

2. Serve the salad in individual bowls and top each serving with alfalfa sprouts and sunflower seeds. Pass the salad dressing at the table in a sauceboat.

note:
Any leftover dressing can be covered and refrigerated up to 5 days, or used as a dip for vegetables or as a sandwich spread in pocket bread.

baked chickpeas provençale

Here is an exquisite-flavored dish that is topped with a mixture of bread crumbs and garlic and baked until crispy. Be sure to use the amount of garlic indicated; it mellows with baking and lends a subtle flavor to the sauce.

serves 4–6

1 1/2 cups dried chickpeas
  (about 4 cups cooked)*
1/3 cup olive oil
12 cloves garlic, minced
1/2 teaspoon rosemary, crumbled
1/4 teaspoon oregano
2 bay leaves
1 1/2 cups chopped peeled tomatoes
  with their juice (from 16-ounce can)
1 tablespoon tomato paste
1 cup dry red wine
3 medium-size potatoes, peeled and
  diced (1/2-inch dice)

3/4 pound cabbage,
  chopped (4 cups chopped)
1/2 teaspoon salt
Liberal seasoning freshly ground pepper

topping:
1/2 cup bread crumbs
  (preferably whole wheat, p. 278)
2 cloves garlic, minced
1/2 cup minced fresh parsley
1/4 cup grated Parmesan cheese

* If you want to use canned cooked beans, then rinse them in a strainer under cold running water and drain very well. Proceed with step 2.

1. Pick through the chickpeas and discard any stones or foreign substance. Rinse them in a strainer under cold running water, then soak them overnight in water to cover, or use the quick-soak method: Cover the beans with water, boil covered for 2 minutes, then let soak in their cooking water for 1 hour. Drain thoroughly, then cover the beans with plenty of water, and cook, uncovered, until perfectly tender (neither crunchy nor mushy), about 1–1 1/2 hours. Drain again very well.

2. Preheat the oven to 350 degrees. Heat the olive oil in a large (10-by-10-inch) flameproof casserole over medium heat, then add the garlic, rosemary, oregano, and bay leaves, and sauté for 2 minutes.

(Note: If your casserole is not flameproof, then sauté everything in a large skillet and put in a large casserole.)

3. Add the chopped tomato and tomato paste, stir to blend, then add the chickpeas and all of the remaining ingredients except the topping, and stir to mix. *May be prepared to this point up to 24 hours in advance, covered, and chilled.*

4. Cover the casserole, bring to a simmer, then bake for 45 minutes, or until the potatoes are tender. (Occasionally remove the dish from the oven and toss the mixture to ensure even cooking.)

baked chickpeas provençale (continued)

5. Meanwhile prepare the topping. Combine the bread crumbs, garlic, parsley, and Parmesan cheese in a small bowl.

6. Remove the casserole from the oven and sprinkle the topping evenly over the top. Return to the oven and bake, *uncovered,* for 15 more minutes. If you desire a browner, crisper crust run the casserole under the broiler for 1 minute, or until golden. Serve immediately.

---

almond butter cookies

Crisp, light, buttery, and richly flavored, these cookies could perhaps be equaled but not surpassed. I think they make a wonderful dessert, especially when served on a decorative platter with a side dish of fresh fruit or Chocolate-Dipped Strawberries (p. 207).

makes 4 dozen

    1 cup (2 sticks) unsalted butter, softened
    1/2 cup sugar
    1/4 cup firmly packed light brown sugar
    1 teaspoon vanilla extract

    1 cup *coarsely* ground almonds
       (about 4 ounces)
    2 1/4 cups unbleached white flour
    1/4 teaspoon salt

1. Cream the butter with the 2 sugars in a large bowl until fluffy. Add the vanilla and almonds and beat until well blended. Gradually beat in the flour and salt just until combined. Do not overbeat the dough.

2. Lightly flour a large sheet of wax paper. Turn the dough onto the wax paper and shape into a log 2 inches in diameter. Roll to cover completely with the wax paper; then refrigerate for at least 1 hour or up to 1 week.

3. When ready to use, cut the log into slices 1/4 inch thick. (For an easy method mark off 1/4-inch spaces with a ruler on the whole log and then slice.)

4. Preheat the oven to 350 degrees. Place on an ungreased cookie sheet about 1 inch apart and bake for 12–15 minutes, or until lightly golden on the edges. These cookies do not spread during baking. Cool on a wire rack before serving. Store in a covered tin up to 2 weeks.

note:
You can freeze the dough and use it whenever you wish, although it does lose some flavor when frozen. Slice it frozen, or just barely frozen, and cook as directed.

menu twenty-two

mozzarella, roasted pepper, and black olive salad
risotto of brown rice and mushrooms
braised broccoli with wine and garlic
fresh fruit with honey zabaglione sauce

Risotto is a special dish that is made with simple ingredients, yet becomes something truly aristocratic. I like to make risotto with brown rice because it is equally delicious yet more nutritious than when made with white rice. Although it demands your full attention when it is cooking, you will be able to cook the broccoli simultaneously during the last 10 minutes if you set the prepared broccoli ingredients before you when you begin the risotto. This menu is good for any season because you can improvise with the variety of fruit you use in the dessert, and select the best that is available.

mozzarella, roasted pepper, and black olive salad

This "salad" has an intriguing array of flavors and textures. Roasting the peppers until the skin is charred provides a nice smokiness. I prefer olives that are cured in brine—Kalamata are my favorite—although, admittedly, one does have to get accustomed to their saltiness. American-style canned black olives have been dipped in ferrous gluconate to make them evenly black, and then treated with lye. They are really quite tasteless and unpalatable, particularly after you've developed a taste for the real thing.

mozzarella, roasted pepper, and black olive salad (continued)

serves 4

1 large red bell pepper
1 large green pepper
6 ounces mozzarella cheese (see Note)
16 black olives (preferably Kalamata)

1 teaspoon oregano
Freshly ground pepper to taste
¼ cup plus 2 tablespoons olive oil
    (preferably extra-virgin)

1. Roast the peppers on a long-handled fork over a gas flame or on the burner of an electric stove until they are blackened. (Or you can put them on a cookie sheet and broil until charred.) Place them in a paper or plastic bag, tightly closed, for 10 minutes; the steam will make the skin peel off more easily. Under cold running water scrape off the skin with your fingers or a knife, then core the peppers and cut into strips about ¾ inch wide.

2. Slice the mozzarella into thin strips also about ¾ inch wide.

3. On 4 serving plates or 1 large platter place the pepper strips, mozzarella strips, and olives in a nice arrangement. Sprinkle the oregano and black pepper evenly over everything, then drizzle on the olive oil. Let sit for 30 minutes at room temperature before serving in order to soften the oregano and let it absorb some of the olive oil.

note:
It is better to buy fresh mozzarella cheese in a cheese store rather than the packaged variety. The texture is creamier and the flavor is sweeter.

risotto of brown rice and mushrooms

Risotto is a creamy rice dish cooked in such a way that the rice makes its own creamy, lush sauce. Although preparing it does take time and patience, I think you'll find that it is well worth the effort. It is important to regulate the heat so that you cook the risotto at just the right pace, and you should have everything else for your meal prepared in advance, for risotto must be served immediately.

serves 4

4 cups water
1 cup brown rice
3½ cups Vegetable Stock,
    homemade (p. 267) or store-bought
5 tablespoons butter

6 ounces (2 cups) mushrooms,
    quartered or cut into eighths
    if very large
¾ cup grated Parmesan cheese
Freshly ground pepper to taste

1. Bring 4 cups of water to a boil in a medium-size saucepan. Meanwhile rinse the rice in a sieve under cold running water. Add to the boiling water. Cook, partially covered, for 20 minutes. Drain in a colander.

2. Bring the stock to a simmer in a small saucepan and keep at a very low simmer throughout the cooking of the risotto.

3. Melt 4 tablespoons of the butter in a medium-size saucepan over medium heat, and sauté the mushrooms for 3 minutes. Add the drained rice and stir to coat all over. Add 1 ladleful (about 3/4 cup) of simmering stock and stir the risotto continuously until the stock is absorbed. The heat should be regulated so that it takes about 5 minutes for the stock to be absorbed.

4. Now add another ladleful of stock and again stir continuously until absorbed. Repeat this process until all but one ladleful of the stock has been used; this will take about 25 minutes. The rice at this stage should be tender yet still *slightly* firm to the bite; if it is too hard add an extra cup of water or stock to the simmering stock, and when it begins to simmer add another ladleful of stock to the risotto and stir until it is absorbed.

5. After the next to the last ladleful has been absorbed, add the Parmesan cheese and remaining tablespoon of butter, and stir to blend. Add the last ladleful of stock and stir until absorbed. Season with freshly ground pepper and serve immediately.

braised broccoli with wine and garlic

serves 4

1 bunch broccoli
4 tablespoons butter
6 cloves garlic, chopped

1/2 teaspoon basil
1/2 cup dry white wine

1. Cut the broccoli florets into bite-size pieces. Peel the stalks (if you wish) and cut them into bite-size pieces.

2. Melt the butter in a large skillet over medium heat. Add the garlic and cook 1 minute. Do not let it get brown. Add the broccoli and basil, and sauté for 7 minutes, tossing occasionally.

3. Add the wine and toss; then cover the skillet and reduce the heat to a simmer. Cook 2–3 minutes, or until the broccoli is tender yet still crunchy. Spoon into a warm serving dish and pour over any remaining sauce. Serve immediately.

fresh fruit with honey zabaglione sauce

Chilled zabaglione with whipped cream folded in makes a heavenly sauce for fresh fruit. Choose whatever fruit is in season — the best quality you can get —

serves 6

> 4 egg yolks
> 4 tablespoons honey
> 5 tablespoons dry Marsala
>   or Grand Marnier

1. In the bottom part of a double boiler bring to a simmer enough water to barely touch the bottom of the pan that rests in it. Have ready a large bowl to scrape the custard into when done.

2. Meanwhile, off the heat put the egg yolks and 3 tablespoons of the honey in the top part of the double boiler and whip them with a wire whisk until they are pale and creamy. Add the Marsala or Grand Marnier and place this pan over the pan with the simmering water. Continue whisking the mixture until it begins to swell into a custardlike texture, about 7 minutes. Be very careful at this point not to overcook or you will end up with scrambled eggs. The mixture is ready when it can form soft mounds. With a rubber spatula immediately scrape the custard into the reserved bowl. Cool it slightly, then cover and refrigerate until well chilled, about 2 hours.

although I don't recommend apples because I find them too crunchy for this delicate sauce.

> 2/3 cup heavy or whipping cream, well chilled
> Fresh ripe fruit (berries, melon, plums,
>   peaches, pears, bananas, oranges,
>   mangos, kiwis, pineapple)

3. Meanwhile whip the cream with the remaining tablespoon of honey until it is very stiff. (The cream will whip better if you chill your beaters beforehand.) Fold into the chilled zabaglione until blended. *May be prepared to this point up to 4 hours in advance and chilled.*

4. Decoratively arrange some fruit (it should be at room temperature) on each serving plate and top with a generous spoonful of sauce. Garnish each serving with a piece of attractive fruit.

note:
If you do not have a double boiler, then you can make one by fitting a bowl over the bottom of the pan that contains the water.

menu twenty-three

indian eggplant dip
cashew nut curry
curried cauliflower and peas
fried bananas
perfect brown rice (p. 266)
(plain yogurt)
ice cream sprinkled with espresso

This menu is in keeping with the Indian tradition of serving many different smaller dishes rather than a large main course. None of these recipes is time-consuming, yet the result will be an exotic array of enchanting flavors and textures worthy of a special occasion. Serve the eggplant dip as the appetizer, then present the remaining dishes (except the dessert) in serving bowls, and let each person put a little bit from each bowl on his or her plate in a circular fashion. The Cashew Nut Curry is particularly good served on the rice, and if you want to include a quick homemade chutney, try Raisin Chutney (p. 157).

indian eggplant dip

This is a richly flavored, spicy dip that is very easy to prepare. It is one of my favorite appetizers, and a good choice to acquaint newcomers to the flavors of curry. I highly recommend serving it with hot pita bread triangles so you can scoop it up, but it also works well as a spread on crackers, if need be.

indian eggplant dip (continued)

serves 4–6

1 medium-size eggplant (1 1/4 pounds)
3 tablespoons butter or Ghee (p. 272)
2 teaspoons ground coriander
1/2 teaspoon turmeric
1/4 teaspoon cumin seeds
1/8 teaspoon cayenne pepper
1 clove garlic, minced

1/2 cup finely chopped,
    drained canned or fresh tomatoes
1/2 teaspoon salt
3 tablespoons yogurt (preferably low-fat)
2 tomato wedges for garnish
Fresh coriander or parsley sprigs
    for garnish

1. Preheat the oven to 400 degrees. Cut the top stem end off the eggplant and discard. Prick the eggplant with a fork in a few places to prevent it from exploding when cooking, and place it on a pie plate or baking dish. Bake for 1–1 1/2 hours, or until the eggplant collapses and is very soft. Let sit for 10 minutes or so, or until cool enough to handle.

2. Meanwhile, heat the butter or ghee in a medium-size skillet. Add the coriander, turmeric, cumin seeds, cayenne, and garlic, and "toast" these spices for

2 minutes, stirring often. Add the tomato and cook 2 minutes more. Remove from the heat.

3. Scoop out the pulp of the eggplant into a medium-size bowl and mash very well. Add the spice mixture, salt, and yogurt, and mix well. Cover and chill at least 1 hour or overnight.

4. Spoon into a serving dish and garnish with the tomato wedges and the coriander or parsley sprigs. Serve with hot pita bread triangles.

cashew nut curry

The cashews in this quick Sri Lanka–style curry become very tender, and the sauce is delicate enough not to overpower their subtle flavor. Raw cashews (they can be purchased at a natural foods store) are the ones to use for this dish.

serves 4

2 tablespoons oil
1 medium-size onion, diced
1/2 red chili, seeded and minced,[G]
    or 1/8 teaspoon cayenne pepper

1 teaspoon turmeric
1 teaspoon ground coriander
1/4 teaspoon ground cardamom
2 cloves garlic, minced

1/2 teaspoon minced gingerroot
1 cinnamon stick
1/2 teaspoon salt
8 ounces (about 2 cups) raw cashews

2 medium-size potatoes,
   peeled and diced (1/2-inch dice)
2 cups coconut milk G

G See Glossary of Ingredients about handling chilies and making coconut milk.

1. Heat the oil in a medium-size saucepan over medium heat and add the onion, chili, turmeric, coriander, cardamom, garlic, gingerroot, and cinnamon stick. Cook for 2 minutes, stirring constantly.

2. Add all of the remaining ingredients and bring to a boil. Lower the heat, and simmer, partially covered, for 20 minutes, or until the potatoes are tender and the sauce is thickened. Serve alone or over rice.

curried cauliflower and peas

serves 4

1 large head cauliflower
6 tablespoons Ghee (p. 272) or butter
1 1/2 teaspoons turmeric
1 1/2 teaspoons ground cumin

1 1/2 teaspoons cumin seeds
1/4 teaspoon cayenne pepper
1 1/2 cups fresh or frozen peas
1/4 teaspoon salt

1. Wash the cauliflower and cut it into small florets.

2. Melt the ghee or butter in a large skillet over medium-low heat. Add the spices, stir to blend, and "toast" them for 30 seconds.

3. Add the cauliflower and toss to coat evenly. Add 2 tablespoons of water, then cover and cook for about 15 minutes, or until the cauliflower is almost but not quite tender, stirring occasionally. If you are using fresh peas add them after 7 minutes.

4. Add the frozen peas (if you are using them) and the salt, and cook uncovered until the peas and cauliflower are tender, about 3–5 additional minutes. *May be prepared up to 24 hours in advance and refrigerated. Reheat, then taste to adjust seasoning.*

fried bananas

This Indonesian dish is a sweet and unique-textured accompaniment that complements hot and spicy dishes. Don't let its simplicity fool you; it is unusually flavorful.

serves 4

    4 medium-size firm but ripe bananas
    Oil for frying

1. Peel the bananas and slice into quarters on the diagonal.

2. Fill a large skillet with oil to a depth of 1 inch. Heat until it is hot but not smoking. Fry the bananas until golden brown on all sides. Drain on paper towels and serve immediately.

ice cream sprinkled with espresso

This is a simple yet distinguished way to serve ice cream. Espresso coffee grounds add a delightful flavor and texture to ice cream when sprinkled lightly on top. I use Medaglia d'Oro coffee grounds and prefer a rich vanilla ice cream, but regular coffee grounds are also delicious, and chocolate and coffee ice cream work well also. Just place a scoop or two of ice cream in an attractive dish or large wine glass and sprinkle about 1/2 teaspoon coffee grounds on top. You could even add some shaved chocolate for a mocha flavor.

menu twenty-four

crudités with yogurt herb dip (p. 76)
cuban black beans and rice
marinated oranges in grand marnier sauce

This highly nutritious menu has a nice balance of light and heavy dishes. After eating the Cuban Black Beans and Rice, you'll find that the dessert of succulent oranges finishes the meal with a nice light touch.

---

cuban black beans and rice

The Cubans, along with many other nationalities, made a significant contribution to the culinary world by combining two nutritionally complementary foods —beans and rice. I enjoy all the different variations: Louisiana red beans and rice, Indian dal on rice, Mideast lentils and rice, and various Latin American and Caribbean dishes, but ı find this Cuban version the most attractive and flavorful. Black beans in a richly flavored sauce are mounded on rice, then garnished with minced hard-boiled egg, sour cream, and chopped red onion.

serves 4

1 1/2 cups dried black beans
3 tablespoons olive oil
3 medium-size onions, diced
4 cloves garlic, minced
2 bay leaves
1/2 teaspoon oregano
1/2 teaspoon thyme
1 tablespoon tomato paste
1/4 teaspoon Tabasco, or to taste
1 tablespoon vinegar
   (preferably red wine vinegar)

1 cup water
2 green peppers, cored and diced
Salt to taste
Freshly ground pepper to taste
Perfect Brown Rice (p. 266)*
1 hard-boiled egg, minced
2/3 cup sour cream
1/2 small red onion, diced

*About 40 minutes before the beans are done you can begin cooking the rice in a separate pan, or you can cook it in advance and reheat it in the oven (350 degrees).

cuban black beans and rice (continued)

1. Rinse the black beans in a strainer under cold running water and pick out and discard any blemished ones, stones, etc. Soak overnight in water to cover. Or put in a saucepan with water to cover and boil for 2 minutes; turn off the heat, cover, and let the beans sit for 1 hour. Drain very well.

2. Combine the olive oil, onions, and garlic in a medium-size saucepan and sauté for 2 minutes.

3. Add the drained beans, bay leaves, oregano, thyme, tomato paste, Tabasco, vinegar, and cup of water. Cover, bring to a boil, and simmer on low heat for 1–1 1/2 hours, or until the beans are tender yet still retain their shape. Stir occasionally. (You might have to add a bit more water before they are done, depending on how long the beans take to cook.

In any event, the sauce should be thick, not dry or watery.)

4. About 10 minutes before they are done, add the diced green peppers, and cook until tender.

5. Taste to adjust the seasoning; it will probably need salt and some freshly ground pepper. *May be prepared in advance to this point, covered, and refrigerated for up to 24 hours.* (In this case you will probably have to add a little water when you reheat it to thin the sauce.)

6. Serve on individual portions of hot brown rice. Garnish with minced hard-boiled egg, top with a spoonful of sour cream, and finally garnish with some diced red onion. Serve immediately.

marinated oranges in grand marnier sauce

If top-quality sweet oranges are available, this fat-free, simple dessert is just the thing to serve as a light finale to a rich or heavy meal, or as a sweet conclusion to a brunch.

serves 4

> 6 navel (seedless) oranges
> 1 teaspoon honey
> 1 tablespoon water

> 1/4 teaspoon cinnamon
> 2 slices lemon peel (1 inch long)
> 1/4 cup Grand Marnier

1. Section the oranges in the following manner: Cut the skin off with a sharp knife, then carefully cut each orange section out of the orange by cutting between the membranes right to the core. Let the orange sections and any juice fall into a medium-size bowl.

2. After all of the oranges have been sectioned, strain the accumulated juice into a small saucepan. Add the honey, water, cinnamon, and lemon peel to the saucepan. Boil over medium heat until reduced by half, about 3 minutes. It should look syrupy.

3. Remove the saucepan from the heat and take out the lemon peel. Add the Grand Marnier and stir to blend. Let the sauce cool until barely warm.

4. Pour over the oranges and toss to coat. Cover and chill for at least 1 hour, or up to 24 hours. Bring to room temperature before serving.

5. Serve the orange sections on small serving plates in decorative patterns such as a circular sun design, or one behind the other in a vertical row. Pour equal amounts of the syrup over each serving. Or serve in decorative goblets.

menu twenty-five

baked stuffed artichokes with pine nuts
and lemon herb sauce
cauliflower and pasta soup (p. 240)
rhubarb cobbler

I serve this menu in the spring when artichokes and rhubarb are plentiful. Spring artichokes are mostly green, in contrast to fall artichokes, which have a bronze cast to them. Both are delicious, and to test their freshness you should squeeze the top of the artichoke and listen for a squeaky sound. If it sounds dull, then it is past its prime.

Some people advise against serving wine with artichokes, because supposedly their flavors conflict and the artichokes cause dry wine to taste sweet. I haven't found this to be so, and I love to drink a crisp white wine with this menu.

baked stuffed artichokes with pine nuts and lemon herb sauce

These scrumptious artichokes are not difficult to prepare, and they look stunning. They resemble open flowers because some of the stuffing is pushed between the leaves and it keeps the petals apart.

Since they are rather filling, I like to serve them just before a hearty soup rather than a regular main course.

serves 4

4 medium-large artichokes
1/2 lemon
1/4 cup pine nuts
6 slices white bread, or 4 slices white
    bread and 2 slices whole wheat bread
1/4 cup minced fresh parsley
1/2 teaspoon tarragon
1/4 cup grated Parmesan cheese
1/2 teaspoon salt
Freshly ground pepper to taste
2 cloves garlic, minced
1 tablespoon butter

1/4 cup olive oil
1/2 cup dry white wine

sauce:
1/2 cup yogurt (preferably low-fat)
1/2 cup mayonnaise
3 tablespoons lemon juice
1/2 teaspoon mixed herbs
    (I like tarragon, basil, thyme,
    and oregano)
Freshly ground pepper to taste

1. Bring a large (6-quart) pot of water to a boil. Meanwhile rinse the artichokes under cold running water, then cut off the stems so they can sit upright. With a sharp knife (preferably serrated) slice off 1 1/2 inches from the top of each artichoke. Rub the newly exposed area with the lemon half to prevent discoloration. With scissors trim 1/2 inch off the top of each leaf, and continue to rub each newly exposed area with the lemon. Drop the artichokes into the boiling water and cook, covered, for 20 minutes.

2. Meanwhile make the stuffing. Preheat the oven to 375 degrees. Toast the pine nuts in one layer in a shallow pan for about 10 minutes, tossing occasionally. Be careful not to burn them; they should be

a pale golden color. Put them in a medium-size bowl and keep the oven on.

3. Put some water in a large bowl and soak half of the bread slices for 10 seconds. Drain out the water then squeeze the bread in your hands to remove *all* of the remaining water. Add the squeezed bread to the pine nuts and crumble with your fingers. Repeat with the remaining bread.

4. Stir in the parsley, tarragon, Parmesan cheese, salt, and pepper. Sauté the minced garlic in the butter for 2 minutes—do not let it brown—and add to the stuffing mixture, tossing to mix.

5. After the artichokes have cooked for 20 minutes, remove them from the pot and invert onto a paper towel until cool enough to handle. Gently make an opening in the center of each artichoke and pull out a few of the innermost leaves, then scoop out the choke — the fuzzy, hairy center — with a teaspoon until it is completely removed. Discard the choke and those innermost leaves.

6. Divide the stuffing into 4 equal portions and stuff the center of each artichoke with some stuffing, and also push bits of stuffing between the leaves in a symmetrical fashion. *May be prepared to this point up to 8 hours in advance, covered, and chilled.*

7. Place the stuffed artichokes in a medium-size baking dish or a pie plate and pour the oil over them. Pour the wine into the dish, then cover the dish with foil. Bake for 45 minutes, then remove the foil and baste the artichokes. Bake *uncovered* for an additional 15 minutes, or until a leaf near the center pulls out easily when grasped with the fingertips.

8. Meanwhile make the sauce. Combine all of the ingredients in a small bowl and beat until smooth. Let sit for at least 30 minutes before serving. (You can cover and chill it.) Serve cool or at room temperature, but not cold.

9. When the artichokes are done, let them sit for 10 minutes before serving; they will be easier to handle and more flavorful if not served piping hot. To eat the artichokes spoon some sauce onto the side of your plate. Pull a leaf out of the artichoke and dip the end that was attached into the sauce. Pull the artichoke leaf through your teeth and the tender meat will easily come off. When all of the leaves have been "scraped" in this manner you will be left with the artichoke bottom, the peak experience of this endeavor. Dip the bottom into the sauce and enjoy! Of course, don't forget to eat the stuffing as you go along.

rhubarb cobbler

This is a dessert for fruit lovers. Warm biscuit dough covers a rich-flavored, soupy rhubarb filling, and is then topped with lightly sweetened whipped cream.

serves 6

filling:
6 cups (about 1¾ pounds)
    diced rhubarb (½-inch dice)
1 cup honey
2 teaspoons cornstarch
Grated rind of 1 orange
¼ teaspoon cinnamon
¼ teaspoon ground cloves
3 tablespoons butter

biscuit dough:
1¾ cups unbleached white flour
2 teaspoons sugar
1 tablespoon baking powder
¼ teaspoon cinnamon
4 tablespoons chilled butter
⅔ cup milk
1 beaten egg

Lightly sweetened whipped cream

1. Preheat the oven to 375 degrees.

2. In a medium-size saucepan combine all of the ingredients for the filling. Simmer until the rhubarb is tender but not mushy, about 10 minutes. Pour into an 8-by-8-inch cake pan.

3. To make the biscuit topping: In a large bowl combine the flour, sugar, baking powder, and cinnamon. Mix well. Cut the butter into bits and add. Cut it into the flour mixture with a pastry cutter or work it in with the tips of your fingers until it resembles coarse meal. Add the milk and stir just to mix. Gather the dough into a ball. If it is too dry add a bit more milk.

4. Knead the dough 3 or 4 times just to make it manageable. On a lightly floured surface roll it to fit the 8-by-8-inch pan. Cover the filling with the dough, and brush the top with some of the beaten egg.

5. Bake for 30 minutes. If the dough is browned before the 30 minutes is up then cover lightly with a piece of foil to prevent further browning. Let cool somewhat before serving. Serve warm with whipped cream.

note:
To reheat, place into a 375-degree oven for 10 minutes, or just until evenly warm.

menu twenty-six

mixed green salad (p. 21)
cauliflower and cashew croquettes
green beans provençale
glazed pear cake

I think this menu is a shining example of how well dishes can enhance one another. The tomato-based Green Beans Provençale are an ideal partner to the rich and creamy croquettes, both because the beans have their own sauce and the dish isn't rich. This flavorful Glazed Pear Cake is one of my favorite desserts, particularly when served with whipped cream.

cauliflower and cashew croquettes

These croquettes are rich and luscious, with a crisp coating on the outside and a creamy filling of cauliflower and cashews within. Leftover cold croquettes make a great picnic food; they are eaten with the fingers and go with almost anything—such as cold soups, salads, and marinated pasta dishes.

cauliflower and cashew croquettes (continued)

serves 4

4 cups finely chopped cauliflower
　(not minced)
1 cup raw cashews*
3 tablespoons butter
5 tablespoons flour
3/4 cup milk
1 egg yolk plus 1 egg
1/2 cup grated Parmesan cheese
1/2 teaspoon salt

Liberal seasoning freshly ground pepper
1 1/4 cups bread crumbs
　(preferably whole wheat, p. 278)
Oil

*Raw cashews can be purchased at health food stores. If you cannot get them, you can substitute roasted, unsalted cashews, in which case you do not have to toast them.

1. Steam the cauliflower until very tender, then put it into a large bowl to cool. (If you do not steam it be sure to drain it very well after it is boiled.)

2. Toast the cashews in a 350-degree oven in a shallow dish such as a pie plate, stirring often until they are golden, about 10 minutes. Be careful not to burn them. With a large knife chop them into small pieces. (Do not put them in a blender or food processor; they will be chopped too fine.) Add to the cauliflower and mix.

3. Melt the butter in a small saucepan, then whisk in the flour and cook this roux over low heat for 2 minutes, whisking constantly. Whisk in the milk and cook another 3–4 minutes, or until the mixture is very thick. Remove from the heat and let cool for 5 minutes.

4. Beat in the egg yolk, Parmesan cheese, salt, and pepper. Scrape this mixture into the cauliflower and cashews and stir until well mixed. Cover and chill until cold, at least 1 hour, or up to 24 hours.

5. Lightly beat the egg in one bowl and put the bread crumbs into another. Form about 1/4 cup of the cauliflower mixture into an oblong shape about 2 inches by 3 1/2 inches. Don't worry about its shape being perfect at this point; it will be easier to form once it is coated with the bread crumbs. Roll in the egg, then the bread crumbs. Repeat with the remaining mixture; you should get 12 croquettes. (They can be breaded up to 1 hour in advance and kept at room temperature. Don't chill once they are breaded or moisture will collect and they won't fry well.)

6. Heat about 1/4 inch of oil in a large skillet until it is hot but not smoking. Fry the croquettes in batches until they are golden all over, then drain on paper towels. Serve immediately or keep hot in a 350-degree oven.

note:
Although I prefer them fried, you can bake the croquettes instead. Lightly grease a baking dish and place them in one layer. Bake in a 425-degree oven for 30 minutes, or until golden all over. Turn the croquettes over after the first 15 minutes.

green beans provençale

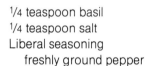

So often green beans are picked too mature and are, consequently, thick and tough. This method of cooking ensures tender results for green beans that are thin or thick, but it is preferable, of course, to choose the thinnest and youngest beans available.

serves 4

1 pound green beans
3 tablespoons olive oil
2 large onions, diced
1 1/2 cups chopped peeled tomatoes
    with their juice (from 16-ounce can)

1/4 teaspoon basil
1/4 teaspoon salt
Liberal seasoning
    freshly ground pepper

1. Snap the ends off the green beans and cut into 1 1/2-inch lengths.

2. Heat the oil in a medium-size saucepan over medium heat. Add the onions and cook, stirring often, for 10 minutes, or until tender.

3. Add the tomatoes, basil, salt, and pepper and bring to a boil.

4. Add the green beans and toss. If there is not enough liquid add a few tablespoons of leftover tomato juice. Cover and bring to a boil, then reduce the heat to a simmer and cook, stirring occasionally, for 20–30 minutes, or until the green beans are tender.

note:
If you want to prepare this in advance, then slightly undercook the green beans. When you are ready to serve them, reheat and cook until tender.

glazed pear cake

Here is a buttery upside-down pear cake that can be made with apples instead of pears—in which case you'd have apple pandowdy—but I find that pears make the most delectable version. Dark brown sugar creates a vivid glaze, so be sure to use that if you can.

serves 6–8

4 tablespoons butter
1/3 cup firmly packed dark brown sugar
4 medium-size ripe but slightly firm pears (preferably Bosc), peeled, cored, and thinly sliced

cake:
4 tablespoons butter, softened
2/3 cup sugar

1 teaspoon vanilla extract
1 egg
2 cups unbleached white flour
1/2 teaspoon cinnamon
3 teaspoons baking powder
1/2 teaspoon salt
1 cup milk

Sweetened whipped cream (optional)

1. Preheat the oven to 375 degrees. Melt 4 tablespoons of butter in a small saucepan over low heat, then brush some of it on the *sides* of an 8-by-8-inch cake pan. Mix the brown sugar with the butter in the saucepan and stir until melted. Pour into the cake pan and spread evenly.

2. Arrange the pear slices in neat rows on top of the glaze. If you have any leftover slices, chop them and evenly distribute them over the first layer.

3. With an electric beater cream 4 tablespoons butter, the sugar, and vanilla in a large bowl until blended. Add the egg and beat again until creamy.

4. In a separate bowl mix the flour, cinnamon, baking powder, and salt together thoroughly. Alternately add this dry mixture and the milk to the butter mixture and beat until well blended.

5. Pour the batter over the pears and spread evenly. Bake for 30–35 minutes, or until a knife inserted in the center of the cake comes out clean.

6. Cool on a wire rack for 10 minutes, then loosen the edges by inserting a knife all around. Lay a platter over the cake and invert. Serve warm or at room temperature, as is or with sweetened whipped cream.

note:
Leftover cake can be reheated in a slow oven (300 degrees) for 15 minutes or so, or until warm.

menu twenty-seven

spicy buddha's delight
(lo mein or linguine)
coconut macaroons

Buddha's Delight is a traditional Chinese dish, of which no two versions are alike. You can substitute any number of other vegetables, such as green peppers, dried mushrooms, cauliflower, water chestnuts, asparagus, and green beans, but be sure to strive for an attractive color combination. Although this dish must be cooked just before serving, you can prepare all of the ingredients a few hours in advance, arrange them in order on a platter, cover with plastic wrap, and keep well chilled. It will then take only 10 minutes or so to cook it.

The honey in the soft, chewy macaroons I've chosen for dessert helps to preserve them, so you can make them a few days in advance and they will still taste fresh.

spicy buddha's delight

Here is a spicy version of the traditional dish, which is usually too bland for my taste. I prefer serving it over noodles, although rice works well also. To serve it with noodles such as lo mein, linguine, or spaghetti (about 12 ounces for 4 people) it is best to cook them before you begin stir-frying. Drain them very well, then put them in a baking dish and toss with a little oil and soy sauce. Cover and keep warm in a preheated 300-degree oven.

spicy buddha's delight (continued)

serves 4

3 tablespoons tamari soy sauce
1/2 teaspoon cornstarch
1 tablespoon Chinese rice wine
   or dry sherry
1 1/2 teaspoons hot spicy oil^G
5 tablespoons oil (preferably peanut oil)
1 large carrot, cut diagonally
   into 1/4-inch slices
3 cloves garlic, minced
1 tablespoon minced gingerroot
2 cups (6 ounces) sliced mushrooms
2 cups bite-size broccoli florets*
1 large red bell pepper,
   cut into 1-inch squares
1 large onion, quartered and
   pieces pulled apart

5 cups diced Napa cabbage or bok choy
   (10 ounces)
4-ounce can sliced bamboo shoots,
   rinsed and patted dry
1/2 cup raw or dry-roasted cashews
1/2 pound fresh snow peas,
   tips removed and strung**
4 scallions, sliced diagonally into
   1 1/2-inch pieces
2 teaspoons Oriental sesame oil^G

 *Use the broccoli stalks in Lemon-Glazed Broccoli Stalks Julienne
  (p. 30).
**Frozen snow peas may be used but they will not have the nice
  crunchy texture of fresh ones. Thoroughly defrost them and pat
  very dry before adding.

1. Set all of the ingredients in front of you in the order that they are listed so you can stir-fry this dish quickly. Mix the soy sauce, cornstarch, rice wine, and hot spicy oil together in a cup and set aside.

2. Heat a wok or large skillet over medium-high heat, then pour in the oil. When the oil is hot add the carrot and stir-fry for 1 minute, then cover and cook 1 minute more.

3. Remove the cover then add the garlic, gingerroot, and mushrooms, and stir-fry for 30 seconds. Add the broccoli and red pepper, and stir-fry for 1 more minute. Add the onion and cook for 1 minute, then add the cabbage, bamboo shoots, and cashews, and stir-fry for 2–3 minutes, or just until the cabbage is wilted.

4. Add the snow peas, toss, and cook for 1 minute, then add the scallions and toss. Give the soy sauce mixture a stir, then pour it over the vegetables. Toss and cook for 30 seconds, then turn off the heat and add the sesame oil. Toss well and serve immediately.

coconut macaroons

makes 24 cookies

3 egg whites, at room temperature
Pinch cream of tartar
1 teaspoon vanilla extract

1/2 cup honey
2 cups unsweetened desiccated coconut
(purchased at health food stores)

1. Preheat the oven to 275 degrees. Line a cookie sheet with aluminum foil and butter the surface of the foil.

2. Put the egg whites in a large bowl with the cream of tartar, and beat them until they hold stiff peaks. Add the vanilla and continue beating. Slowly pour in the honey, and continue beating until the meringue is very stiff, about 5 minutes.

3. Fold in the coconut with a rubber spatula until it is thoroughly blended. Drop the batter by teaspoonfuls onto the cookie sheet, using the back of the spoon to help shape the cookies into attractive mounds.

4. Bake for 30–35 minutes, or until golden. (If you would like the macaroons to be darker, slide them under the broiler for 30 seconds.) Allow to cool completely on a rack before serving.

note:
When storing these macaroons, put sheets of wax paper between the layers to prevent them from sticking together. Store in a covered tin.

---

menu twenty-eight

mixed green salad (p. 21)
spaghetti squash with broccoli butter sauce
brandied fruit compote

Spaghetti squash is a deceptively light vegetable for its size, and it isn't as filling as pasta. With it I like to serve this fruit compote, which is very filling and satisfying, yet not too rich.

spaghetti squash with broccoli butter sauce

Spaghetti squash is a large egg-shaped squash in which the pulp, when cooked, separates like strands of spaghetti. It is delicious, has considerably fewer calories than spaghetti, and adapts well to most pasta sauces. I prefer it with a delicate sauce, such as this broccoli butter sauce, so as not to overpower its mild flavor. If spaghetti squash is overcooked it will be mushy and lose the texture of individual spaghetti strands. The best way to control this is to undercook when you boil it, then separate it into strands and sauté until tender.

serves 2–3

1 medium-size spaghetti squash
   (about 3½ pounds), rinsed off
1 large bunch broccoli
4 tablespoons butter
2 tablespoons olive oil
2 cloves garlic, minced

1 tablespoon minced fresh basil,
   or 1 teaspoon dried basil
1 tablespoon water
Salt to taste
Freshly ground pepper to taste
Grated Parmesan cheese

1. Bring a large pot of water to a boil, drop in the spaghetti squash, then cover the pan and cook over medium heat for 45 minutes. Remove from the pot and cut it in half crosswise (surprisingly this will give you longer strands). Let sit until cool enough to handle, about 10 minutes, then scoop out the seeds and discard them. With a fork scoop out the pulp and separate it into strands, then put it in a medium-size bowl. *May be prepared up to 24 hours in advance, covered, and chilled.*

2. Cut the florets off the broccoli, then cut them into small pieces. Save the stalks for another use (such as Lemon-Glazed Broccoli Stalks Julienne, p. 30).

3. Melt the butter and olive oil in a large skillet over medium heat, then add the garlic and cook for 2 minutes. Add the broccoli and basil, toss to coat well, then add 1 tablespoon of water and cover the pan. Cook for 2 minutes, or until the broccoli is about half cooked.

4. Discard any accumulated liquid in the bottom of the squash bowl, then add the squash to the broccoli and toss to blend. Cook, uncovered, for about 10 more minutes, or until the squash is crunchy but not hard. Season with salt and pepper, and serve with grated Parmesan cheese to pass at the table.

brandied fruit compote

You could substitute different fruits in this delicious compote, such as oranges, pears, or figs; the idea is to have a mixture of dried and fresh fruit (all-dried fruit is too heavy), and be sure to include the sliced banana. I love the combination of brandy and fruit flavors, and although it is not essential that you serve it with crème fraîche, I highly recommend it.

serves 4

1 cup dried apricots
    cut into bite-size pieces
1/2 cup pitted prunes cut into quarters
1/2 cup golden raisins
1 medium-size apple, peeled, cored,
    and diced
2 strips orange peel or lemon peel,
    1 inch wide

1 cinnamon stick
1 cup apple cider or water
1 tablespoon honey
1 medium-size banana,
    sliced 1/2 inch thick
3 tablespoons brandy
Crème Fraîche (p. 271)
    (optional)

1. Put everything in a medium-size saucepan except the banana, brandy, and crème fraîche, bring to a boil, then reduce the heat to a simmer and cook for 5 minutes.

2. Remove the orange peel and discard. Pour the compote into a bowl and add the sliced banana and brandy. Toss, then chill at least 1 hour. (If you are going to chill it longer, then cover the bowl.) *May be prepared up to 24 hours in advance. In this case don't add the banana until 1 hour before serving. When you are ready to serve, add a little more brandy if it has been completely absorbed.* Serve, as is or with a spoonful of crème fraîche, in decorative goblets or small dishes.

menu twenty-nine

mixed green salad (p. 21)
buttermilk herb and onion tart
sesame broccoli
chocolate-chip walnut squares

The Pâte Brisée with Whole Wheat Flour is a light, flaky crust with a nutty flavor, and it is a good match for the tangy buttermilk filling in the tart. Because this tart, like quiche, is better served warm rather than hot, you can begin cooking the broccoli once the tart has been removed from the oven.

buttermilk herb and onion tart

Buttermilk, which has the same caloric content as skim milk, adds a delicious piquancy to this tart, and significantly reduces the calories, which would be very high if cream were used. This is a wonderful way to use leftover buttermilk.

serves 4

Pâte Brisée with Whole Wheat Flour (p. 275)
2 1/2 tablespoons butter
3 medium-size onions, diced
4 eggs
1 1/2 cups buttermilk
2 cloves garlic, minced
1/2 teaspoon basil

1/4 teaspoon thyme
1/4 teaspoon tarragon, crumbled
1/4 teaspoon oregano
1/2 teaspoon salt
Freshly ground pepper to taste
1 1/2 cups (6 ounces) grated
    Monterey jack or Muenster cheese

1. Prebake the pie crust according to the recipe for Pâte Brisée (p. 275). Remove from the oven and set aside on a wire rack. Reduce the oven temperature to 375 degrees.

2. Melt 1½ tablespoons of the butter in a medium-size skillet, add the onions, and sauté for 10 minutes, or until tender but not mushy. Remove from the heat.

3. Beat the eggs in a large bowl until well blended, then beat in the buttermilk, garlic, basil, thyme, tarragon, oregano, salt, pepper, and reserved onions.

4. Evenly distribute the grated cheese over the bottom of the pie crust, then carefully pour in the custard mixture and shake gently to distribute. Cut the remaining tablespoon of butter into bits and place evenly on top of the tart.

5. Bake for 25–30 minutes, or until a knife inserted in the center comes out clean. Let sit on a wire rack for 20 minutes before serving. Serve warm not hot.

sesame broccoli

Here is a simple, low-fat way to prepare broccoli, and although it has an Oriental character I find that it goes well with most entrées. You could also mix broccoli and sliced carrots for a colorful combination.

serves 4

1 large bunch broccoli
1 tablespoon sesame seeds

2 teaspoons Oriental sesame oil[G]
1 tablespoon tamari soy sauce

1. Cut the broccoli into bite-size florets. Peel the stalks and cut them into comparable-size pieces. Steam both the florets and the stalks in a vegetable steamer until crisp yet tender. The broccoli should retain its bright green color.

2. Meanwhile toast the sesame seeds in a small saucepan or skillet over medium heat until they begin to smoke lightly and become fragrant. Shake the pan often and be careful not to burn them. Immediately remove from the heat and put in a small bowl.

3. Drain the broccoli well. Return it to the pot over the heat, then mix the sesame oil and soy sauce together and pour over the broccoli. Toss well. Add the sesame seeds and toss again. Serve immediately.

chocolate-chip walnut squares

These squares should be cut into small pieces, for they are very sweet and rich.

makes 16 squares

1/2 cup whole wheat flour
1/4 teaspoon baking soda
1/4 teaspoon salt
1 egg

3/4 cup firmly packed light brown sugar
1 teaspoon vanilla extract
1/2 cup semisweet chocolate chips
1/2 cup chopped walnuts

1. Preheat oven to 350 degrees. Butter an 8-by-8-inch pan and set aside. (If your baking dish is glass, then preheat oven to 325 degrees.)

2. Thoroughly mix the flour, baking soda, and salt in a medium-size bowl.

3. Beat the egg in another medium-size bowl, then beat in the sugar and vanilla until blended.

4. Stir the flour mixture into the eggs until blended. Stir in *half* the chocolate chips and all the walnuts.

5. Scrape the batter into the prepared pan and spread evenly. Sprinkle on the remaining chocolate chips.

6. Bake for 18–20 minutes, or until golden brown. The center should still be soft. Cool on a wire rack. When cool, cut into 16 squares. Store in a covered tin.

menu thirty

ricotta basil spread (p. 13)
(on crackers or french bread)
collards mornay
barley pilaf
ginger cookies

I occasionally like to serve a meal comprised of vegetable and grain side dishes with no main course per se. The Barley Pilaf nicely contrasts with the rich and creamy Collards Mornay, and together they provide an ample amount of protein, calcium, and iron, which is further increased by the Ricotta Basil Spread.

If collards aren't available, you could substitute kale, which has a similar nutritional makeup and an equally delicious flavor.

collards mornay

Collards, which have a flavor reminiscent of kale, are one of the most nutritious greens available. They are filled with vitamin A, calcium, and potassium, and are a good source of iron. I don't feel that they should be cooked to death as many Southern recipes suggest. I like them to retain their bright green color, crunchy texture, and mild flavor, so I cook them briefly, as I would most other greens.

collards mornay (continued)

serves 4

1 large bunch collards
2 tablespoons butter
2 large shallots, minced
3 tablespoons flour
1 cup milk
1/2 cup heavy or whipping cream

1/4 teaspoon salt
Dash cayenne pepper
1/8 teaspoon nutmeg
1 cup (4 ounces) grated Cheddar cheese
1 egg yolk
1 1/2 tablespoons grated Parmesan cheese

1. Preheat the oven to 350 degrees. Cut the stems off the collards and discard. Peel the coarser ribs off the leaves by folding the leaves in half lengthwise (right sides together) and pulling the ribs upward until they are released. Rinse the collards off by dunking them in a pot of cold water until they are clean. Change the water several times if necessary. Chop them into bite-size pieces and put them in a medium-size saucepan with a few tablespoons of water. Cook until they wilt and begin to get tender, about 5 minutes; they should still have a slight crunch to them. Drain very well in a colander and press out the excess liquid with a spoon or your hands.

2. To make the Mornay sauce: Melt the butter in a medium-size saucepan over medium heat, add the shallots, and sauté for 2 minutes. Add the flour and whisk until smooth, then cook this roux for 2 minutes, whisking constantly. Do not let it get brown. Whisk in the milk, cream, salt, pepper, and nutmeg, and cook, whisking often, until thickened, about 5 minutes.

3. Remove the sauce from the heat and stir in the Cheddar cheese. When the cheese has melted, stir in the egg yolk until blended, then stir in the drained collards.

4. Spoon the mixture into a medium-size shallow baking dish and top with the Parmesan cheese. *May be prepared, covered, and chilled up to 8 hours in advance. Bring to room temperature before baking.* Bake for 15 minutes, or until bubbly. Run the dish under the broiler for a browner crust, if desired. Serve immediately.

barley pilaf

Barley has a unique nubby texture and is very filling, so I prefer to serve it with a vegetable side dish rather than a hearty main course. Mushrooms have a natural affinity to barley and lend a distinct flavor, so be sure to include them.

serves 4

1 cup barley
2 tablespoons butter
2 cups (6 ounces) quartered
  mushrooms
1 large onion, minced
1/4 teaspoon thyme

1 2/3 cups Vegetable Stock,
  homemade (p. 267) or store-bought
2 teaspoons tamari soy sauce
1/2 teaspoon salt
Freshly ground pepper to taste

1. Rinse the barley in a strainer under cold running water, then put it in a medium-size saucepan and cover it with water. Bring to a boil and cook for 2 minutes, then turn off the heat and cover the pan. Let sit for 1 hour, then drain thoroughly.

2. Preheat the oven to 350 degrees. Melt the butter in a medium-size flameproof baking dish over medium heat. Add the mushrooms, onion, and thyme, and sauté for 10 minutes, or until the mushrooms begin to brown. Remove from the heat.

3. Add the drained barley, vegetable stock, soy sauce, salt, and pepper, and toss to mix. Cover the baking dish and bake undisturbed for 1 hour, or until all of the liquid is absorbed. Do not stir until just before serving. Serve immediately or keep warm in the oven until you are ready. *May be prepared up to 48 hours in advance and chilled. To reheat, add a few tablespoons of water or stock and place in a 350-degree oven until hot, about 20 minutes.*

note:
If you do not have a flameproof baking dish, sauté the mushrooms, etc., in a skillet, then spoon them into a buttered baking dish and add the barley, etc. You can make this pilaf on top of the stove in a saucepan, but it inevitably sticks to the bottom of the pan, so I recommend the oven method.

ginger cookies

Cookies to me are a great dessert as long as they are rich and flavorful. These ginger cookies are crisp and buttery with a good dose of spiciness. They are quick to make, and you can prepare the dough up to one week in advance, or make it a few months in advance and freeze it, although there is a little flavor lost when frozen. Sometimes I serve them alongside a dish of rich vanilla ice cream, but that is by no means essential.

makes about 4 dozen

1 cup (2 sticks) butter, softened
1/2 cup firmly packed light brown sugar
1/2 cup white sugar
2 cups unbleached white flour
1 1/2 tablespoons ground ginger
1/4 teaspoon cinnamon
1/4 teaspoon ground cloves
1/4 teaspoon salt
Sugar to sprinkle on top

1. Cream the butter and sugars in a large bowl with an electric beater until well blended and fluffy. In a smaller bowl mix the remaining ingredients until well blended.

2. Gradually add the flour mixture to the butter mixture and beat until blended, but do not overbeat the dough. Gather it into a ball; it will be crumbly. (You can gather it into 2 balls and shape each into a log, then freeze 1 for future use.)

3. Lightly flour a sheet of wax paper about 12 inches long. Put the dough on it and shape it into a log 2 inches in diameter. Roll up the log so that it is covered with wax paper. Chill it for 1 hour or up to 1 week, or freeze until ready to use. (If you keep it longer than a day or if you freeze it, wrap it in a plastic bag.) If frozen, thaw slightly before slicing.

4. Preheat the oven to 350 degrees. Slice the log into 1/4-inch-thick slices—no thicker. An easy way to do this is to use a ruler as a guide and mark off 1/4-inch spaces across the log. Place them on the cookie sheet 1 inch apart.

5. Bake 8–10 minutes, or until evenly golden. Be careful not to burn them. When done, immediately sprinkle some sugar on each cookie, then cool completely on a wire rack. Store in a covered tin.

elegant menus

When the occasion calls for a special meal that will delight the senses and be adventurous for cook and guest alike, choose a menu from this section. Although planning a meal that includes a number of carefully prepared courses is undoubtedly a time-consuming endeavor, it need not tax you so that you're exhausted by the time the guests arrive. You should relax before dinner, and the only way to do this is to prepare a great part of the meal in advance. Take advantage of the suggestions noted in most of the recipes for planning ahead, and you will enjoy the fruits of your efforts—and the company of your guests—a lot more.

menu one

pâté de légumes
(french bread)
sautéed tofu in french sweet butter
and vinegar sauce
perfect brown rice with peas (p. 266)
maple custard with maple pecan sauce

This menu would be a good choice for a very special occasion. I sometimes like to serve a salad with it; however, since there is pâté with French bread for the first course, I prefer to have the salad *after* the main course. If you want to serve a salad try Arugula and Boston Lettuce Salad (p. 84) or Mixed Green Salad (p. 21).

The tofu dish requires last minute preparation, but everything else can be prepared well in advance. I have found that it is a good idea to make the Perfect Brown Rice with Peas a few hours beforehand, and then to heat it in a covered dish in a 350-degree oven; that way your full attention can be turned toward preparing the tofu.

pâté de légumes

Here is a luscious pâté that resembles a meat pâté in texture, but it is much more nutritious and lower in fat. It can be served sliced with crusty French bread on the side, or used as a sandwich spread. Because this recipe makes a large loaf, I like to freeze a portion of it; but whatever you do it is so delicious you can be sure none will go to waste.

serves 8–10

6 cups water
2 cups lentils, rinsed and picked over
    for stones, etc.
2 cups diced green beans
1/4 cup olive oil (mild-flavored)
4 medium-size onions, diced
4 cloves garlic, minced
1 cup bread crumbs
    (preferably whole wheat, p. 278)

1/2 cup minced fresh parsley
3 eggs, beaten
1 1/2 tablespoons dry sherry
1 tablespoon tamari soy sauce
1/2 teaspoon salt
A few dashes cayenne pepper
Pinch thyme
Liberal seasoning freshly ground pepper

1. In a medium-size saucepan bring about 6 cups of water to a boil. Add the lentils and cook, uncovered, for 20 minutes. Stir occasionally.

2. Add the diced green beans and cook 20 minutes more, or until the green beans are very tender. Stir occasionally. Drain this mixture very well in a colander and return it to the pot (off the heat).

3. Heat the olive oil in a medium-size skillet over low heat. Add the onions and garlic and sauté, stirring often, for 20 minutes, or until the onions are very tender.

4. Add the onions to the pot containing the lentils, and mix. Add all of the remaining ingredients and mix well.

5. Preheat the oven to 375 degrees. Purée the lentil mixture in the blender or processor until very smooth. This will have to be done in batches. Scrape down the sides of the blender as necessary. Transfer each batch to a bowl when puréed. Taste to adjust seasoning.

6. Generously butter a 1 1/2-quart loaf pan. Line with wax paper and generously butter the wax paper. Pour in the pâté and smooth over the top. Cover with buttered wax paper or aluminum foil.

7. Set the pan into a larger baking dish and fill the outer dish with enough hot water to reach one-third up the sides of the loaf pan. (This bain-marie ensures gentle, moist cooking.)

8. Place the pans in the oven and bake for 1 1/2 hours, or until a knife inserted in the center comes out clean.

9. Remove from the oven, and lift out the loaf pan. Uncover and let it sit for 20 minutes.

10. Place a large plate or platter over the pâté and invert it onto the plate. Lift off the pan, then carefully remove the wax paper. Let the pâté cool for 15 minutes or so, then wrap it in foil and chill for at least 4 hours or up to 4 days. Serve chilled or at room temperature, but not warm. You can also freeze the pâté for up to 2 weeks, wrapped in foil and placed in a plastic bag.

serving suggestions:
Place a slice of pâté on a small serving plate and garnish with a few parsley or watercress sprigs. Serve with crusty French bread or melba toast. In addition, serve some chopped raw onion and mayonnaise on each plate. You could also serve it spread on warm toast with mayonnaise spread on top.

sautéed tofu in french sweet butter and vinegar sauce

This memorable dish was inspired by a classic French chicken dish taught by Lydie Marshall, a superb New York cooking teacher. Instead of chicken I use tofu that is sautéed and cooked with chopped tomatoes and mushrooms, then I deglaze the pan with vinegar and thicken the sauce with sweet butter. To simplify the preparation of this dish, have all of the ingredients prepared and set out before you, as you would for a Chinese stir-fry dish.

serves 4

4 tablespoons oil
1 pound firm tofu, cut into 1-inch cubes
    and patted dry
3 cups (8 ounces) sliced mushrooms
2 medium-size onions, minced
3 cloves garlic, minced
16-ounce can imported plum tomatoes,
    chopped and thoroughly drained
    (1 cup drained tomato pulp)

1/2 teaspoon salt
Liberal seasoning freshly ground pepper
2 tablespoons red wine vinegar
5 tablespoons sweet (unsalted) butter,
    cut into 5 pieces and brought to
    room temperature
Parsley sprigs for garnish

1. Preheat the oven to 350 degrees. Heat a large skillet over medium-high heat with 2 tablespoons of the oil. When the oil is hot add the tofu. Toss often and sauté until golden. With a slotted spoon remove the tofu from the pan and place in a medium-size baking dish. Cover the dish and keep the tofu hot in the oven.

2. Add 2 more tablespoons of oil to the skillet. When hot add the mushrooms and sauté until brown, about 10 minutes. With a slotted spoon remove the mushrooms and add to the tofu. Return the dish to the oven.

3. Put the onions and garlic in the skillet. Sauté for 5 minutes. Add the drained chopped tomatoes, salt, and pepper, and toss to blend. Cook for 10 minutes, or until most of the liquid has evaporated.

4. Add the vinegar and any accumulated juices from the tofu and mushrooms. Boil for 2 minutes.

5. Pour this sauce into the blender and purée until smooth. Immediately return it to the skillet but keep the skillet *off* the heat. Whisk in 1 tablespoon of the butter. When it has melted, whisk in another one. Repeat until all of the butter has been added. (The sauce will thicken with the addition of butter as long as it does not cook.)

6. Pour the sauce over the tofu and mushrooms and toss. Garnish with parsley sprigs and serve immediately.

maple custard with maple pecan sauce

This is a rather rich dessert in which delicate custards are topped with a chunky pecan sauce. You can present them on one large platter or serve individually. Either way looks attractive.

serves 6

6 eggs
1/3 cup pure maple syrup
Dash cinnamon
1 3/4 cups milk

sauce:
1/2 cup pecans
2/3 cup pure maple syrup
1 tablespoon water

1. Preheat the oven to 325 degrees. In a large bowl beat the eggs, maple syrup, and cinnamon together until well blended. Pour in the milk and stir just to blend.

2. Divide the mixture equally among 6 custard cups and thump each cup on the counter to break any air bubbles.

3. Place the custard cups in a larger baking dish and add enough hot water to the baking dish to reach halfway up the sides of the custard cups.

4. Bake for 30 minutes, or until a knife inserted in the center of a custard comes out clean. Remove the custard cups from the baking dish and cool completely. Keep the oven on.

5. To make the sauce: Raise the oven heat to 350 degrees. Chop the pecans coarse and scatter into a pie tin or baking dish. Toast in the oven, tossing occasionally, until lightly golden and fragrant, about 10 minutes.

6. In a small saucepan combine the maple syrup, water, and toasted pecans. Bring to a boil and immediately remove from the heat. Stir occasionally and let the sauce cool.

7. To serve the custards unmold each one onto a serving dish. Spoon equal portions of the sauce over each one.

note:
If there is any leftover sauce and it hardens when chilled, then heat gently just until it thins before serving it.

menu two

arugula and boston lettuce salad (p. 84)
rolled stuffed lasagne with kale
in a tomato cream sauce
linzertorte

If you have very hearty eaters, you might want to serve a good French or Italian bread with the salad course, although the lasagne dish is very filling and would satisfy most appetites without adding anything else to this menu.

For so stunning a dessert, Linzertorte is not that time-consuming to make. You just have to spend a modest amount of time preparing the crust, but the filling requires no work at all.

rolled stuffed lasagne with kale
in a tomato cream sauce

A luscious alternative to the traditional tomato sauce–laden version of lasagne. In this dish strips of lasagne are covered with a flavorful kale and cheese mixture, then rolled, and finally topped with a delicate tomato cream sauce. The slightly crunchy texture and definite flavor of kale give this lasagne a special character. It is perfect for a special occasion because it can be made in advance and then baked with no fuss. Note—avoid kale leaves that are very large and have thick stems; the smaller the leaves the more delicate the flavor and texture. Kale leaves shouldn't be longer than 7 inches or so. If you wish, you can substitute spinach or other greens. See note at end of recipe.

serves 4

1 pound kale (weight with stems)
1 tablespoon oil
8 lasagne noodles

2 tablespoons butter
2 cloves garlic, minced
1 medium-size onion, minced

1 1/2 cups ricotta cheese
1 cup (about 4 ounces) finely diced
    mozzarella cheese
1/2 cup grated Parmesan cheese
3/4 teaspoon salt
Freshly ground pepper to taste

sauce:
4 tablespoons butter
4 tablespoons flour
3 cups milk
2/3 cup tomato purée
1/8 teaspoon ground nutmeg
1/2 teaspoon salt
Freshly ground pepper to taste

1. Rinse the kale well by dunking it in a large bowl of cold water. Cut off the stems and discard. If the ribs attached to the leaves are thick then rip the leaves off and discard the ribs. Roughly chop the kale, then place in a large (6-quart) saucepan with a few table-spoons of water. Cover the pot and steam the kale until it wilts and is tender, about 5 minutes. Do not overcook it or it will turn olive brown and develop a strong taste. Drain it in a colander and let cool.

2. Meanwhile fill the same large pot with water and bring to a boil with the 1 tablespoon of oil. Add the lasagne and cook until tender, not mushy. Drain and rinse under cold water to cool quickly. Drain again and toss with a little oil to prevent sticking. Set aside. (Note: You can cook the lasagne noodles the night before and chill.)

3. When the kale is cool enough to handle, squeeze out all of the remaining moisture with your hands. Chop the kale so that it has a fine texture, but not so that it is minced. In a large skillet melt the 2 table-spoons of butter. Add the garlic and onion and sauté for 5 minutes. Add the kale and cook for 5 additional minutes.

4. Place the kale mixture in a large bowl and stir in the ricotta, mozzarella, 1/4 cup Parmesan cheese, salt, and pepper until well blended. Set aside. Pre-heat the oven to 350 degrees.

5. To make the sauce: In a medium-size saucepan over medium heat melt the 4 tablespoons butter. Add the flour and whisk until blended. Cook this roux for 2 minutes, whisking frequently. Add the milk, tomato purée, nutmeg, salt, and pepper, and whisk to blend. Cook for 5 minutes, or until the sauce comes to a boil, whisking often. Remove from the heat.

6. To assemble the lasagne: Pour a little of the sauce in a large baking dish to coat the bottom. Lay a strip of lasagne on a work surface and spread one-eighth of the kale mixture evenly over it. It doesn't have to be perfectly covered; the filling will spread when it melts. Roll the lasagne loosely, then lay it seam side down in the baking dish. Repeat with the remaining 7 strips of lasagne. Pour the remaining sauce over and sprin-kle on the remaining 1/4 cup of Parmesan cheese. *May be prepared to this point up to 24 hours in advance, then covered and refrigerated. Bring to room temperature before baking.*

7. Bake, uncovered, for 30 minutes, or until hot and bubbly.

note:
You can substitute 1 pound loose spinach, collards, or mustard greens if desired. If you are using pack-aged spinach, then a 10-ounce bag is fine.

linzertorte

Here is a classic dessert that deserves its grand reputation. A buttery almond lattice crust reveals glistening raspberry preserves, and although it seems rather complicated to construct it really isn't that difficult. You can serve it plain, but it is especially good served with whipped cream or rich vanilla ice cream, and for the perfect finale, follow it with a demitasse of piping hot espresso.

serves 8

3/4 cup (1 1/2 sticks) butter,
    softened
3/4 cup sugar
1 teaspoon grated lemon peel
2 egg yolks
1 1/2 cups unbleached white flour
1 teaspoon cinnamon
1/2 teaspoon ground cloves

1/4 teaspoon salt
1 1/2 cups (about 6 1/2 ounces)
    ground almonds
1 1/4 cups raspberry preserves
1 tablespoon lemon juice
1 egg white
Lightly sweetened whipped cream or
    vanilla ice cream (optional)

1. Cream the butter with the sugar in a large bowl until smooth, then add the lemon peel and egg yolks, and mix until well blended.

2. Combine the flour, cinnamon, cloves, salt, and almonds in a separate bowl, and stir until mixed. Pour into the butter mixture and mix just until combined and smooth; do not overwork the dough. Gather two-thirds of the dough into one ball and flatten it into a disk, then make a ball out of the remaining third of the dough and flatten that into a disk. Wrap individually in plastic and chill for 30 minutes. *May be prepared up to 2 days in advance and chilled, or frozen up to 2 weeks in advance. Thaw before proceeding with step 3.*

3. Remove the dough from the refrigerator; if it has chilled for longer than 30 minutes and is hard then let it sit at room temperature for 15 minutes, or until it is slightly firm. Butter an 8- or 9-inch springform pan, and with your fingers press the large ball of dough into the pan to cover the bottom and 1 inch up the sides.

4. Mix the preserves with the lemon juice and spread evenly over the bottom of the crust.

5. Roll out the remaining ball of dough between 2 pieces of wax paper until it is 8 or 9 inches in diameter, depending on the size of your pan. Slide the whole thing onto a plate and chill for 20 minutes, or freeze for 10 minutes.

6. Remove the top sheet of wax paper from the dough, then cut the dough into 1/2-inch-wide strips, cutting right through the wax paper. Take the center strip and lay it across the center of the torte with the wax paper side up, then peel off the wax paper. Place the second longest strip across the center in the opposite direction to make a cross, then peel off the wax paper. Press the ends of the strips into the sides of the crust as you go along. Place a strip on *each*

side of *both* of these strips, and continue in this manner until the top is covered with the lattice.

7. Preheat the oven to 350 degrees. Carefully brush some of the egg white over the lattice. Bake for 45 minutes, or until the crust is evenly golden. Cool on a wire rack for 20 minutes before removing the sides of the pan. Serve at room temperature, with lightly sweetened whipped cream or vanilla ice cream if desired.

menu three

miso soup
moo shoo vegetables with mandarin pancakes
chilled green beans with sesame sauce
maple-glazed baked stuffed apples
with crème fraîche

Here is a very different kind of Chinese menu because everything can be prepared in advance, which is unusual for Chinese food. Actually, Miso Soup is a Japanese soup, but its flavor is compatible with all Chinese dishes, and it enhances this menu superbly.

The Moo Shoo Vegetables with Mandarin Pan-cakes are eaten with the hands, so choose an occasion to serve this when everyone will feel comfortable eating this way. I don't think wine goes well with Oriental food, and so I suggest you serve beer, or mixed drinks, or sparkling water with a lemon or lime wedge.

miso soup

A very nutritious and attractive light soup that could be part of a light meal with a salad, or could serve as a first course to an Oriental meal. Boiling soup with tofu is poured over fresh raw spinach, thereby quickly cooking it and allowing it to retain its bright green color. If you aren't familiar with miso read about it in the Glossary of Ingredients to become acquainted with this wonder food of the soybean family.

serves 4–6

1/4 pound spinach
  (5–6 cups spinach leaves
  loosely packed)
6 cups water
1/2 cup miso G

1 tablespoon peanut oil
Freshly ground pepper to taste
1/2 pound firm tofu,
  cut into 1/2-inch dice
2 scallions, very thinly sliced

1. Wash the spinach very well by dunking it into a pot of cold water. Remove the stems and discard. Cut the spinach into shreds and divide it evenly among the serving bowls.

2. Bring the water to a boil in a medium-size saucepan. Remove about a cup of the water (a coffee mug is easy to use) and mix the miso into it until it is dissolved. (You must dilute the miso this way or it will remain lumpy.) Return the liquid to the pot and stir to blend.

3. Add the oil and the pepper. Bring to a boil again and add the tofu. Cook 1 minute. *May be prepared to this point up to 24 hours in advance and chilled.*

4. Ladle the boiling soup into the serving bowls over the raw spinach and stir lightly. Top each serving with sliced scallions. Serve immediately.

moo shoo vegetables with mandarin pancakes

This shredded egg and vegetable dish served with Mandarin Pancakes is an irresistible adaptation of the traditional Chinese dish usually made with pork or shrimp. The recipe works well for entertaining because, unlike most Chinese dishes, both the filling and the pancakes can be prepared in advance and reheated. To help organize yourself, it is a good idea to prepare the vegetables while the tiger lily buds and cloud ears are soaking.

serves 4

Mandarin Pancakes (next recipe)

sauce:
1/4 cup tamari soy sauce
1/2 cup water
2 tablespoons Chinese rice wine or
    dry sherry
2 slices gingerroot (1 inch wide)

filling:
1/2 cup dried tiger lily buds G
1 tablespoon dried cloud ears (tree ears) G
1 tablespoon Chinese rice wine or
    dry sherry
2 tablespoons tamari soy sauce

1 teaspoon cornstarch
1 teaspoon sugar
1/4 cup peanut oil
4 eggs, well beaten
2 teaspoons minced gingerroot
2 cups (6 ounces—about 1/4 of a
    small head) finely shredded cabbage
2 cups (6 ounces) thinly sliced
    mushrooms
1/2 cup (about 1/2 of an 8-ounce can)
    finely chopped water chestnuts
6 scallions, shredded
2 teaspoons Oriental sesame oil G
Salt to taste
Freshly ground pepper to taste

1. Make the Mandarin Pancakes and set them aside. To make the sauce boil the soy sauce, water, rice wine, and gingerroot in a small saucepan for 1 minute. Remove the gingerroot and discard. Pour into individual small dishes and set aside.

2. To make the filling: In a small bowl cover the tiger lily buds with enough hot water to cover. Soak for 30 minutes, then rinse in a sieve under cold running water and drain. Cut off and discard any hard ends on the buds, and cut the buds in half. Set aside.

3. In the meantime cover the cloud ears with hot water and soak for 30 minutes. Rinse in a sieve under cold running water and drain. Finely chop and set aside.

4. In a small bowl mix together the rice wine, soy sauce, cornstarch, and sugar and set aside. Keep the Mandarin Pancakes warm by folding them into quarters and placing them in a steamer, or putting

them in a covered baking dish and warming them in a 300-degree oven.

5. Place the prepared gingerroot, cabbage, mushrooms, water chestnuts, and scallions within easy reach of the stove. Heat a wok or large skillet over medium heat until hot but not smoking. Pour in 2 tablespoons of the oil, and when hot but not smoking add the eggs. Cook, tossing constantly, until set, about 3 minutes. Transfer the eggs to a plate and set aside.

6. Add 2 more tablespoons of oil to the pan, and when hot add the gingerroot and cook for 15 seconds. Add the cabbage and stir-fry for 2 minutes. Add the mushrooms and stir-fry another 2 minutes. Continue stirring and add the water chestnuts, reserved tiger lily buds, and cloud ears. Stir-fry 2 minutes more.

7. Roughly chop the reserved eggs and add. Toss to

moo shoo vegetables with mandarin pancakes (continued)

mix. Stir the soy sauce mixture, pour it in, and continue tossing for another 2 minutes. Add the scallions, toss, then remove from the heat and scrape into a serving bowl. Drizzle on the sesame oil, toss; season with salt and pepper to taste. *May be prepared to this point up to 24 hours in advance, covered, and chilled. Reheat gently in a skillet or wok just until hot.*

8. To serve, each person spoons 1–2 tablespoons of the moo shoo mixture onto an open pancake, then rolls the pancake over the mixture, folding in one side as he/she goes along. Eat with your hands, and dip the unfolded end into the dipping sauce.

mandarin pancakes

Most countries have to their credit some type of dish using the ubiquitous pancake. In China, Mandarin pancakes are used as wrappers for Peking duck or a moo shoo dish made with shredded ingredients. They are similar to Mexican tortillas but are thinner and chewier. They are easy to make, and the ones you don't use freeze very well. Rolling out and cooking them in pairs ensures the thinnest and most delicate pancakes possible.

makes 12 pancakes

1 cup unbleached white flour
1/2 cup boiling water

1 tablespoon Oriental sesame oil[G]

1. Put the flour in a medium-size bowl. Make a well in the center and pour in the boiling water. Gradually incorporate the water into the flour by stirring with a wooden spoon from the center outward. When the flour and water are mixed, turn the dough onto a lightly floured board or work surface.

2. Knead the dough until it is smooth and elastic, at least 7 minutes. Leave the dough on the board or work surface, cover it with a damp cloth or towel, and let rest for 15 minutes.

3. Cut the dough in half. Roll each half into a 6-inch log. Cut each log into 6 equal pieces. Roll each piece into a round ball, then flatten each ball into a 3-inch circle. Lightly brush some sesame oil on 6 of the circles. Place each oiled circle face down on an unoiled circle. You should now have 6 pairs.

4. On a lightly floured board roll each pair into 6-inch circles, turning the dough occasionally as you roll in order to keep the circles as round as possible.

5. Heat a medium- or large-size skillet over medium heat. Cook the pancakes, 1 pair at a time, for 30 seconds on each side; they should have a few brown flecks on them when they are done. After each pair is cooked, gently separate the halves and stack them. Keep them covered with a dry towel.

6. Serve immediately, or reserve and reheat by folding each pancake into quarters and steaming them in a steamer for about 3 minutes. (A vegetable steamer works well.)

to freeze:
Thoroughly wrap the stack of pancakes in aluminum foil, then place in a plastic bag. Defrost before using. Reheat as in step 6.

chilled green beans with sesame sauce

serves 4

1 pound green beans
3 tablespoons peanut oil
1 tablespoon tamari soy sauce
2 teaspoons Chinese rice vinegar
   (or other vinegar)

1 teaspoon Oriental sesame oil[G]
Freshly ground pepper to taste
1 tablespoon sesame seeds

1. Snap the ends off the green beans. Wash and drain them.

2. Fill a medium-size saucepan with water and bring to a boil. Blanch the green beans for 5 minutes, or just until tender yet still crisp. Test by tasting one.

3. Drain and immediately immerse them in cold water for a few minutes to stop further cooking. Drain again very well.

4. In a small jar with a tight-fitting lid combine the peanut oil, soy sauce, vinegar, sesame oil, and pepper. Shake well.

5. Put the green beans in a serving dish and pour over the sauce. Toss well.

6. Place the sesame seeds in a small saucepan. Cook over medium heat, stirring constantly, until fragrant and lightly toasted, about 5 minutes. (Be careful not to burn them. Once they become hot they smoke slightly and exude a noticeable aroma— at this point they are done.)

7. Immediately pour onto the green beans and toss well again. Cover and chill for at least 1 hour, or up to 24 hours before serving. Serve cool, *not* cold.

maple-glazed baked stuffed apples
with crème fraîche

A dessert that is relatively simple to prepare yet tastes so rich and satisfying. The apples are coated with maple syrup and filled with a mixture of walnuts, raisins, and spices that puffs up during baking. The sweetness of the apples and maple syrup is nicely contrasted by the tartness of the crème fraîche.

serves 4

4 large tart apples (such as Cortland
   or McIntosh)
1/2 cup pure maple syrup
1/3 cup finely chopped walnuts
   (not ground)
2 tablespoons raisins
1/2 teaspoon cinnamon

Pinch allspice
Pinch nutmeg
1 egg white
1 tablespoon butter
1/4 cup water
1 recipe Crème Fraîche (p. 271)

1. Butter a baking dish large enough to fit the 4 apples. Preheat the oven to 425 degrees.

2. Peel one-third of the skin off around the tops of the apples, leaving the remaining two-thirds of the peel intact. Core the apples. (If you do not have an apple corer the easiest way to do this is to cut two-thirds down from the top of the apple around the core, going around the core a number of times until a smooth cut has been made, then repeating this from the bottom of the apple. Push the core out from the bottom through the top.)

3. Put the maple syrup in a small bowl. Roll each cored apple in the syrup, making sure to coat thoroughly both inside and out. Place the apples upright in the baking dish and reserve the syrup.

4. In a small bowl combine the walnuts, raisins, and spices. Add 1 tablespoon of the reserved maple syrup. Add the egg white and mix well. Spoon an equal amount of the mixture into each apple.

5. Pour the remaining maple syrup equally over each apple. Cut the butter into bits and place on top of each apple.

6. Cut 4 small pieces of aluminum foil—just large enough to cover the filling in each apple to prevent the raisins from burning—and lightly butter each one. Place one on top of each apple. (The filling will puff up during baking.)

7. Pour the water into the dish and move the dish around to blend the liquids. Bake the apples for 30–35 minutes, or until tender when gently pierced with a knife. Do not overcook them or the apples will burst. Baste occasionally with the syrup.

8. Serve warm or at room temperature, and pour any remaining syrup over the apples. Top each apple with some crème fraîche.

menu four

mango and avocado salad with raspberry vinaigrette
spinach custard ring with tomato cream sauce
bulghur almond pilaf (p. 25)
prune tart with orange almond crust

Here is a very special menu with an intriguing medley of sumptuous flavors and textures, and not too much time demanded for their preparation. This meal would make a good choice for avid fruit and vegetable lovers.

mango and avocado salad with raspberry vinaigrette

Mango and avocado complement each other nicely in this delectable salad. If you aren't familiar with mangoes, this is a good way to become acquainted. When ripe, they will be tender to the touch and will have a rose or yellow blush on them.

serves 4

vinaigrette:
3 tablespoons Raspberry Vinegar (p. 273)
    or red wine vinegar
1/3 cup vegetable oil (not olive oil)
1/4 teaspoon salt
Freshly ground pepper to taste

2 ripe avocados (preferably black
    pebbled-skin variety)
1 ripe mango
8 red leaf lettuce leaves
1/4 cup diced red onion

mango and avocado salad with raspberry vinaigrette (continued)

1. To make the vinaigrette put the vinegar, oil, salt, and pepper in a small jar with a tight-fitting cover, and shake vigorously. Pour the vinaigrette into a medium-size bowl.

2. Cut the avocados in half vertically. Remove the seeds and discard. Insert the handle of a teaspoon between the skin and the flesh of each avocado and gently move it all around the circumference until the flesh is free from the skin. Slice each half into 4 lengthwise slices, then add the slices to the vinaigrette. Toss gently to coat well.

3. Peel the mango with a small sharp knife. The seed of the mango does not free itself from the flesh as the avocado seed does, so cut 12 lengthwise slices cutting toward the seed, then gently cut them away from the seed.

4. Lay 2 lettuce leaves on each of 4 serving plates. Remove the avocado from the vinaigrette and alternate slices of avocado and mango (4 avocado, 3 mango) on the lettuce leaves. Sprinkle on a horizontal row of the diced onion. Pour an equal amount of the vinaigrette over each serving. Serve immediately.

spinach custard ring with tomato cream sauce

This is a stunning dish that is very easy to make. If you don't have a ring mold, you can substitute a loaf pan or soufflé dish, although the ring mold looks especially elegant. When you purchase spinach, check to see that it is free of yellow spots, which are a sign of old age. Loose fresh spinach weighs more than packaged fresh spinach because it generally has much longer stems. One pound is equivalent to a 10-ounce package. I buy the packaged kind when loose spinach is extremely dirty.

serves 4

2 pounds loose fresh spinach
   (weight with stems), or two 10-ounce
   packages fresh spinach, or
   two 10-ounce packages frozen
   chopped spinach, thawed
4 large eggs
1 cup heavy or whipping cream
1 1/2 teaspoons minced fresh basil,
   or 1/2 teaspoon dried basil

1/2 teaspoon salt
Liberal seasoning freshly ground pepper

sauce:
3/4 cup tomato purée
3/4 cup heavy or whipping cream
1/4 teaspoon salt
Freshly ground pepper to taste
1/4 cup grated Parmesan cheese

1. Remove the stems from the fresh spinach and discard. Clean the spinach thoroughly by dunking it into a large pot of cold water and lifting it out, leaving the dirt behind. Discard the water, and repeat the process until the spinach is completely free of dirt.

2. Put the spinach in a large pot with just the water that clings to it. Cover the pot and cook, over low heat, just until it wilts. Drain in a colander and let cool. When cool enough to handle, squeeze out *all* of the water from the spinach with your hands. Mince it on a cutting board and set aside. (If you are using frozen chopped spinach then, when thawed, squeeze out *all* of its moisture with your hands. Set aside.)

3. Preheat the oven to 375 degrees. Beat the eggs very well in a large bowl and stir in the cream, basil, salt, pepper, and spinach. *May be prepared to this point up to 8 hours in advance, covered, and refrigerated. Bring to room temperature before proceeding with the next step.*

4. Generously butter a 1 1/2-quart ring mold (or loaf pan or soufflé dish), and fill with the spinach custard. Place this dish in a larger baking dish. Pour enough hot water into the larger dish to reach halfway up the sides of the mold. (This must be done to ensure gentle cooking.)

5. Bake for 20–30 minutes, or until a knife inserted in the center of the custard comes out clean. Let sit for 10 minutes before unmolding.

6. While the ring mold is resting, turn the oven up to 450 degrees. Combine the tomato purée, cream, salt, and pepper, and mix well.

7. Run a knife around the mold and carefully unmold it onto a quiche dish (not a quiche pan with a removable bottom), or any other attractive shallow baking dish. Pour the tomato cream sauce evenly over it, and sprinkle on the Parmesan cheese.

8. Bake for another 15 minutes, or until golden brown.

prune tart with orange almond crust

For some unfortunate reason prunes have a lowly reputation in this country. In Europe they are appreciated as a delectable fruit. This tart is one of my favorite desserts, and because it is rather intensely flavored, only a small piece is needed.

makes one 10-inch tart

12 ounces pitted prunes
Juice of 1 large orange (grate the orange
    rind first for the crust)
¾ cup water
⅓ cup honey
¼ teaspoon ground cloves
1 recipe Orange Almond Crust (p. 277)
2 egg whites (at room temperature)

1. To make the filling: Combine the prunes, orange juice, water, honey, and cloves in a medium-size saucepan. Bring to a boil, then reduce the heat to a simmer. Cook for 15 minutes, or until the prunes are very soft. Purée in a blender or food processor until very smooth. Scrape down the sides as necessary. Spoon into a large bowl and set aside to cool.

2. To prebake the crust: Preheat the oven to 400 degrees. Line a pie plate or tart pan as directed. Cover the pastry with foil and press it into the edges. Be sure to cover all the edges. Fill the foil with dried beans to weight it down—you must do this or the pastry will shrink. Bake the pastry "blind" for 10 min-utes. Remove from the oven and remove the foil and beans. Reduce the oven heat to 350 degrees. Set the pastry aside.

3. In a large bowl beat the egg whites until stiff but not dry. (They will beat better if they are at room temperature or slightly warm.) Fold them into the prune mixture until blended.

4. Spoon this into the prebaked pie shell and smooth over the top. Bake for 25 minutes, or until golden brown on top. Thoroughly cool on a wire rack before serving.

menu five

puris
vegetable kofta
red lentil dal
perfect brown rice (p. 266)
orange raita
raisin chutney
kheer

Here is a menu that will fascinate your guests with its beauty, symmetry, and exotic character. Indians are very much concerned with achieving a balance of flavor, texture, and color in their splendidly laid out meals. In India all of the courses are brought out at once and placed on the table in numerous attractive serving bowls and plates, and guests take a portion of each dish—including the dessert, which is called a "sweet"—and arrange them around their plates with rice mounded in the center (if it is being served). Then they proceed to eat (with their fingers), alternating among the spicy, sweet, bland, bitter, and soothing dishes.

I like to serve this menu in a similar fashion, although I still cling to the Western customs of eating with utensils and serving the dessert at the end of the meal. I always serve beer with Indian food, and to those who prefer something else I offer sparkling water on ice with lemon or lime wedges. Fine dry red or white wines do not go well with spicy food because they accentuate the hotness rather than soothe the palate.

Everything can be prepared in advance except the Puris, which require last minute attention. So take advantage of the do-ahead suggestions and make this a relaxed affair.

puris
(deep-fried puffed bread)

Once cooked, these flaky breads must be served immediately, which means that you'll be at the stove while everyone else is seated at the table. This works out all right for Indian women because they usually don't eat with the men, but in our case it is a change of routine. It actually isn't too troublesome because Puris take only a few minutes to cook, and if you are well organized you can do it with great aplomb. The method of making the dough for Puris is the same as that for tortillas, samosas, and Mandarin Pancakes, though Puris are cooked differently. Once you discover how easy it is to handle the dough, you'll want to try all of these breads.

makes twelve 5-inch breads

2 cups whole wheat flour
1/2 teaspoon salt
3 tablespoons Ghee (p. 272) or oil

3/4 cup warm water
    minus 1 tablespoon
Oil for frying

1. Blend the flour and salt in a medium-size bowl. Add the ghee or oil and rub it into the flour with the tips of your fingers until it resembles a coarse, flaky meal.

2. Make a well in the center and pour in the water, then stir with a spoon until blended. Turn the dough onto a lightly floured board or work surface and knead for 7 minutes. Place the dough back in the bowl and cover with a slightly damp towel. Let rest for 30 minutes, or wrap in plastic and chill overnight. Bring to room temperature before rolling.

3. Divide the dough in half, roll each half into a cylinder, then cut each cylinder into 6 even-size pieces. Roll a piece of the dough into a ball between your hands, then flatten it into a disk. With a rolling pin roll the disk on a lightly floured surface into a 5-inch circle, turning the dough as necessary to keep the circle evenly round. Lightly flour the work surface as necessary. Repeat with the remaining dough and unevenly stack the Puris as you go along, then cover with a slightly damp towel.

4. Pour enough oil into a medium-size skillet to reach a depth of 2 inches, and heat over medium heat until hot but not smoking. To test if the oil is hot enough drop a tiny piece of dough into it; it should sizzle immediately and rise to the surface. Slide one Puri into the oil and press it down with a slotted spatula to keep it below the surface. It will immediately begin to puff up. Cook for 30 seconds, then turn over and cook another 30 seconds, or until lightly golden. Drain on paper towels and serve immediately, or you can keep them in a 250-degree oven for the few minutes it takes you to finish the batch.

note:
Do not be surprised if all of the Puris don't puff up perfectly. Sometimes that happens, but they are still delicious. If *many* of them don't puff up then perhaps they are not evenly round, or perhaps they have been rolled larger than 5 inches. In either case, form the uncooked dough into a ball again and reroll into a circle.

vegetable kofta

These fried Indian vegetable balls in a fragrant coconut sauce are one of the most delectable Indian dishes.

serves 4–6

10-ounce package fresh spinach, or 1 pound
   loose spinach, or 10-ounce package
   frozen chopped spinach, thawed
2 large potatoes, peeled, boiled, and mashed
2 medium-size carrots, finely diced and cooked
1 tablespoon whole wheat flour
1 tablespoon ground coriander
1/2 teaspoon turmeric
1/4 teaspoon ground cumin
1/4 teaspoon cayenne pepper
2 teaspoons sugar
3/4 teaspoon salt
2 eggs, lightly beaten
1 1/2 cups bread crumbs
   (preferably whole wheat, p. 278)
Oil for frying

sauce:
1/4 cup Ghee (p. 272) or butter
1 medium-size onion, minced
1 1/2 teaspoons minced gingerroot
1 cinnamon stick
1 bay leaf
1/2 teaspoon ground cardamom
1/2 teaspoon turmeric
1 1/2 teaspoons ground coriander
1 1/2 teaspoons ground cumin
1/4 teaspoon cayenne pepper
1 large tomato, peeled, seeded,
   and chopped G
2 1/2 cups coconut milk G
1/2 teaspoon salt

1. Wash the fresh spinach by dunking it in a pot of cold water. Drain off the water and repeat until there is no sandy residue. Remove the stems from the spinach and discard.

2. Put the spinach in a large pot with just the water that clings to it. Cook just until wilted. When cool, squeeze out *all* of the moisture in the spinach with your hands. Mince it. (If you are using frozen spinach, when thoroughly defrosted, squeeze out *all* of the moisture with your hands. Mince.)

3. To make the koftas: Combine the spinach, mashed potatoes, cooked carrots, flour, and all of the flavorings (up to the eggs) in a large bowl and mix well.

4. Put the beaten eggs and bread crumbs in separate bowls and place them in front of you. One by one form the mixture into 1 1/2-inch balls, then roll in the eggs, then the bread crumbs.

5. Pour enough oil into a large skillet to reach 1/2 inch up the sides of the pan. Heat the oil over medium heat until hot but not smoking. Fry the balls, turning them often, until they are golden brown and very crisp on the outside. Drain on paper towels and set aside. Discard the oil.

6. To make the sauce: In the same skillet heat the ghee. When hot add the onion and all of the spices, and sauté for 2 minutes.

vegetable kofta (continued)

7. Add the tomato and stir to blend. Add the coconut milk and salt, stir, and boil the mixture for 3 minutes. *May be prepared in advance to this point; cook within 8 hours. Chill the sauce and koftas separately.*

8. Preheat the oven to 350 degrees. Place the koftas in a shallow baking dish (a 10-by-10-inch dish works well) and pour the sauce over them. Cover and bake for 20 minutes. Alternatively, add the koftas to the sauce in the skillet and cook together, covered, on top of the stove for 20 minutes, or until the sauce has thickened.

red lentil dal

Dal is a thick saucelike mixture of puréed lentils or split peas and spices. It is usually served on rice and is the protein component of an Indian vegetarian meal. I think that red lentils make the most delicious dal. When cooked, they turn a rich golden color, and have a buttery, nutlike flavor.

serves 4–6

1 1/4 cups red lentils*
3 cups water
1/2 teaspoon salt
2 tablespoons Ghee (p. 272) or oil
1/4 teaspoon black mustard seeds**
1/4 teaspoon turmeric
1/4 teaspoon cayenne pepper
1/4 teaspoon ground cumin

1/4 teaspoon ground coriander
1/2 teaspoon minced gingerroot
Thin lemon slice for garnish

*Red lentils are available at health food stores and Indian food shops.
**Black mustard seeds can also be purchased in Indian food shops and some health food stores. They have a milder and nuttier flavor than yellow mustard seeds. Omit them if you cannot get them.

1. Rinse the lentils in a sieve under cold running water. Pick out any stones or foreign substances. Put the lentils in a medium-size saucepan along with the water and salt. Cook, uncovered, over medium-low heat for about 25 minutes, or until the lentils are almost completely smooth.

2. Heat the ghee or oil in a separate small skillet over medium heat and add the mustard seeds. After the seeds have stopped popping and spattering add all the spices and stir. Cook 1 minute. Very carefully add this mixture to the dal. Stir, then simmer the dal 2 minutes more. (If you used oil to cook the spices, then stir in 1 tablespoon of butter.) *May be prepared to this point up to 24 hours in advance. Cover and chill. Reheat over low heat.* Scrape the dal into a warm serving dish and garnish with lemon slices.

orange raita

Raitas are the "salad" component of an Indian meal. Their cool, refreshing character serves to contrast with the spiciness of many dishes.

serves 4–6

    1 large seedless navel orange
    1 1/2 cups yogurt (preferably low-fat)
    1/2 teaspoon ground cumin
    1/4 teaspoon salt

1. Wash the orange and dry very well. Grate half of the orange peel on the fine side of a grater. Put *half* of the grated rind into a medium-size bowl. Set aside the remaining grated rind for garnish.

2. Cut away the remaining peel and pith from the orange with a small, sharp knife and discard. Over a bowl, holding the orange in one hand, with the knife cut away each segment of fruit from the membrane on either side; the sections will fall out easily. Cut each segment in half.

3. Put half of the slices in the bowl and mash lightly to release their juice. Add the remaining orange pieces and mix.

4. Stir in the yogurt, ground cumin, and salt. Pour into a serving dish and garnish with the reserved orange rind. Cover and chill for at least 1 hour or up to 2 hours before serving.

---

raisin chutney

This is my favorite chutney. It has an intense flavor — both sweet and spicy. It can be made well in advance and would make a wonderful gift for a chutney lover.

serves 4–6

    1 cup raisins
    2 teaspoons minced gingerroot
    1/4 cup water
    Dash cayenne pepper
    1/2 teaspoon salt
    Juice of 1/2 lemon

1. Place all the ingredients in the container of a blender or food processor and blend until you have a coarse paste. You will probably have to turn off the machine and scrape down the sides a few times.

2. Scrape into a container with a tight cover. This will keep for up to 2 weeks in the refrigerator.

kheer
(rice, almond, and cardamom pudding)

This creamy pudding, fragrant with cardamom, adds a nice balance to a spicy Indian meal. It is rich; therefore, small portions will be very satisfying. Although it is simple to prepare it does demand a lot of stirring; so read a book, or prepare other parts of your meal while you are tending to this task.

serves 6

5 cups milk
1/4 cup white rice
   (preferably converted rice)
1/3 cup honey
1/4 cup chopped almonds, toasted
1/3 cup raisins

1/4 teaspoon ground cardamom
1/2 teaspoon rosewater (optional)*
Chopped almonds for garnish

*Rosewater can be purchased at specialty food shops and some pharmacies.

1. Bring the milk to a boil in a heavy-bottomed medium-size saucepan. Stir frequently to prevent a skin from forming. Reduce the heat to medium and cook the milk at a lively simmer for 15 minutes, stirring often.

2. Add the rice and continue to cook over medium heat for 30 more minutes, or until the rice is very soft. You must continue to stir frequently to prevent the mixture from overflowing or sticking to the bottom. If any skin forms, remove and discard it.

3. Add the honey, almonds, raisins, and cardamom. Cook 5 more minutes, or until the pudding is thick enough to lightly coat a spoon. (It gets very thick when chilled.)

4. Remove from the heat and stir in the rosewater. Pour the mixture into a large bowl or shallow pan (for quick cooling), cover with foil or plastic wrap, and chill at least 1 hour or up to 24 hours. Stir occasionally to prevent a skin from forming.

5. Serve in goblets or custard cups and garnish with some chopped almonds.

menu six

three-layered vegetable pâté
with herb mayonnaise
skillet tofu and vegetables
in brandy cream sauce
brussels sprouts with
lemon soy glaze
fine egg noodles
with light garlic sauce (p. 5)
mocha walnut torte

The pâté and the torte can be made up to a few days in advance, so this very impressive menu need not turn away timid or busy cooks by its luxuriousness. You can cook the noodles in advance and reheat them. All that will require last minute attention will be the tofu dish and the Brussels sprouts—neither of which is taxing.

three-layered vegetable pâté
with herb mayonnaise

Here is a delicious and stunning pâté made up of layers of carrot purée, minced leeks, and minced spinach. It is not as complicated to prepare as it appears, and a little goes a long way. I like to simplify the preparation by cooking the vegetables on one day and assembling the pâté on the next day. Whichever way you choose to do it, this beautiful pâté is well worth the effort. In addition to serving it as an appetizer, I also like to serve it for lunch along with a cup of soup and a well-made crusty bread, either homemade or store-bought. Read about purchasing spinach under Spinach Custard Ring with Tomato Cream Sauce (p. 150).

three-layered vegetable pâté (continued)

makes 1 large loaf

carrot layer:
1 pound carrots (9 medium-size),
    thinly sliced
2 eggs
1/4 cup heavy or whipping cream
1 tablespoon honey
1/2 teaspoon ground coriander
1/8 teaspoon cinnamon
1/2 teaspoon salt
Liberal seasoning freshly ground pepper
1/2 cup bread crumbs

leek layer:
4 medium-large leeks
    (with 2 inches of green top)
2 tablespoons butter
2 eggs
1/4 cup bread crumbs
1/4 cup heavy or whipping cream
1/2 teaspoon salt
Liberal seasoning freshly ground pepper

spinach layer:
2 pounds loose fresh spinach (weight with
    stems), or two 10-ounce packages
    fresh spinach, or two 10-ounce
    packages frozen chopped spinach
2 eggs
1/2 cup heavy or whipping cream
1/4 cup bread crumbs
1/4 cup grated Parmesan cheese
1 tablespoon minced fresh basil,
    or 1 teaspoon dried basil
1/2 teaspoon salt
A few dashes cayenne pepper

herb mayonnaise:
1 cup mayonnaise
    (preferably homemade, p. 269)
3/4 cup yogurt (preferably low-fat)
1/4 cup minced fresh parsley
1/2 teaspoon mixed herbs (I like crushed
    fennel seed, basil, thyme, and tarragon)
Freshly ground pepper to taste

Parsley sprigs for garnish

1. Butter a 1 1/2-quart loaf pan and line with wax paper. Butter the wax paper.

2. Cook (preferably steam) the carrots until very tender, then drain thoroughly. Purée them in a blender or food processor along with the eggs, cream, honey, coriander, cinnamon, salt, and pepper until very smooth. Stir in the bread crumbs, then spoon into the loaf pan and smooth over the top.

3. Cut the roots off the leeks and cut off all but 2 inches of the top green part. Slit each one length-wise almost all the way through to the other side, then open each leek and thoroughly rinse under cold running water to rid them of all of their dirt. Finger through the leaves to find hidden dirt. Pat dry and then thinly slice; you need 6 cups sliced.

4. In a large skillet melt the butter and sauté the leeks for 10 minutes, or until tender. Beat the eggs in a medium-size bowl, then add the leeks, bread crumbs, cream, salt, and pepper, and mix well. Spoon this mixture over the carrot layer, then smooth over the top.

5. Remove all of the stems from the fresh spinach, then dunk the leaves in a large pot of cold water to rid them of all their dirt. Lift the leaves out of the water and repeat the procedure until the water in the bottom of the basin is free of any dirt. Put the spinach in a large pot with just the water that clings to it, and cook until it wilts. Drain in a colander and let sit until cool enough to handle. Squeeze the spinach in your hands until *all* of the liquid is removed. (If you are using frozen spinach then either let it thaw completely and squeeze dry, or cook until thawed and squeeze dry.) Mince the spinach very fine (do not purée it).

6. Beat the eggs in a medium-size bowl, then add the spinach, cream, bread crumbs, Parmesan cheese, basil, salt, and cayenne pepper, and mix well. Spoon this mixture over the leek mixture and smooth over the top.

7. Preheat the oven to 350 degrees. Cover the top of the pâté with a sheet of buttered wax paper, then cover that with a sheet of foil. Place the loaf in a larger baking pan, and pour in enough hot water to reach halfway up the sides of the loaf pan. Bake for 1 1/2 hours, or until a knife inserted in the center of the pâté comes out clean. Remove the loaf pan from the water bath, peel away the foil and wax paper, then cool on a wire rack for 1 hour. To unmold place a large plate or platter over the pâté and invert. Remove the loaf pan, then peel away the wax paper. Let sit for 20 minutes at room temperature, then cover with foil and chill for at least 2 hours or up to 48 hours before serving.

8. Meanwhile make the herb mayonnaise. Combine all of the ingredients (except the parsley sprigs) in a medium-size bowl and stir until well blended. Cover and chill at least 1 hour before serving to thicken and develop the flavors.

9. To serve, slice the pâté into 3/4-inch-thick slices and place each slice on a small serving plate. Spoon a few spoonfuls of herb mayonnaise next to the pâté and garnish the sauce with a sprig of parsley.

---

skillet tofu and vegetables in brandy cream sauce

I think it is unfortunate that most people first become acquainted with tofu (bean curd) in Oriental dishes where it has been simmered in a bland sauce, because the texture seems soft and unpalatable, and the flavor is nondescript. If you've never particu- larly liked tofu, try it lightly fried in oil and then seasoned well, as it is in this dish. You'll find that its crisp texture makes it very appetizing, and the tofu will have absorbed the flavors of the sauce.

serves 4

1 pound firm tofu
3 tablespoons oil
3 tablespoons butter
2 cloves garlic, minced
1 medium-size onion, finely diced
3 cups (8 ounces) sliced mushrooms
1 1/2 teaspoons flour
1 bay leaf

1 medium-size carrot, grated
1 teaspoon fresh tarragon, or 1/2 teaspoon dried tarragon, crumbled
1/4 cup brandy (or dry sherry)
1/2 cup heavy or whipping cream
1/4 teaspoon salt
Freshly ground pepper to taste
1 tablespoon minced parsley

skillet tofu and vegetables (continued)

1. Cut the tofu into 1-inch cubes and pat very dry.

2. Heat the oil in a large skillet over high heat until it is hot but not smoking. Add the tofu and sauté, tossing often, until it is golden, about 10 minutes. Remove to a platter and set aside. Discard any remaining oil.

3. Reduce the heat to medium and melt the butter. Add the garlic, onion, and mushrooms, and sauté

for 10 minutes, tossing often. Sprinkle on the flour, toss, and cook 1 more minute.

4. Reduce the heat to a simmer and add the reserved tofu and all of the remaining ingredients except the parsley. Stir to blend and simmer for 5–10 minutes, or until the sauce has thickened. Add the parsley just before serving and toss to mix. Tofu gets too firm when reheated so it is best to serve this immediately.

brussels sprouts
with lemon soy glaze

This recipe has won over many confirmed Brussels sprouts haters. I find that Brussels sprouts are infinitely more delicious and attractive if they are halved or quartered when cooked. They become more deli-

cate and are more colorful because they expose a yellow-and-white interior. Try this method even if you want to serve them plain with butter.

serves 4

1 pound Brussels sprouts
3 tablespoons butter

Juice of 1/2 lemon (about 1 1/2 tablespoons)
1 tablespoon tamari soy sauce

1. Trim off any yellow leaves from the Brussels sprouts, and cut each one in half (unless they are tiny), and cut the large ones into quarters. Steam them until tender, not mushy, about 10 minutes. They should still retain a bright green color. Remove from the steamer.

2. Melt the butter in a large skillet over medium heat, then add the Brussels sprouts and sauté for 3 minutes, tossing often. Push them to the periphery of the pan, then pour the lemon juice and soy sauce into the center. Let it boil rapidly until the liquid is reduced by half, then toss the Brussels sprouts in it and cook another minute. Serve immediately.

mocha walnut torte

This very quick torte is unusually light and smooth, with the ground walnuts being barely discernible. It is covered with my favorite icing — a heavenly chocolate cream coating — and the entire torte can be assembled up to 3 days before serving with no noticeable loss in texture or appearance.

serves 6–8

cake:
5 eggs
1 cup sugar
1 cup walnuts
1/4 cup unbleached white flour
2 1/2 teaspoons baking powder
1/8 teaspoon cinnamon

icing:
1 1/2 cups heavy or whipping cream
4 ounces semisweet chocolate, chopped
2 tablespoons sugar
1 tablespoon instant coffee

Chocolate curls for decoration (see Note)
   (I use a Baker's German's Sweet
   chocolate bar)

1. Preheat the oven to 350 degrees. Butter two 8-inch round cake pans and line the bottoms with wax paper, then butter the wax paper.

2. Blend the eggs and sugar very well in a blender or food processor. Add the walnuts and blend until they are very fine. Mix the flour with the baking powder and cinnamon, add to the batter, and blend until smooth.

3. Pour into the prepared pans and bake for 15 minutes, or until golden on top and springy to the touch. Cool on a wire rack for 5 minutes, then invert the pans and peel away the wax paper. Cool the cakes completely, about 1 hour.

4. Meanwhile make the icing. Combine the cream, chocolate, sugar, and coffee in a medium-size saucepan, and whisking steadily, bring to a boil over medium heat. Remove from the heat as soon as the mixture begins to boil and continue to whisk until the chocolate is melted. Pour into a large bowl (metal is best for quick cooling) and chill, uncovered, until ice cold, or cover and chill up to 24 hours. Occasionally stir the mixture for even cooling and to prevent hard chocolate from developing along the sides. It is a good idea to chill your beaters at this time also.

5. Whip the frosting with the chilled beaters until very stiff. To ice the torte: Spread 4 strips of wax paper around the edges of your cake plate or platter. Place the first layer top side down and adjust the wax paper so it will protect the plate from icing. Spread some icing over the top of this layer. Place the second layer on top so the bottom side is up, then spread the remaining icing over the entire torte and smooth as evenly as you can. Garnish with the chocolate curls, then remove the wax paper strips. Insert a few toothpicks into the top of the torte to prevent the icing from getting messy, then cover with plastic wrap and chill until ready to serve.

mocha walnut torte (continued)

note:
To make chocolate curls place a semisweet or bitter-sweet chocolate bar over a flame or hot electric burner for a few seconds, or just long enough to slightly warm the surface. Do not let the flame get near it. With a vegetable peeler peel off a few curls onto the top of the torte. Repeat until the torte is nicely decorated.

menu seven

hummus
tabbouleh
spanakopita
honey-glazed sugar snap peas
with carrots
banana rum roll cake

This is a good menu for a buffet; it looks very appealing, and it is easy for guests to help themselves to these dishes. The Hummus should be offered first as the appetizer, and a Greek red or white wine (such as the brand "Demestica") can be served with it for a nice touch. Because Tabbouleh is such a nutritious and substantial salad, the Honey-Glazed Sugar Snap Peas with Carrots will be sufficient to accompany the Spanakopita. Everything can be prepared in advance except the vegetable side dish, which only takes a few minutes to prepare and cook.

hummus

Hummus is a rich and exotic Middle Eastern dip or spread that is especially good served with warm pita bread triangles. For a delicious lunch, try spooning leftover hummus over sautéed vegetables that have been stuffed into pita bread.

makes about 2½ cups

1⅓ cups dried chickpeas,
    or 16-ounce can (2 cups) cooked
    chickpeas, drained, rinsed,
    and drained again
3 cloves garlic, minced
½ cup fresh lemon juice (about 3 lemons)
1 cup tahini*
1 teaspoon salt

1 cup cold water
Olive oil
Paprika

*Tahini is a sesame butter, which can be purchased in some supermarkets, specialty food shops, or Middle Eastern grocery stores. It is not the same thing as Oriental sesame paste. Tahini must be mixed well before using because the oil usually separates and rises to the surface.

1. If using dried chickpeas cook them as follows: Soak overnight covered with plenty of water, or boil for 2 minutes in a large potful of water and let sit covered for 1 hour. Drain thoroughly. Add enough water to cover by 2 inches and cook until very tender, about 1½ hours. Drain very well and chill until cool.

2. In a blender or food processor combine the chickpeas, garlic, lemon juice, tahini, and salt. Blend and slowly pour in the water. Turn off the machine and scrape down the sides as necessary. Add a tablespoon or so more of water if the hummus is too thick.

3. Pour into a serving dish, cover, and chill until ready to serve. Just before serving drizzle a little olive oil on top (don't mix) and sprinkle on some paprika. Serve with warm pita bread triangles.

tabbouleh
(bulghur wheat salad)

serves 6–8

1 1/2 cups bulghur G
2 medium-size tomatoes,
    seeded and diced
3 tablespoons minced fresh parsley
3 scallions, thinly sliced
1 teaspoon minced fresh mint (optional)

3 tablespoons lemon juice
1/2 cup olive oil
Salt to taste
Freshly ground pepper to taste
12–16 small lettuce leaves
    (not iceberg lettuce)

1. Rinse the bulghur in a sieve under cold running water. Empty it into a medium-size bowl and cover with boiling water. Let soak for 30 minutes, or until tender when tasted.

2. Line a sieve with cheesecloth and drain the bulghur into it. (This might have to be done in batches.)

Bring up the edges of the cheesecloth and squeeze to extract all of the moisture.

3. Put the bulghur into a mixing bowl and add all of the remaining ingredients except the lettuce. Toss to blend thoroughly. Cover and chill for at least 1 hour or up to 48 hours. To serve, arrange 2 lettuce leaves on each small serving plate and spoon on the tabbouleh.

spanakopita
(spinach cheese pie)

This is one classic dish that cannot be improved upon. The spinach, feta, and dill filling enclosed in crisp, buttery filo leaves is a superb marriage of flavor and texture. It is not as difficult to prepare as it seems—just follow these directions and you can't go wrong. If you are entertaining, take advantage of the fact that the pie can be prepared up to 24 hours in advance; it will be just as crisp.

serves 6–8

2 pounds loose fresh spinach (weight with
stems) or two 10-ounce packages
fresh spinach, washed and thoroughly
drained, or two 10-ounce packages
frozen chopped spinach, thawed
1/4 cup olive oil
3 medium-size onions, finely diced
1/4 cup minced fresh dill,
or 2 tablespoons dried dill weed

3/4 teaspoon salt
Freshly ground pepper to taste
1/3 cup milk
1/4 pound feta cheese, finely crumbled
1 cup small curd cottage cheese
4 eggs, well beaten
1 cup (2 sticks) butter, melted
16 sheets filo (about 3/4 pound),
each 12 inches by 16 inches

1. If using fresh spinach remove the stems and discard. Cook the leaves, covered, in a large skillet with just the water that clings to them (when washed) until the spinach is completely wilted. Put it in a strainer, press out *all* of the liquid with the back of a spoon, and chop the spinach on a cutting board until minced. If using frozen spinach, squeeze it dry to remove *all* the moisture.

2. In a large skillet heat the olive oil over medium heat until hot but not smoking. Add the onions and cook until golden, about 5 minutes, then add the cooked spinach and heat through.

3. Add the dill, salt, and a liberal seasoning of freshly ground pepper, and cook, stirring often, until all of the liquid has evaporated and the spinach has begun to stick to the pan, about 3 minutes.

4. Scrape the mixture into a large bowl and stir in the milk. Cool to room temperature. Add the feta cheese, cottage cheese, and eggs, and mix well.

5. Preheat the oven to 300 degrees. With a pastry brush coat the sides and bottom of a 12-by-7-by-2-inch rectangular baking dish with some of the melted butter. Line the dish with a sheet of the filo dough and press it firmly into the corners and sides of the dish. There will be some overlap.

6. Brush the entire surface of the filo dough with a little of the melted butter (don't drench it), then lay another sheet of filo on top. Brush this layer with some melted butter and continue this procedure until 8 sheets have been used.

7. With a rubber spatula spread the spinach mixture evenly over the top layer of the dough. Place another layer of filo over the spinach mixture, coat it with some melted butter, and repeat this procedure until the remaining 8 sheets have been used on top.

8. With scissors or a small sharp knife trim the edges of the filo close to the pie (leave 1/4-inch rim around it) and brush the top layer of the filo with the remaining melted butter. Make shallow cuts through the first few layers to mark off where you will cut at serving time. (This prevents the top layer from flaking too much afterward.) *May be prepared to this point, covered, and chilled up to 24 hours in advance.*

9. Bake for 1 hour, or until the pastry is evenly golden and crisp. It is best to let the pie sit for 30 minutes or so before serving, for, like quiche, it is more flavorful and has a better texture when served warm rather than hot. To serve cut into squares. Leftover Spanakopita is great reheated and served as an appetizer, and it is also delicious served room temperature at a picnic.

honey-glazed sugar snap peas with carrots

Sugar snap peas look just like fresh peas in their pods, but they are slightly smaller and more tender, so you can eat the whole thing—pod and all. They are sweet and tasty and are also delicious served raw—try them on your next crudités platter. If you cannot get them, then try this dish with snow peas; they also make a wonderful side vegetable. Snow peas take less time to cook than sugar snaps so if you are using them, cook them for only 3 minutes along with the final cooking of the carrots.

serves 6–8

1 1/2 pounds sugar snap peas
4 medium-size carrots, peeled

4 tablespoons butter
1 1/2 tablespoons honey

1. Rinse the sugar snap peas under cold water and pat very dry. String them by grasping the top stem end and pulling down toward the *flat* side of the pea. This will string both sides at once. Cut the carrots crosswise into thirds. Cut each third into quarters vertically so that they resemble the shape of the sugar snap peas.

2. Bring about 1 inch of water to a boil in a large skillet. Add the carrots and cook, covered, for 3–5 minutes, or until they are tender yet still a little crisp. Drain thoroughly and dry the pan.

3. In the same skillet melt the butter over medium heat. Sauté the sugar snap peas for 5 minutes, stirring frequently, then add the carrots and cook 3 more minutes, or until the peas are tender yet still crisp and bright green. Drizzle on the honey and stir to coat. Cook for 1 minute, stirring constantly. Serve immediately.

banana rum roll cake

This cake is made like a jelly roll—in this case a banana sponge cake is spread with a filling of rum-flavored whipped cream and sliced bananas, and is then rolled and dusted with powdered sugar. Don't be apprehensive about trying this, it isn't difficult at all; in fact, it's fun to do and it makes an impressive, delicious dessert. I recommend presenting the cake on the most attractive platter you have, and even surrounding it with a few loose flowers if they are in season.

serves 8

4 eggs, separated
1 cup sugar
1 teaspoon vanilla extract
1 medium-size ripe banana, mashed
Pinch salt
2/3 cup unbleached white flour
2 tablespoons cornstarch

filling:
2 medium-size ripe bananas
2 teaspoons lemon juice
1 cup heavy or whipping cream, well chilled
1/3 cup powdered (confectioners') sugar
1/4 cup rum, light or dark
Powdered (confectioners') sugar to coat

1. Preheat the oven to 375 degrees. Butter a 10½-by-15½-inch jelly roll pan and line it with wax paper. Butter the wax paper and set the pan aside.

2. Beat the egg yolks with ½ cup of the sugar in a large bowl until very pale and thick. Add the vanilla and mashed banana, and beat until blended.

3. Clean the beaters very well and dry thoroughly. In a separate large bowl beat the egg whites with the salt until soft peaks form. (The egg whites will beat better if they are slightly warm.) Add the remaining ½ cup of sugar and beat until they are stiff and glossy.

4. Sift the flour with the cornstarch (on a sheet of wax paper is a good idea). Add the egg whites to the yolks and sprinkle on the flour mixture. With a rubber spatula gently fold the mixtures together until blended. Use a light hand—you want the batter to be blended but you don't want the egg whites to deflate.

5. Scrape the batter into the prepared pan and spread very evenly. Bake for 12 minutes, or until a cake tester inserted in the center comes out clean. Cool on a wire rack for 5 minutes.

6. Meanwhile, lightly dust a cotton or linen kitchen towel with powdered sugar. Invert the cake onto it and remove the pan. Peel away the wax paper. Roll up the long side of the cake with the towel inside.

Twist the towel ends. Lay the roll on a wire rack and let cool completely, about 1 hour.

7. Meanwhile, make the filling. Slice the bananas ¼ inch thick into a medium-size bowl and toss with the lemon juice to prevent darkening.

8. In another medium-size bowl whip the cream until it begins to thicken. Add the powdered sugar and beat until stiff. Add the rum and beat again just until blended. Fold in the sliced bananas.

9. Unroll the cake. Spread the filling all over it to within 1 inch of the edges. Roll it again, but this time *without* the towel. Lay it seam side down. Put some powdered sugar in a sieve and dust it all over the roll. Slightly turn it on its sides to get at them also.

10. Diagonally cut a thin slice off each end to make the roll a neater shape. (If no one is looking eat these slices with pleasure.) Carefully place the roll on a decorative platter seam side down. Serve immediately, or insert toothpicks on the top and cover with plastic wrap. Chill. If by the time you are ready to serve it the powdered sugar has melted into the cake, lay a few sheets of wax paper around the platter and dust the cake lightly with more powdered sugar. Remove the wax paper (of course) and toothpicks. Serve sliced on the diagonal.

menu eight

arugula and boston lettuce salad (p. 84)
noodle timbales with pesto cream sauce
zucchini, red pepper, and snow pea sauté
raspberry almond torte

Here is a luscious combination of superb dishes, which are very harmonious together. Because the timbales are so rich, I like to serve them with a light accompaniment such as this Zucchini, Red Pepper, and Snow Pea Sauté. A nice dry red wine would be particularly good with the timbales and their garlic-scented sauce.

noodle timbales with pesto cream sauce

Timbales are little custards that are so named because their shape resembles a kettledrum—*timbale* in French. These noodle timbales are especially rich and luscious, and need only a salad and side vegetable as accompaniments. They are virtually foolproof and reheat very well.

serves 4

2 cups (2 ounces) fine egg noodles
6 eggs, well beaten
1/2 cup heavy or whipping cream
1/3 cup milk
1/2 cup grated Parmesan cheese
1/4 teaspoon salt
Freshly ground pepper to taste

sauce:
2/3 cup Pesto (p. 270) or
　Winter Pesto (p. 271)
1/3 cup heavy or whipping cream

1. Fill a medium-size saucepan with water and bring it to a boil. Add the noodles and cook until al dente—that is, tender yet slightly firm to the bite. Drain very well, then put in a large bowl and cool slightly.

2. Add the beaten eggs, cream, milk, Parmesan cheese, salt, and pepper, and mix well. *May be prepared to this point up to 8 hours in advance, covered, and refrigerated.*

3. Preheat the oven to 375 degrees. Butter eight 1-cup custard cups or small soufflé dishes and fill evenly with the mixture. (Smaller cups can be used but be sure to adjust the cooking time accordingly.) Place the custard cups in a large baking dish and fill the dish with enough hot water to reach one-third up the sides of the cups. (This bain-marie ensures gentle, moist cooking and is essential.) Bake for 20–25 minutes, or until a knife inserted in the center of one comes out clean.

4. Meanwhile, make the sauce. Combine the pesto and cream in a small saucepan and heat over low heat until piping hot, stirring constantly.

5. Remove the cups from the baking dish, and loosen the timbales by inserting a knife around the edges. Invert them onto a platter (or dry the baking dish they were in and use that if it is suitable), and spoon the sauce over them. Serve immediately.

note:
If you are not going to serve all of the timbales at one sitting, you can keep them in the cups and they will reheat very well the next day. Place them in a saucepan with about an inch of water, cover the pan, and heat over medium heat until hot throughout, about 10–15 minutes.

zucchini, red pepper, and snow pea sauté

serves 4

2 small to medium zucchini
2 large red bell peppers
1/4 pound fresh snow peas
2 tablespoons butter

1 tablespoon oil
1 teaspoon tamari soy sauce
Juice of 1/2 lemon

1. Wash the zucchini and pat dry. Cut the ends off and slice in half lengthwise. Cut each half lengthwise again and slice into 1/2-inch-thick slices.

2. Wash and dry the red peppers. Core them and remove all the seeds. Cut into strips 1 inch wide, then cut the strips into 1-inch squares. The point is to have the vegetables approximately the same shape.

3. String each snow pea by grasping its stem and pulling down until the string is released. Cut the snow peas into thirds or about 1 inch wide.

4. Heat 1 tablespoon of the butter and the oil in a large skillet over medium-high heat until hot. Add the zucchini and sauté for 2 minutes, stirring frequently.

zucchini, red pepper, and snow pea sauté (continued)

5. Add the red peppers and cook 3 minutes, stirring frequently.

6. Add the snow peas and toss. Mix the soy sauce with the lemon juice and add to the vegetables. Cook for 1–2 minutes, or just until the snow peas are heated through and the liquid is absorbed. (Do not overcook the vegetables; they should be crunchy.)

7. Remove the pan from the heat. Cut the remaining tablespoon of butter into bits and add. Stir until blended and serve immediately.

note:
This dish should be cooked just before serving, but the vegetables can be cut up the day before.

raspberry almond torte

Tortes are cakes made with ground nuts or bread crumbs and little or no flour, and they are usually only about 2 inches high. But there are many exceptions to this definition, and tortes look very different from one another. Unlike the Mocha Walnut Torte (p. 163), which is very light and delicate, this torte has a delightful and distinct nutty texture, and is filled with a layer of raspberry preserves, then covered with whipped cream. Serve it with a demitasse of piping hot espresso for a spectacular combination.

serves 6–8

torte:
5 eggs, separated
1 teaspoon vanilla extract
1 cup sugar
1 teaspoon baking powder
1 cup bread crumbs
2 cups (9 ounces) ground almonds*
1/8 teaspoon salt

icing:
1 cup heavy or whipping cream, well chilled
2 tablespoons sugar

1/4 teaspoon almond extract
2/3 cup raspberry preserves
1 tablespoon lemon juice

Chocolate curls for decoration** (I use a bar of Baker's German's Sweet chocolate)

*Grind the almonds—a handful at a time—in a blender or food processor, and spoon into a measuring cup. Do not pack.
**To make chocolate curls place a semisweet or bittersweet chocolate bar over a flame or hot electric burner for a few seconds, or just long enough to slightly warm the surface. Do not let the flame get near it. With a vegetable peeler shave off curls onto the top of the torte until the cake is nicely decorated.

1. Preheat the oven to 325 degrees. Butter two 8-inch round cake pans and line the bottoms with wax paper, then butter the wax paper.

2. With an electric beater beat together the egg yolks, vanilla, and sugar in a large bowl until very pale and thick.

3. Mix the baking powder with the bread crumbs and add to the egg mixture along with the almonds. Beat until blended; it will be very thick and crumbly. After beating use a knife to break up the clumps into small pieces.

4. Clean the beaters thoroughly. In a separate large bowl beat the egg whites until they begin to foam. Add the salt, then beat until they are stiff but not dry. (They will beat better if they are warm or at room temperature.)

5. Stir one-third of the egg whites into the almond mixture to lighten the batter, then fold in the remaining egg whites with a rubber spatula until evenly blended. The batter will look somewhat clumpy.

6. Scrape into the prepared pans and smooth the tops. Bake for 25 minutes, or until lightly golden and springy to the touch. The cakes should also have begun to shrink from the sides of the pans. Cool on wire racks for 10 minutes, then invert and peel away the wax paper. Cool thoroughly, about 1 hour.

7. Meanwhile, whip the cream with the sugar and almond extract until very stiff. To assemble the torte place one layer top side down on a plate. Mix the raspberry preserves with the lemon juice and spread on evenly to within 1/2 inch of the edge. Top with the other layer top side down. Spread all over with the whipped cream and smooth it on evenly. Garnish with the chocolate curls.

menu nine

guacamole
black bean and cream cheese enchiladas
sautéed greens with garlic (p. 51)
sangría (p. 52)
pear tart with almond nut crust

This is a great menu for a party. Everything can be easily doubled and all can be made in advance. For a special addition, you could serve with the tart mugs of hot coffee mixed with Kahlua (or another liqueur of your choice) and topped with whipped cream and a dash of cinnamon.

guacamole

This dip deserves the current popularity that it has gained. Though it's delicious served with crackers or crudités, I think it's even more appetizing when served with corn chips.

2 ripe avocados (preferably the black
   pebbled-skin variety)
Juice of 1/2 lemon or lime
1 tomato, seeded and minced
1 tablespoon minced onion
2 tablespoons sour cream
Salt to taste

1/2 jalapeño pepper, seeded and minced,[G]
   or Tabasco to taste
Lemon slice, lime slice,
   or tomato wedges for garnish

[G] See Glossary of Ingredients about handling chilies.

1. Slice the avocados in half vertically and remove the pit. Insert the handle of a spoon between the skin and the flesh and move it around to separate them.

2. In a medium-size bowl mash the avocado with a fork until smooth. Add all of the remaining ingredients (except the garnish) and mix. Cover and chill for at least 1 hour.

3. Spoon into a serving dish and add the garnish of your choice.

black bean and cream cheese enchiladas

When I want a hearty, stick-to-the-ribs dish I make these luscious enchiladas. Delicate wheat tortillas are filled with black beans and cream cheese and rolled, then topped with a flavorful tomato chili sauce and baked until bubbly.

serves 4

1 1/2 cups (9 ounces)
   dried black beans

2 medium-size onions, diced
2 cloves garlic, minced

1 teaspoon oregano
1 teaspoon ground cumin
2 bay leaves
1/2 teaspoon salt
Freshly ground pepper to taste

sauce:
1/4 cup olive oil
2 medium-size onions, diced
2 cloves garlic, minced
28-ounce can imported plum tomatoes,
    finely chopped with all their liquid
1/4 cup tomato paste
1/3 cup water

1 small can (4 ounces) mild green
    chilies, drained and finely diced
1 large jalapeño pepper (fresh, pickled,
    or canned), seeded and minced G

8 Wheat Tortillas (p. 277), or store-bought
    wheat tortillas (10 if they are 6-inch)
8 ounces cream cheese, cut into 8
    (or 10) slices
1 1/2 cups (6 ounces) grated
    Monterey jack cheese

G See Glossary of Ingredients about handling chilies.

1. Rinse the beans in a colander or strainer under cold running water. Pick out any stones, etc. Put the beans in a medium-size saucepan and cover with water plus 2 inches. Cover the pan, bring to a boil, and cook for 2 minutes. Turn off the heat and let the beans soak for 1 hour.

2. Drain the beans very well by tilting the pan to its side with the cover ajar. Pour in just enough water barely to cover the beans, and add the onions, garlic, oregano, cumin, bay leaves, salt, and pepper. Cover the pan, bring to a boil, then reduce the heat to a simmer. Cook the beans until they are tender, about 1 hour, stirring occasionally. (Note: The point is to have the beans absorb *most* of the liquid by the time they are done so that they have a thick saucelike consistency. If they aren't done and more water is needed, add just a little and check the beans again when most of it is absorbed. The beans should still retain their shape when they are done.) Discard the bay leaves.

3. Mash about one-quarter of the beans against the sides of the pot and stir to blend them. Set aside to cool.

4. To make the sauce: In a large skillet heat the olive oil. Add the onions and garlic and cook over medium heat for 10 minutes, or until tender and limp, stirring often. Add the chopped tomatoes and all their juice, tomato paste, water, chilies, and jalapeño pepper, and stir to blend. Cook for 5 minutes, or until the sauce has thickened. *May be prepared to this point up to 24 hours in advance. Cover and chill the sauce and beans separately.*

5. Preheat the oven to 350 degrees. To assemble the enchiladas: Spoon a little of the sauce into the bottom of a large baking dish or 2 medium-size dishes. Place a tortilla on your work surface and spoon about 2 tablespoons of the bean mixture down the center. (It is good to divide the filling beforehand.) Cut a slice of the cream cheese into 2 or 3 pieces and place on top of the beans. Roll the tortilla and place seam side down in the baking dish. Repeat with the remaining tortillas.

6. Spread the sauce evenly over the enchiladas. Top each enchilada lengthwise with some of the grated cheese. This helps to identify the enchiladas when you are dishing them out. *May be prepared to this point up to 2 hours in advance. Keep covered to prevent the tortillas from drying out.* Bake for 20–25 minutes, or until hot and bubbly.

pear tart with almond nut crust

I especially like this tart because it is not too rich, and the fruitiness of the filling is very pronounced. Any ripe pears will do, but I find that Boscs are particularly sweet and juicy.

makes one 10-inch tart

1 recipe Almond Nut Crust (p. 277)
7 ripe but slightly firm pears, peeled, cored, and vertically sliced
2 tablespoons unbleached white flour
¼ cup honey

glaze:
⅓ cup apricot preserves
1 teaspoon water

1. To prebake the crust: Preheat the oven to 400 degrees. Cover the crust with aluminum foil and press it into the sides. Line the crust with dried beans to weight it down. Bake for 10 minutes. Remove from the oven and remove the foil and beans. (Save the beans for future use.) Reset the oven to 350 degrees.

2. Meanwhile in a large bowl toss the pear slices with the flour. Add the honey and toss again very well. Turn the pear filling into the crust and smooth over the top.

3. When the oven is at 350 degrees bake the tart for 25 minutes.

4. Meanwhile heat the preserves and water together until the mixture begins to boil. Pour into a strainer and press through into a small bowl.

5. Spread the glaze over the tart and return it to the oven to bake 10 more minutes. Cool thoroughly on a wire rack before serving.

menu ten

deep-fried cheese-filled polenta balls
tofu francese with artichoke hearts
rutabaga gratin
perfect brown rice pilaf (p. 266)
poached honey pears topped with ginger custard

Organization is important in putting together this menu. You could make the polenta mixture, the pilaf, the gratin (up to step 4), and the custard the day before. Frying the polenta balls and cooking the tofu will require your full attention just before mealtime, but they can be relatively trouble-free if you have everything else in order.

---

deep-fried cheese-filled polenta balls

This is a sumptuous appetizer that is richly varied in texture, with a crispy coating on the outside, light and moist polenta within, and a creamy center of melted cheese. I like to serve these with a nice dry red or white wine before dinner so they can be relished on their own.

makes 12 balls

1 1/2 cups water
1/2 cup cornmeal
1 egg, beaten
1/2 cup grated Parmesan cheese
1/4 cup plus 2 tablespoons unbleached
  white flour

1/4 teaspoon salt
3 ounces semisoft cheese (such as Italian
  fontina, Muenster, or Monterey jack)
1/2 cup bread crumbs
  (preferably whole wheat, p. 278)
Oil for frying

deep-fried cheese-filled polenta balls (continued)

1. To make the polenta: Bring the water to a boil in a small saucepan, then very slowly add the cornmeal, beating with a wire whisk all the while. Reduce the heat to a simmer and cook, whisking constantly, until the polenta tears away from the sides of the pan, about 10 minutes. Pour onto a plate and chill until cold, about 20–30 minutes.

2. Put the polenta in a medium-size bowl and mash with a fork. Add the egg, Parmesan cheese, flour, and salt, and mix well. *May be prepared to this point up to 24 hours in advance, covered, and chilled.*

3. Cut the cheese into 12 cubes. Form the polenta mixture into balls about 1½ inches in diameter and insert a cube of cheese into the center, making sure to cover the cheese completely. This will be messy but manageable. Roll the balls in the bread crumbs to coat completely. You can let them sit at room temperature for up to 30 minutes before cooking.

4. Pour enough oil into a medium-size saucepan to reach a depth of 2 inches and heat until it is very hot but not smoking. (The best way to test if the oil is hot enough is to drop in a bread crumb; it should immediately rise to the top.) Fry 4 or 5 balls at a time, turning occasionally to brown all over. It should take about 3–4 minutes to brown them. Remove with a slotted spoon and drain on paper towels. Serve immediately.

tofu francese with artichoke hearts

The northern Italian lemon and butter sauce is a favorite of mine, and I have found that it works wonderfully with tofu. In this dish tofu is dipped in an egg batter then sautéed with artichoke hearts and served in a light lemon, butter, and white wine sauce. If you are going to serve Brown Rice Pilaf as an accompaniment, then cook the pilaf in advance and keep it warm in the oven while you prepare this.

serves 4

1 pound firm tofu
⅓ cup unbleached white flour
1 egg, beaten
Oil for frying
4 tablespoons butter
14-ounce can artichoke hearts,
    drained and quartered

Juice of 1 lemon
½ cup dry white wine
Freshly ground pepper to taste
4 thin slices lemon for garnish
4 parsley sprigs for garnish

1. Set all of the ingredients before you to ensure relaxed cooking. Slice the tofu into rectangular slices about 2 1/2 inches long by 2 inches wide by 1/4 inch thick—no thicker. Pat thoroughly dry with paper or cotton towels. Put the flour in one small bowl and the beaten egg in another. One by one dip the tofu slices into the flour to coat them completely, and lay them on a platter in front of you.

2. Pour enough oil into a large skillet to reach 1/4-inch depth and heat it over medium-high heat until it is hot but not smoking. One by one dip a few slices of tofu into the beaten egg, then place them carefully in the hot skillet. Fry on both sides until golden brown. Remove and set aside on a platter covered with paper towels. Repeat with the remaining tofu.

3. Pour any remaining oil out of the skillet. Melt the butter, then sauté the quartered artichokes 3–5 minutes, or until they are heated through. Add the lemon juice, wine, and pepper, and bring to a simmer. Add the tofu and spoon some sauce over it. Cook, basting occasionally, 3–5 minutes more, or until the sauce has thickened slightly and the tofu is hot. Serve immediately and garnish each serving with a lemon slice and parsley sprig.

rutabaga / yellow turnip gratin

Rutabagas are the large yellow-fleshed root vegetables that are usually waxed, and are oftentimes called "yellow turnips." Actually, turnips are small and white-fleshed, and they have purple tops. I prefer rutabagas for their stronger, spicier flavor. Here is my favorite way of preparing them, which makes the most luscious side vegetable dish I know of. They are grated and sautéed, then baked with heavy cream and topped with a crisp crust.

serves 4 as a side dish

1 small to medium rutabaga
　　(about 1 1/2 pounds)
1 large carrot
3 tablespoons butter
Salt to taste

Freshly ground pepper to taste
1 cup heavy cream
1/4 cup bread crumbs
　　(preferably whole wheat, p. 278)

1. Peel the rutabaga with a vegetable peeler or a paring knife and cut it into chunks. Grate it on a grater or shred it in a food processor. You should have 7–8 cups grated. Peel and grate the carrot.

2. Melt 2 tablespoons of the butter in a large skillet over medium-high heat. Add the rutabaga and carrot and sauté for exactly 10 minutes, stirring regularly. Do not brown.

rutabaga gratin (continued)

3. Preheat the oven to 375 degrees. Scrape the mixture into a medium-size shallow baking dish and season with the salt and pepper. *May be prepared to this point up to 24 hours in advance, covered, and refrigerated. Bring to room temperature before proceeding with the next step.*

4. Pour on the heavy cream, coating as much of the mixture as possible. Sprinkle on the bread crumbs and dot with the remaining tablespoon of butter. Bake for 20–25 minutes, or until the cream is thickened and mostly, not completely, absorbed. Serve immediately.

poached honey pears topped with ginger custard

This variation of the classic French dessert combines the sweet succulence of pears with a rich, ginger-laced custard. It is not difficult to make, nor does it take much time, yet it bears a simple elegance.

serves 4

> 4 large pears, ripe but still slightly firm
>   (preferably Bosc, Anjou, or Comice)
> 1/3 cup honey
> 1/4 cup water
>
> custard:
> 1 1/2 cups milk
> 4 egg yolks
> 1/4 cup honey
> 2 tablespoons cornstarch
> 1 1/2 tablespoons pear brandy,
>   or 1 teaspoon vanilla extract
> 2 tablespoons minced crystallized ginger

1. Peel the pears and cut them in half vertically through the center. Carefully cut out the cores and the remaining stems.

2. In a large skillet mix the honey and water and bring to a boil over medium heat. Slip the pears in, flat side down, and cover the pan. Cook 5 minutes. Remove the cover, and cook uncovered for an additional 5 minutes, basting the pears frequently, or until they are tender when pierced with a skewer or cake tester. Do not overcook.

3. Remove the pears and place them in a shallow serving dish flat side up. Boil the syrup down until it is very thick and only 3 tablespoons remain. Pour onto the pears. Cover and chill until ready to serve.

4. To make the custard: In a medium-size saucepan over medium heat bring the milk almost to a boil.

5. Meanwhile in a medium-size bowl whisk the egg yolks and honey with a wire whisk until well blended. Add the cornstarch and whisk well again until perfectly smooth.

6. Slowly whisk in the hot milk, then pour the mixture into the saucepan. Over medium heat bring the mixture to a boil, whisking constantly, and boil 1 minute, or until it has thickened to the consistency of custard.

7. With a rubber spatula immediately scrape the custard into a bowl. Stir in the pear brandy or vanilla. Stir

in 1 tablespoon of the ginger. Cover the custard with plastic wrap and press it directly on the custard to prevent a skin from forming. Chill until cold, about 1 hour. *May be prepared to this point up to 24 hours in advance, covered, and refrigerated until ready to serve.*

8. To serve the pears, arrange them in one large serving dish or in individual dishes. Spoon equal amounts of custard into the cavity of each pear. Garnish with the remaining tablespoon of minced crystallized ginger.

menu eleven

moroccan tomato and roasted pepper salad
vegetarian b'stilla
braised celery
mocha walnut torte (p. 163)

Here is a menu for those who like to make eating and cooking an adventure. Moroccan food is little known in this country, and it's interesting to become acquainted with this cuisine's use of spices—such as cinnamon and ground ginger—in main course dishes. Because the torte can be made the day before,

and the salad can be prepared in the morning, you can set aside an hour or so in the afternoon to make the B'Stilla at a leisurely pace, and allow yourself a few hours to relax before serving time. All that will remain for last minute preparation is the celery, and that needs very little attention.

moroccan tomato and roasted pepper salad

This colorful "salad" has a refreshing soupy consistency, and is redolent of cumin and lemon.

serves 6

    3 medium-size green peppers
    5 medium-size ripe tomatoes, peeled,
        seeded, and cubed G
    2 tablespoons minced onion
    1/4 teaspoon dried
        red pepper flakes
    2 cloves garlic, minced
    2 tablespoons minced parsley
    Juice of 1 lemon
    1/4 cup olive oil
    1 teaspoon ground cumin
    Salt to taste
    Freshly ground pepper to taste

1. Roast the peppers over the flame on a gas stove or on the burner of an electric stove until the skin is evenly charred all over. (Roasting the peppers under the broiler cooks them too much for this dish.) Place them in a plastic or paper bag, close it, and let them sit for 10 minutes to facilitate removing the skin. Scrape the skin off with a knife under cold running water, then pat the peppers very dry. Core them, cut into bite-size pieces, and put in a medium-size bowl.

2. Add all of the remaining ingredients and toss gently. Marinate at least 1 hour before serving and serve at room temperature. If you are going to marinate the salad longer, cover and chill, and bring to room temperature before serving. Because of its soupy consistency, I like to serve this salad in bowls, although it is traditionally eaten with the fingers.

---

vegetarian b'stilla

I became interested in Moroccan cooking after reading Paula Wolfert's recipes and writings on Moroccan food. B'Stilla is a classic dish, which is traditionally made with pigeon. I didn't want to miss out on such a wonderful mixture of exotic flavors so I created this vegetarian version, which has an unforgettable combination of sweetness and spiciness. Do try eating it with your fingers—Moroccan style.

serves 6

    1 1/2 pounds mushrooms
    6 tablespoons butter

    1 large onion, minced
    2 teaspoons cinnamon

1/2 teaspoon freshly ground pepper
1 teaspoon ground ginger
1/4 teaspoon turmeric
1/4 cup lemon juice
(about 1 1/2 lemons)
10 eggs, well beaten
Salt to taste

2 tablespoons oil
1 1/2 cups almonds
1/4 cup powdered (confectioners') sugar
7 tablespoons melted butter
8 sheets filo dough
Powdered (confectioners') sugar for garnish
Cinnamon for garnish

1. Wipe each mushroom off with a damp towel or paper towel to remove the dirt, then chop them into medium-size pieces. Melt 6 tablespoons of butter in a large skillet, then add the onion, 1/2 teaspoon of the cinnamon, the pepper, ginger, and turmeric, and sauté for 1 minute. Add the mushrooms and cook for about 5 minutes, or until they give off their juice. Remove with a slotted spoon to a platter and leave the remaining juice in the skillet.

2. Add the lemon juice to the skillet and heat these juices until bubbling. Add the beaten eggs and cook them, stirring constantly, until they resemble moist scrambled eggs. Do not allow them to become dry. Remove them to a platter, add salt to taste, and chill, uncovered, until the eggs are cool.

3. Meanwhile heat the oil in a small skillet, and when hot add the almonds and sauté until golden all over. Be careful not to let them burn. Put them in a blender or food processor and blend until finely chopped. (The almond meal should not be as fine as powder.) Add the remaining 1 1/2 teaspoons of cinnamon, the 1/4 cup powdered sugar, and 2 tablespoons of the melted butter, and blend until well mixed.

4. To assemble the B'Stilla: Place the filo in front of you and cover with a piece of wax paper and then a damp towel to prevent the dough from drying out. Also set a pastry brush and the remaining 5 tablespoons of melted butter in front of you.

5. Preheat the oven to 425 degrees. Lightly brush the bottom and sides of a pie plate or 9-inch round

cake pan with some melted butter. Lay 1 sheet of filo in the plate, then gently press it into the sides and allow the dough to overlap the edges. (Immediately cover the pile of filo again after removing each sheet.) Quickly and lightly brush the surface of the filo with melted butter; you need not do it perfectly but be sure to cover the overlapping edges. Repeat this procedure with 4 more sheets of filo.

6. Spoon in the mushroom mixture, top with the cooked eggs, then finely crumble the almond mixture over it.

7. Gather the overlapping edges of the filo and fold over the filling, making sure to keep the round shape of the pie. Now cover the pie with a sheet of filo, allowing it to drape over the sides. Brush lightly with melted butter and repeat with the 2 remaining sheets. Tuck the edges in around the pie, keeping the circular shape, then pour any remaining butter over the top and spread it on evenly. *May be prepared to this point up to 4 hours in advance and chilled.*

8. Bake for 15 minutes, or until evenly golden on top. Remove the pie from the oven, top with a cookie sheet, and invert. Lift off the pie plate and bake the pie on the cookie sheet an additional 15–20 minutes, or until golden and crisp.

9. Invert the pie onto a circular plate or platter and sprinkle on some powdered sugar through a sieve. Top with some cinnamon in a lattice pattern.

braised celery

Properly cooked celery has a delicate and distinctive flavor, and it is particularly delicious as a side vege-table braised as it is here in a little liquid. An easy, no-fuss dish.

serves 6

> 8 celery ribs
> 3 tablespoons butter
> Freshly ground pepper to taste
>
> 4 tablespoons Vegetable Stock,
>   homemade (p. 267) or store-bought,
>   or water

1. If the celery ribs are large and possibly stringy, then string them: Make an incision in the top of the ribs and pull down on the strings to remove. Cut each rib on the diagonal into pieces no thicker than 1/4 inch.

2. Melt the butter in a large skillet over medium-high heat. Sauté the celery for 10 minutes, tossing often.

3. Add the vegetable stock or water, cover the pan, and reduce the heat to a simmer. Cook slowly for 5–7 minutes more, or until the celery is tender and the liquid is absorbed. Remove the cover and toss again until the excess liquid has evaporated. Season liberally with freshly ground pepper.

---

menu twelve

stuffed mushrooms with blue cheese
leek timbales with white wine sauce
bulghur pilaf (p. 25)
pear tart with almond nut crust (p. 176)

I like to serve this menu in the fall and winter when leeks and pears are at their prime. You could accompany it with a salad—such as Watercress and Jerusalem Artichoke Salad with Sweet Mustard Dressing (p. 49) or Mixed Green Salad (p. 21)—served before or after the main course, but I have found that the stuffed mushrooms are rich and satisfying enough to make a salad unnecessary.

stuffed mushrooms with blue cheese

The toasted flavor of the sunflower seeds nicely complements the blue cheese in this stuffing.

serves 4

2 tablespoons sunflower seeds
12 large mushrooms
1/4 cup crumbled blue cheese

1/4 cup cream cheese
2 tablespoons milk
2 tablespoons fine bread or cracker crumbs

1. Preheat oven to 400 degrees. Put the sunflower seeds in a baking dish large enough to hold the 12 mushrooms (to save you from dirtying an extra pan) and toast them in the oven until lightly golden, about 7 minutes.

2. Remove the stems from the mushrooms and reserve for another use. Wipe the mushroom caps clean with a damp cloth.

3. Mash the blue cheese, cream cheese, and milk in a medium-size bowl until smooth. Stir in the toasted sunflower seeds and bread crumbs.

4. Fill each mushroom cap with this mixture. Butter the baking dish and arrange the mushroom caps within. Bake for 15–20 minutes, or until golden on top and juicy. Serve immediately.

leek timbales with white wine sauce

Leeks and onions are not interchangeable; the leek has a sweetness that is one of the most captivating of flavors. We make this dish in one of my classes and I have yet to meet a fledgling cook who wasn't won over by this vegetable. When you purchase leeks, choose firm, unblemished ones with healthy-looking tops. Beware of spring leeks; they have often-times been wintered over and have developed hard cores. These timbales (small savory custards) are virtually foolproof to make and the leeks give a delicious flavor. The custard can be made a day in advance, and leftover timbales reheat very well. What more could you ask of a dish?

leek timbales with white wine sauce (continued)

serves 4

6 medium-large leeks
   (with 2 inches of their green tops)
4 tablespoons butter
4 eggs, well beaten
1/2 cup heavy or whipping cream
1/3 cup milk
1/2 teaspoon salt
Freshly ground pepper to taste

sauce:
2 tablespoons butter
2 tablespoons flour
1–2 teaspoons tomato paste (for color)
1 1/2 cups Vegetable Stock (p. 267)
1/2 cup dry white wine
Freshly ground pepper to taste
Parsley sprigs for garnish

1. Cut the roots off the leeks, then slice them length-wise down their centers almost through to the other side. Rinse them under cold running water, being careful to clean out *all* of the dirt that is lodged between the leaves. (Leeks are very dirty, so use your fingers to separate the leaves and look for hidden dirt.) Pat them dry and slice very thin. You need 7 cups.

2. Melt the butter in a large skillet and sauté the leeks until tender, about 15 minutes. Spoon them into a large bowl, add the eggs, cream, milk, salt, and pepper, and mix well. *May be prepared to this point up to 24 hours in advance, covered, and chilled.*

3. Preheat the oven to 375 degrees. Butter eight 1-cup custard cups or small soufflé dishes and divide the leek mixture evenly among them, filling them no more than three-fourths full. (Of course if your molds are smaller or larger divide the mixture accordingly.)

4. Place the custard cups in a large baking dish and carefully pour in enough hot water to reach halfway up the sides of the cups. Bake for 20–30 minutes,

or until a toothpick inserted in the center of a timbale comes out dry.

5. Meanwhile make the sauce. Melt the butter in a small saucepan over low heat. Whisk in the flour and cook this roux for 2 minutes, whisking constantly. Be careful not to let it burn.

6. Add a teaspoon of the tomato paste, the vegetable stock, and wine, and whisk until smooth. Bring to a boil and cook an additional 10 minutes, whisking occasionally. If the sauce needs more color add the additional teaspoon of tomato paste. Season with freshly ground pepper and taste to see if it needs salt. If the sauce isn't perfectly smooth, then strain it. *May be prepared up to 24 hours in advance, covered, and chilled. If it is too thick when reheated, thin with a little stock.*

7. Unmold the timbales onto a serving platter and top with the sauce. Garnish the periphery of the platter with parsley sprigs.

menu thirteen

—a thanksgiving feast to serve six—

yogurt herb cheese
walnut loaf with burgundy sauce
chestnut purée
braised red cabbage with apples
roasted potatoes with rosemary
cranberry fruit tart

This menu has all the wonderful associations one has with the fall season—herbs, nuts, chestnuts, fall vegetables, and fruits. I have served this meal to many non-vegetarians on Thanksgiving Day, and everyone has admitted that they didn't miss the turkey.

The chestnuts can be prepared well in advance and frozen, the pie crust can be prepared and cooked 2 days before, and the yogurt cheese, walnut loaf, and pie filling can be prepared the day before. What will remain on Thanksgiving Day will be cooking the loaf, making the gravy, puréing and heating the chestnut purée, preparing the cabbage and potatoes, and assembling the pie. None of these tasks demands much time, so you won't be a slave to the kitchen, as is oftentimes the case on Thanksgiving Day.

yogurt herb cheese

This Middle Eastern method of making fresh cheese out of yogurt is easy and fun to do. You simply hang yogurt in a cheesecloth bag and let it drip until the yogurt reaches the consistency you want; the longer it drips, the firmer it gets. To make a creamy dip let it hang for 1 hour; for a ricotta cheese (spread) consistency 4 hours; and for a cream cheese consistency let it hang at least 12 hours or overnight. My recipe makes a tangy, creamy spread that is delicious on crackers or thin toasts. It doesn't take long to prepare, although it must hang for at least 4 hours, then after it is mixed with the herbs it should sit a few hours to blend the flavors.

yogurt herb cheese (continued)

makes about 1 cup

2 cups yogurt (preferably low-fat)
1 clove garlic, minced
1 tablespoon olive oil
1/4 teaspoon thyme

1/4 teaspoon basil
1/4 teaspoon oregano
Salt to taste
Freshly ground pepper to taste

1. Line a strainer with a double thickness of cheesecloth about 16 inches by 16 inches. Spoon the yogurt into the center. Gather the corners of the cheesecloth and tie a string around them to hold them tightly together. The yogurt sack must now hang so the whey can drip out. You can either tie the cheesecloth to the faucet, suspending the sack over the sink, or tie the cheesecloth around a dowel (or something similar) and let it hang above a large bowl or pot. Let hang for 4–12 hours. Occasionally untie the cheesecloth to check the consistency. The cheese is ready when it has the consistency of ricotta cheese.

2. When ready untie the cheesecloth and scoop out the cheese into a serving dish. Mix in all of the remaining ingredients. Cover and chill for at least 2 hours before serving. Serve as a spread on toasted French bread slices or crackers.

walnut loaf with burgundy sauce

This loaf makes an impressive entrée for a Thanksgiving feast or any special occasion. Being a great fan of leftovers, I particularly look forward to leftover walnut loaf because it makes superb sandwiches, sliced and topped with mayonnaise or Russian dressing.

makes 1 large loaf

3/4 pound sliced whole wheat bread
   (about 14 slices)
3/4 pound
   (about 2 3/4 cups) walnuts
4 large onions, minced
1 bunch parsley, minced
   (about 2 cups minced)
1 green pepper, minced
1 celery rib, minced

3 eggs, beaten
1 1/2 teaspoons poultry seasoning
1 teaspoon salt
Pinch thyme
Freshly ground pepper to taste
2 tablespoons oil
1 small (16-ounce) can imported plum
   tomatoes, chopped and drained
1 bunch parsley for garnish

burgundy sauce:
7 tablespoons butter
6 tablespoons flour
1/2 cup red Burgundy wine,
  or other dry red wine

1/3 cup tamari soy sauce
31/2 cups Vegetable Stock,
  homemade (p. 267) or store-bought
Freshly ground pepper to taste

1. Preheat the broiler. Lay the slices of bread on a baking sheet and toast under the broiler on both sides until golden. Cool, then grind into bread crumbs in a blender or food processor. Put the bread crumbs in a large bowl.

2. Reduce the oven setting to 375 degrees. Grind the walnuts in the blender or food processor as you did the bread. They should be fine. Add to the bread crumb bowl and mix well.

3. Add all of the remaining ingredients up to the parsley garnish and mix very well.

4. Generously butter a 1 1/2-quart loaf pan and spoon the mixture into it. Press it in firmly and smooth over the top. Cover with foil. *May be prepared to this point up to 24 hours in advance and chilled.*

5. Place the loaf pan in a larger pan or baking dish and fill with enough hot water to reach halfway up the sides of the loaf pan. Bake for 2 hours. Let the loaf sit on a wire rack for 10 minutes before unmolding.

6. To unmold, carefully slide a knife around the loaf to loosen it from the pan. Lay a serving platter on top of the loaf pan and invert. Garnish the loaf with parsley sprigs around the platter. Serve sliced, with Burgundy Sauce.

To make burgundy sauce:
1. In a medium-size saucepan melt 6 tablespoons of the butter, then add the flour and whisk until smooth. Cook this roux over low heat for 2 minutes, whisking constantly.

2. Add the wine, soy sauce, vegetable stock, and pepper, and whisk to blend. Bring to a boil, whisking constantly, then simmer for 5 minutes, or until the sauce is thickened and fragrant. Just before serving add the remaining tablespoon of butter and stir until melted. Do not boil again. Serve in a sauceboat.

---

chestnut purée

Rich, intensely flavored, and naturally sweet, this aristocratic dish is not as time-consuming as it appears to be. You can prepare the chestnuts in advance and freeze them if you like. My method of removing the chestnut meat is by far the easiest I've found. If you want larger chunks (for another recipe) then cook the chestnuts half the time.

chestnut purée (continued)

serves 6

1 1/2 pounds fresh chestnuts
3/4 cup heavy or whipping cream
3/4 cup milk

Dash salt
Pinch sugar
1 tablespoon butter

1. Fill a medium-size saucepan halfway with water and bring to a boil. Add the chestnuts and boil, covered, for 20 minutes.

2. Remove the pan from the heat and spoon out 3 or 4 chestnuts. With a large, sharp knife one at a time slice each chestnut in half and squeeze out the flesh into the container of a blender or food processor. If the flesh doesn't come out easily use the handle of a spoon and scoop it out. Repeat with the remaining chestnuts, removing only 3 or 4 at a time from the hot water. (If the flesh of any chestnut is dark or spoiled, then discard it.) *May be prepared in advance*

to this point and refrigerated for up to 2 days or frozen for up to 1 week.

3. Add the cream, milk, salt, and sugar to the blender or processor along with the chestnut meats, and purée until almost smooth. Scrape down the sides as necessary.

4. Return the purée to the saucepan or a small skillet, and heat over medium-low heat until piping hot. If too thick add a little more milk. Add the tablespoon of butter and stir until melted. Serve immediately.

braised red cabbage with apples

serves 6

1/4 cup olive oil
2 medium-size onions, halved vertically
    and thinly sliced
2 medium-size apples, peeled, cored,
    and thinly sliced
1 small to medium red cabbage
    (1 1/2 pounds), cored, quartered, and
    shredded (8 cups shredded)

1/2 teaspoon salt
1/3 cup red wine vinegar
1/2 cup dry red wine
Minced fresh parsley for garnish

1. Heat the olive oil in a large (6-quart) stockpot over medium heat. Add the onions and apples, toss, and cook for 5 minutes.

2. Add the shredded cabbage, salt, vinegar, and wine, and toss well. Reduce the heat to a simmer, cover the pan, and cook the cabbage slowly, tossing occasionally, for 45–60 minutes, or until tender and flavorful but not mushy. (If too much liquid remains when the cabbage is done, then remove the cover and raise the heat. Cook until most of the liquid is evaporated.) Spoon into a serving bowl and garnish with parsley.

roasted potatoes with rosemary

serves 6

6 medium-size boiling (waxy) potatoes
4 tablespoons melted butter
4 teaspoons fresh rosemary,
    or 2 teaspoons dried rosemary,
    crumbled
Freshly ground pepper to taste

1. Preheat the oven to 375 degrees. Peel the potatoes, slice them in half, and blanch them in a large pot of boiling water for 10 minutes. Drain well.

2. Butter a large shallow baking dish and arrange the potatoes in it in 1 layer.

3. Pour the melted butter over the potatoes to coat evenly. Sprinkle on the rosemary and freshly ground pepper. Bake for 30 minutes, or until the potatoes are tender and brown, turning them occasionally for even browning. Note: If your baking dish can withstand the broiler, you can broil the potatoes for a few minutes for extra crispness and color.

cranberry fruit tart

serves 8

Pâte Sucrée (p. 276)
4 cups fresh cranberries (1 pound)
1 seedless navel orange
1 ripe but slightly firm pear, peeled,
    cored and diced
3/4 cup honey
2 tablespoons raisins
3/4 cup chopped walnuts, toasted

1/4 teaspoon cinnamon
2 teaspoons cornstarch

topping:
1 cup heavy or whipping cream,
    well chilled
2 tablespoons honey

1. Prepare the pie crust and line a 10-inch quiche or tart pan with it. Bake blind as directed (20 minutes total), and allow to cool completely.

2. Wash and pick over the cranberries to remove stems and any spoiled berries, then put them in a medium-size saucepan with 1/4 cup of water. Cook over medium heat just until they begin to burst, about 5 minutes. Remove from the heat.

3. Meanwhile wash the orange and pat dry. Grate it on the fine side of a grater; try not to grate any of the white pith. Here is a good trick: Wind plastic wrap tightly around the grater and grate the orange rind against the plastic wrap. The grating edge will pierce through the wrap. When you've finished, you'll be able to peel off the plastic and with it, the gratings (instead of having to scrape them out of all the interstices). Peel the orange and discard the white pith. Separate the orange into slices, then cut each slice into thirds.

4. Add the orange peel, orange pieces, and all of the remaining ingredients (except the topping) to the cranberries and cook, stirring occasionally for 3 more minutes, or until the juices thicken. Spoon into a bowl, cover, and chill until cold, about 3 hours or up to 24 hours.

5. Spoon the filling into the prepared pie shell and smooth over the top. Whip the cream with the honey until very stiff, then scrape it into a pastry bag with a star tip and pipe it on the tart in a lattice fashion. (Or spread it decoratively over the top.) Chill until ready to serve.

summer menus

During the hot summer months one should be mindful of the value and comfort of preparing dishes that are suited to hot weather cooking and eating. Unfortunately, it took me a long time to learn this lesson. Many a guest has built up a sweat as a result of my unbridled enthusiasm for cooking whatever struck my fancy at the time. If I had an urge to prepare a spicy curry dinner or a particular dish that required baking, then no one could stop me. (I know that spicy food is eaten in many hot climates and the sweating that results from it cools the body, but I think that most people in cooler climates, who aren't used to such practices, would prefer to remain dry while dining.)

But this is a tale of the past. I now look forward to preparing dishes that complement summer weather and require little use of the stove. Marinades, cold soups, rice and pasta salads, and fresh fruit desserts are all delectable and much more compatible with this precious season. With an assortment of fresh vegetables and fruits in abundance and the addition of fruity olive oil, mayonnaise, yogurt, vinegar, lemon juice, and herbs, one can create the most flavorful of dishes, and all with a minimum of cooking. The little amount of cooking that is required can take place in the cooler hours of the night or early morning, and most of the recipes will benefit from being made in advance.

menu one

tzadziki with pita bread
curried rice salad with apples and cashews
peach almond torte

Here is a good example of how foods from different cultures can be compatible with one another. Tzadziki is Greek, the rice salad has an Indian character, and the torte was inspired by Italian desserts. They are a splendid trio, enhancing each other superbly.

---

tzadziki

This is a simple Greek dip that has a pungent garlic flavor. It is especially good served with hot pita bread triangles.

    1/2 medium-size cucumber
    1 cup yogurt (preferably low-fat)
    2 cloves garlic, minced
    1/4 teaspoon salt
    1 teaspoon minced parsley

1. Peel the cucumber and slice in half lengthwise. With a spoon scrape out the seeds and discard. Grate the cucumber on a grater and put in a medium-size serving bowl.

2. Stir in the yogurt, garlic, and salt and garnish with the minced parsley. Chill for at least 30 minutes before serving to develop the flavor.

curried rice salad with apples and cashews

This is a stunning, beautifully colored salad served on contrasting spinach leaves and topped with toasted coconut. It would make a wonderful luncheon, dinner, or buffet dish.

serves 4 as a main course

1 1/2 cups raw brown rice,
  cooked and well chilled
  (about 4 cups cooked, p. 266)
1/3 cup raisins
1/2 cup raw cashews, toasted*
1 medium-size carrot, very thinly sliced
1 small firm, tart apple, cored and diced

dressing:
1/2 cup yogurt (preferably low-fat)
1/2 cup Mayonnaise, homemade
  (p. 269) or store-bought
2 teaspoons curry powder
2 cloves garlic, minced

1/2 teaspoon minced gingerroot
Dash cayenne pepper

3 cups fresh spinach leaves
  (cleaned and stemmed)
1/3 cup Vinaigrette (p. 268)
1/4 cup unsweetened dried coconut, toasted**
  (purchased at health food stores)

* Raw cashews may be purchased in a health food store and toasted in a moderate (350-degree) oven for 10–15 minutes, or until lightly browned. Otherwise dry-roasted, unsalted cashews may be used.
** To toast coconut place in a saucepan and heat over medium heat. Toss often until it is fragrant and begins to get lightly browned. Be careful not to burn it.

1. In a large serving bowl toss the cold cooked rice, raisins, cashews, carrot, and apple together, mixing well.

2. In a medium-size bowl mix together thoroughly the yogurt, mayonnaise, curry powder, garlic, gingerroot, and cayenne pepper. Add to the rice mixture and toss to coat. Taste to correct seasoning; it may need salt. Chill at least 2 hours before serving.

3. Just before serving toss the spinach with the vinaigrette to coat lightly. Serve the rice salad on a bed of spinach either on one large platter or on individual serving plates. Garnish with the toasted coconut.

peach almond torte

During the height of the peach season I love to make this sweet, buttery torte and serve it with espresso as part of a special meal. It is quick to make, and is best served warm or at room temperature. Although it is still delicious on the second day, it tends to get very moist from the juice of the peaches, so plan to make it on the day you will serve it.

serves 8

1/2 cup (1 stick) butter, softened
1 cup sugar
1/2 cup ground almonds
1/2 cup unbleached white flour
1 teaspoon baking powder
2 eggs
1/2 teaspoon almond extract
4 ripe peaches, peeled and sliced
   1/2 inch thick

topping:
1 tablespoon butter, cut into bits
1 tablespoon sugar
2 tablespoons unbleached white flour
1/2 teaspoon cinnamon

1. Preheat the oven to 350 degrees. Butter the bottom of a 9-inch springform pan.

2. In a large bowl cream the butter and sugar together until blended. Add the almonds, flour, baking powder, eggs, and almond extract, and beat until smooth and fluffy.

3. Scrape the batter into the springform pan and smooth over the top. Arrange the peach slices on top in 1 layer (they don't have to be neat).

4. In a small bowl make the topping: Toss together the butter, sugar, flour, and cinnamon. Cut the butter into the mixture until it is the texture of coarse crumbs. Sprinkle evenly over the peaches.

5. Bake for 50–60 minutes, or until golden brown all over. Cool on a wire rack for 10 minutes, then remove the sides of the pan. Serve warm or at room temperature.

menu two

pasta with uncooked tomato and fresh basil sauce
raspberry pie

This is one of my all-time favorite menus. Both dishes are supreme examples of the glory of summer produce. If you feel you'd like to add to the menu, try serving some crusty French bread alongside the pasta.

---

pasta with uncooked tomato and fresh basil sauce

A quick summer dish that is best prepared at the height of the season, when tomatoes are irresistibly plump and red and fresh basil is available in abundance. This is, to me, one of the best pasta dishes, potent yet simple.

serves 4

- 6 ripe plum tomatoes (about 1 pound)
- 3–4 cloves (depending on your taste) garlic, minced
- 1 cup shredded fresh basil leaves (loosely packed)
- 1/2 cup chopped fresh parsley
- 1/2 cup olive oil
- 1/2 teaspoon dried red pepper flakes
- 1/2 teaspoon salt
- Freshly ground pepper to taste
- 2/3 pound (10 ounces) pasta, such as linguine, spaghetti, or vermicelli
- 2/3 cup grated Parmesan cheese

1. Wash the tomatoes and pat them dry. Cut out the cores and discard. Cut each tomato in half horizontally and gently squeeze out the seeds.

2. Dice the tomatoes into 1-inch pieces and place in a medium-size bowl. Add the garlic, basil, parsley, olive oil, red pepper flakes, salt, and pepper to taste. Toss well. Let marinate at room temperature for at least 2 hours. If you marinate it longer then chill it. *May be prepared in advance to this point, covered, and chilled for up to 24 hours.* Bring to room temperature before serving.

pasta with uncooked tomato and fresh basil sauce (continued)

3. Bring a large pot of water to a boil and cook the pasta al dente—slightly firm to the bite. Drain very well in a colander and return to the pot or a large serving dish.

4. Immediately toss the Parmesan cheese on the pasta. Pour on the sauce. Toss well and serve immediately. When the dish is served it tends to be warm rather than hot; this is fine and the flavor will gain as a result.

raspberry pie

My sister Julianne created this memorable pie and it has proven to be one of my favorite desserts. It is beautiful to look at, has a distinct fresh raspberry flavor, and doesn't demand a lot of preparation time.

1 recipe Pâte Brisée (p. 274)
     made with sugar instead of salt
3 cups fresh raspberries
2/3 cup water
3/4 cup sugar

2 1/2 tablespoons cornstarch
2 tablespoons butter
2/3 cup heavy or whipping cream
1 tablespoon sugar

1. Preheat the oven to 400 degrees. Line the chilled pie shell with aluminum foil and fill it with dried beans or rice. (You must do this to prevent shrinkage.) Bake for 10 minutes. Remove from the oven and remove the foil and beans. (Save for future crusts.) Prick the crust all over and return to the oven. Bake 3–5 additional minutes, or until the crust is evenly golden and completely cooked. If it begins to get too dark in some spots, then cover them with pieces of foil. Cool thoroughly on a wire rack.

2. To make the filling: In a medium-size saucepan combine 1 cup of the raspberries with the water, sugar, and cornstarch. Bring to a boil, stirring continuously, and cook until clear and thickened, about

3 minutes. Remove from the heat and stir in the butter. Cool to room temperature and carefully fold in the remaining raspberries. (You should reserve a few of the perfect ones for garnish.) Chill until the pie shell is thoroughly cooled.

3. To assemble the pie: Spread the raspberry filling evenly in the pie shell. Whip the cream and sugar until very stiff. Decorate the top of the pie with the whipped cream and the reserved raspberries. (I like to put the whipped cream in a pastry bag with a star tube and decorate the pie in lattice fashion. Then I place the reserved raspberries where the lattice crisscrosses.) Chill for at least an hour before serving.

menu three

iced plum soup
tempeh salade niçoise
fresh peaches with honey rum sauce

I like to prepare these dishes at the peak of summer when these fruits and vegetables are at their best. With the addition of tempeh in the salad you are getting some complete protein, but if you would like to add more, then serve some bread and cheese (perhaps something soft like Brie) with the salad.

---

iced plum soup

Choose sweet, flavorful plums for this soup and allow them to get perfectly ripe. I often take this on a picnic, transporting it in a glass jar with a screw top and then serving it in cups.

serves 4

9–10 ripe plums (2 pounds), washed
1/2 cup dry red wine
1/2 cup water
1/2 teaspoon ground coriander
1/8 teaspoon allspice

1/4 teaspoon salt
1 tablespoon honey
1/2 cup heavy cream
1 cup sour cream
Mint sprigs for garnish

1. Fill a medium-size saucepan half full of water and bring to a boil. In batches blanch the plums for 10 seconds. Remove them with a slotted spoon to your work surface. Discard the water when all have been blanched. Peel the plums and put the skins in the saucepan along with the red wine and the 1/2 cup of water. Bring to a boil, cook 5 minutes, then remove from the heat.

2. With a slotted spoon remove the skins and put in a strainer and rest it over the pan. Press out as much liquid as you can, then discard the skins. (Cooking the skins flavors and colors the soup.)

3. Make sure the plums don't have any skin adhering to them. Cut them into bite-size pieces and discard the pits. Add them to the wine mixture along

iced plum soup (continued)

with the coriander, allspice, salt, and honey. Bring to a boil and simmer for 10 minutes.

4. In the container of the blender or food processor purée the mixture with the heavy cream. Pour into a large bowl. Chill at least 1 1/2 hours, or until very cold.

5. Before serving whisk in the sour cream until perfectly blended. Serve chilled, garnished with a mint sprig on each serving.

tempeh salade niçoise

This salad, like traditional Salade Niçoise, is a meal in itself. In France, much to my bewilderment, I was often served Salade Niçoise packed in a bowl with its dressing on the side. Served in such a manner it is impossible to toss, or to get at the lettuce without causing the toppings to land in your lap and the olives to roll across the table. To prevent such a disaster in my home, I like to arrange it decoratively on large dinner plates and pour on the dressing before serving it. See if you agree.

serves 4

8 ounces tempeh,G cut into 1/2-inch cubes
Vinaigrette (p. 268), 1 1/2 times the recipe
2 tablespoons mayonnaise
    (preferably homemade, p. 269)
1 1/2 cups diced green beans
1 large head lettuce (Boston, green or
    red leaf, Bibb, or other soft lettuce)

2 hard-boiled eggs, minced or quartered
1 small red onion, sliced
2 medium-size ripe tomatoes
16–20 black olives (preferably Kalamata)
2 teaspoons capers
1 cup alfalfa sprouts

1. Steam the tempeh in a vegetable steamer for 20 minutes. Put in a medium-size bowl and toss with 1/4 cup of the vinaigrette, then toss with the mayonnaise and chill for at least 20 minutes.

2. Blanch the green beans in boiling water for 3 minutes, or until tender yet slightly crunchy. Drain and cool thoroughly in cold water. Drain again, pat dry, then toss with 2 tablespoons of the vinaigrette.

3. Wash the lettuce and pat or spin dry. Tear it into bite-size pieces and divide evenly among 4 dinner plates. Mound one-quarter of the tempeh in the center of each plate.

4. Evenly divide and decoratively arrange the green beans, hard-boiled eggs, onion, tomatoes, and olives on each plate. Top with the capers and sprouts. Drizzle some of the remaining vinaigrette over, and serve immediately with the remaining dressing alongside.

fresh peaches with honey rum sauce

serves 4

2 tablespoons honey
2¹/₂ tablespoons rum
   (preferably dark)
6 ripe peaches

1. In a medium-size bowl mix the honey and rum together thoroughly.

2. Peel the peaches and slice in half. Remove the pits and cut each peach half into 4 slices and place in the bowl. Toss well, cover, and chill at least 1 hour before serving. Serve in decorative goblets or large wine glasses.

menu four

gazpacho
marinated pasta and vegetable salad
summer fruit tart

Here are three dishes that have become very popular, and for good reasons. They are very harmonious together, and beautifully display the good, fresh summer produce.

gazpacho

serves 6

5 medium-size tomatoes, cored
2 medium-size cucumbers
1 small onion, diced
1 large green pepper,
    cored and finely diced
    (1/4-inch dice)
2 cloves garlic, minced
1/3 cup red wine vinegar

1/3 cup olive oil
1/2 cup Vegetable Stock,
    homemade (p. 267) or store-bought,
    tomato juice, or water
A few dashes Tabasco
Salt to taste
Freshly ground pepper to taste
Croutons (see Note)

1. Roughly chop all of the tomatoes. Peel both cucumbers and slice lengthwise. Remove the seeds with a teaspoon and discard them. Roughly chop 1 1/2 of the cucumbers and add to the tomatoes along with the diced onion. In batches purée this mixture in a blender or food processor until almost smooth but not liquefied. Pour into a large serving bowl.

2. By hand finely dice the remaining cucumber half and add to the soup. Add all of the remaining ingredients except the croutons and stir to blend. Chill at least 2 hours before serving. Taste to adjust seasoning. Serve well chilled, garnished with the croutons, in individual soup bowls.

note:
To make croutons remove the crusts from a few slices of bread (preferably whole wheat). Lightly toast them in a toaster. Rub both sides with a garlic half (you will probably need a couple of them). Then, using a pastry brush, brush both sides lightly with olive oil. Cut the bread into 1/2-inch cubes and lay them on a cookie sheet. Dry them out until they are crisp in a 350-degree oven that has just been turned off. Toss occasionally. They will get harder as they come to room temperature.

marinated pasta and vegetable salad

I like the mixture of whole wheat and white pasta in this salad; the whole wheat rotini adds extra flavor and nutrients. You could substitute all white rotini with successful results, but I don't recommend using all whole wheat because its flavor is too strong. When-ever I have served this salad to a large crowd, it has been very popular. Children are attracted to it because of the playful shape of the rotini, which entices them to eat it with their fingers.

serves 6

1/2 pound whole wheat rotini
   (short spiral-shaped pasta)*
1/2 pound white rotini
3 cups sliced mushrooms
1 tablespoon butter
3 cups broccoli florets**
1 cup peas (fresh or frozen)
15 cherry tomatoes
1/2 cup chopped fresh parsley
1/4 cup finely diced red onion

dressing:
1/3 cup olive oil
1/3 cup vegetable oil
3 tablespoons red wine vinegar
4 cloves garlic, minced
1/2 teaspoon basil
1/4 teaspoon oregano
1/4 teaspoon tarragon, crumbled
1/4 teaspoon red pepper flakes
1 teaspoon salt
Liberal seasoning freshly ground pepper

*One-half pound of rotini is about 3 1/2 cups uncooked. Whole wheat rotini can be purchased at health food stores and some specialty food shops.

**The broccoli stalks can be used in Lemon-Glazed Broccoli Stalks Julienne (p. 30).

1. Cook both pastas together in a large pot of rapidly boiling water until al dente — that is, tender yet slightly firm to the bite. Drain in a colander and run under cold water. Drain again thoroughly, then put into a large serving bowl.

2. Sauté the mushrooms in the butter until tender and brown, then add to the pasta and toss.

3. Steam the broccoli until tender yet still bright green. Immerse in cold water to stop further cooking, then drain very well. Pat dry with a towel and add to the pasta.

4. If you are using frozen peas thoroughly defrost them, or place in a sieve and pour hot water over them; they do not need further cooking. Pat dry, then add to the pasta. If you are using fresh peas, steam them just until tender, about 5 minutes, or add them raw for a nice touch if they are particularly young and sweet.

5. Add the cherry tomatoes, parsley, and onion and mix well.

6. Combine all of the ingredients for the dressing in a jar with a tight-fitting lid and shake vigorously. Pour onto the pasta and toss until well coated. Cover and chill for 2 hours or up to 48 hours. Bring to room temperature before serving.

summer fruit tart

A quick tart which demands that the oven be on for only about 15 minutes — a welcome relief during hot summer weather. You can use almost any assortment of fresh fruit for the topping — strawberries, cantaloupe, kiwis, white grapes, etc. — but my favorite is a mixture of peaches, plums, and blueberries, offering a beautiful presentation of shades of yellow, red, and blue.

crust:
14 graham cracker halves
1/4 cup melted butter
2 tablespoons sugar
Dash cinnamon

filling:
8 ounces cream cheese, softened
1/4 cup honey
1 teaspoon vanilla extract

topping:
2 ripe peaches, peeled and
    sliced 1/2 inch thick
3 ripe plums, peeled and
    sliced 1/2 inch thick
2/3 cup blueberries (approximately)

glaze:
2 tablespoons raspberry or
    red currant jelly
1/2 teaspoon water

1. To make the crust: Preheat the oven to 350 degrees. Place the graham crackers in a plastic bag and seal. Roll over the bag with a rolling pin until fine crumbs are formed. Put them in a medium-size bowl and add the butter, sugar, and cinnamon. Toss well. Put this mixture in a 9-inch pie plate and press in place evenly. (It is helpful to use another pie plate to press down on the crumbs.) Bake for 10 minutes, or until evenly golden. Cool thoroughly on a wire rack.

2. To make the filling: In a medium-size bowl beat together by hand the cream cheese, honey, and vanilla until smooth. Spread onto the bottom of the thoroughly cooled pie shell.

3. Make a decorative topping with the fruit, for example: Alternate slices of peaches and plums around the edge of the tart. Make a star out of plum slices in the center. Use the blueberries to make a border around the outer edge of the tart, and fill in the spaces near the star.

4. Make the glaze by heating the jelly and water, stirring constantly, until the jelly is smooth. Carefully brush all the glaze onto the tart. Chill the tart for at least 2 hours, or until the filling and glaze are firm.

menu five

marinated bean curd, cucumber, and radish salad
cold sesame noodles with broccoli and cashews
ginger cookies (p. 134)
chocolate-dipped strawberries

This is a good picnic menu and a nice change from the more common picnic fare. Everything can be easily packed into containers and served without fuss. The Chocolate-Dipped Strawberries add a special touch, so be sure to include them.

---

marinated bean curd, cucumber, and radish salad

Cold bean curd (tofu) is delicious when marinated in a flavorful sauce and mixed with crunchy vegetables. It is not often that you get protein in the salad course and with so little effort.

serves 4

½ pound firm bean curd (tofu),
   cut into ¾-inch cubes
2 cucumbers
8 radishes, thinly sliced
1 tablespoon tamari soy sauce

2 tablespoons Chinese rice vinegar
   (or other vinegar)
2 tablespoons peanut oil
½ teaspoon sugar
Freshly ground pepper to taste

1. Half fill a medium-size saucepan with water and bring to a boil. Toss in the bean curd and blanch for 1 minute. (This improves its texture.) Remove with a slotted spoon to paper towels to drain. Let cool. Put in a medium-size serving bowl.

marinated bean curd, cucumber, and radish salad (continued)

2. Peel the cucumbers. Slice in half lengthwise and scrape out the seeds. Discard them. Cut each half in half again lengthwise and slice into 1/2-inch-thick slices. Add to the bean curd, along with the radishes and toss.

3. Mix together the remaining ingredients and pour over the bean curd mixture. Toss well. Cover and chill up to an hour before serving; the salad gets too soggy if left any longer. Serve cool not cold.

---

cold sesame noodles with broccoli and cashews

This is my version of the traditional Chinese dish. Because it is so rich and satisfying, I prefer to serve it as a main course as one would serve other pasta salads.

serves 4

1 bunch broccoli, florets only,
   cut into small pieces
6 ounces fine egg noodles
   (or vermicelli broken in half)
1 tablespoon plus 1 teaspoon Oriental
   sesame oil[G]
3/4 cup unsalted roasted cashews
   (see Note)

1/3 cup Oriental
   sesame seed paste[G]
1/2 teaspoon hot spicy oil[G]
3 tablespoons tamari soy sauce
1 tablespoon Chinese rice vinegar
   (or other vinegar)
1/4 cup peanut oil
4 cloves garlic, minced

1. In a medium-size saucepan bring water to a boil and blanch the broccoli for 2 minutes. Drain and immerse in cold water until thoroughly cold. Pat dry with a towel until very dry and set aside.

2. Boil the noodles for a few minutes or until al dente, tender yet slightly firm to the bite. Drain in a colander very well and pat with paper towels. Place the noodles in a large serving bowl and add 1 teaspoon of the sesame oil. Toss thoroughly.

3. Add the broccoli and cashews and toss again.

4. In a separate small bowl stir the sesame paste with a fork until smooth (see Note). Add the spicy oil, soy sauce, vinegar, remaining sesame oil, peanut oil, and garlic, and stir to blend.

5. Add the sauce to the noodles and toss well. The salad can be served immediately, or covered and chilled for up to 48 hours. Serve cool not cold.

note:
You can use raw cashews and toast them in the oven (400 degrees) until golden. When you purchase ses-

ame seed paste it will probably have separated in the jar. It is best to put all of it in a bowl and whisk until smooth. Return it to the jar and measure the amount needed.

chocolate-dipped strawberries

These are great served alone or alongside cookies, cakes, or other fruit desserts. They should be made the day you are going to serve them, for the berry "sweats" after a while and changes the texture of the chocolate.

20 strawberries (½ pound)
3 ounces semisweet chocolate
1 ½ teaspoons dark rum

1. Wash the strawberries and dry very well with paper towels. Keep the hulls on. Place a large sheet of wax paper on a platter or cookie sheet and set aside.

2. In a double boiler over low heat melt the chocolate and rum together. Remove from the heat, keeping the chocolate over the double boiler pan. Dip the bottom two-thirds of each strawberry into the chocolate, leaving the top third bare. Place each strawberry on the wax paper and chill until set, about 1 hour. (If the chocolate in the pan begins to harden before you are finished dipping, then return the double boiler to the heat with ½ teaspoon of rum and stir until soft again.)

menu six

cold cucumber and watercress soup
chilled tomatoes stuffed with
white beans and pesto
peaches marsala

This is a very satisfying menu, and the stuffed toma- toes are rather filling. If you'd like to serve bread, though, a crusty Italian or French bread would be delicious served with either the soup or the tomatoes.

cold cucumber and watercress soup

serves 4–6 as a first course

2 tablespoons butter
2 medium-size onions, diced
4 medium-large cucumbers, peeled,
   halved lengthwise and seeded,
   and sliced 1/2 inch thick
2 cups Vegetable Stock,
   homemade (p. 267)
   or store-bought

2 teaspoons fresh tarragon,
   or 1 teaspoon dried tarragon,
   crumbled
1 teaspoon vinegar
1/2 teaspoon salt
Freshly ground pepper to taste
1 bunch watercress
1 cup sour cream

1. In a medium-size saucepan melt the butter over medium heat, and sauté the onions, for 5 minutes.

2. Add the sliced cucumber, vegetable stock, tar- ragon, vinegar, salt, and pepper. Cover the pot and bring to a boil. Cook over medium heat for 20 minutes, or until the cucumbers are very tender. Stir occasionally.

3. Meanwhile wash the watercress by dunking it in cold water several times. Pat dry. Remove a few perfect-looking sprigs for garnish, wrap them, and chill them until ready to use. Tear off all of the water- cress leaves from their stems and discard the stems. Mince the watercress leaves and set aside.

4. When the cucumbers are very tender purée the

soup in a blender or food processor. This will prob- ably have to be done in batches. Pour the soup into a large bowl and stir in the minced watercress. Let cool for 15 minutes.

5. Whisk in the sour cream, and chill the soup until it is ice cold, at least 3 hours. Serve garnished with the reserved watercress sprigs.

note:
This soup becomes more flavorful as time passes, so don't hesitate to make it 24–48 hours in advance.

chilled tomatoes stuffed with white beans and pesto

Use perfectly fresh ripe summer tomatoes that are both flavorful and tender for this dish. It would not be worth making if you have to use the hothouse or commercially grown tomato that is leathery, flavor- less, and juiceless.

serves 4

1 cup dried white beans
    (Great Northern or navy) (see Note)
4 large ripe tomatoes
1/2 cup Pesto (p. 270) or
    Winter Pesto (p. 271)

1/4 teaspoon salt
Freshly ground pepper to taste
1/2 medium-size red onion, minced,
    plus 1 tablespoon for garnish
1/2 celery rib, minced

1. Rinse the beans in a strainer under cold running water, and remove and discard any damaged beans or stones. Put the beans in a bowl and cover with water to soak overnight. (Alternatively, cook the beans for 2 minutes in water to cover, then remove from heat and let soak, covered, for 1 hour.) Drain, then add enough fresh water to cover plus 2 inches. Cook, partially covered, until tender, about 1 hour. Drain again.

2. Meanwhile slice off the top of each tomato and scoop out the pulp with a spoon. Discard. Invert the tomatoes on a plate and allow to drain.

3. Toss the hot cooked beans in a medium-size bowl with the pesto, salt, pepper, onion, and celery. Taste to adjust the seasoning. Chill for at least 1 hour, or until cold.

chilled tomatoes stuffed with white beans and pesto (continued)

4. Stuff equal amounts of the bean mixture into each tomato. Garnish with the remaining onion.

note:
If you wish to use canned beans, try about 2 cups Italian white cannellini beans, rinsed and thoroughly drained.

You can prepare this dish in advance and refrigerate it, but be sure to remove it 30 minutes before serving. Tomatoes lose their flavor if served cold.

---

peaches marsala

serves 4

    4 large ripe peaches
    1/4 cup sweet or dry Marsala
    1 tablespoon sliced almonds

1. Peel the peaches and cut in half vertically. Remove the pit and discard. Cut the peaches into 1/2-inch-thick slices and put in a bowl.

2. Add the Marsala and toss. Cover and let marinate in the refrigerator for at least 1 hour.

3. Bring to room temperature before serving. Divide evenly among 4 small serving dishes and top each portion with sliced almonds.

---

menu seven

bulghur salad with tarragon and vegetables
open-face tomato sandwiches
summer fruit salad

This would be an ideal lunch or light dinner to serve guests because it is so easy to prepare, and it can all be made in advance (but don't assemble the sandwiches until you are ready to serve them). You could improvise with the bulghur salad and try substituting some thinly sliced raw zucchini, cherry tomatoes, blanched fresh peas, or blanched broccoli.

bulghur salad with tarragon and vegetables

serves 4

1½ cups bulghur G
1 cup (4 ounces) diced green beans
2 cups (6 ounces) sliced mushrooms
½ tablespoon butter
1 red bell pepper, cored and
    cut into ½-inch pieces
1 scallion, thinly sliced
2 tablespoons minced fresh parsley

dressing:
½ cup olive oil
2 tablespoons red wine vinegar
3 cloves garlic, minced
2 teaspoons fresh tarragon, or 1 teaspoon
    dried tarragon, crumbled
¼ teaspoon oregano
½ teaspoon salt
Freshly ground pepper to taste
8 lettuce leaves (any variety except iceberg)

1. Rinse the bulghur in a sieve under cold running water, then place in a medium-size bowl and pour boiling water over it to cover by 2 inches. Soak for 30 minutes, or until tender when tasted. Drape a cheesecloth over a sieve and pour in some of the bulghur. Gather up the edges of the cheesecloth and squeeze out all the moisture from the bulghur. Dump it out into a large bowl and repeat with the remainder.

2. Steam the green beans until tender but still slightly crunchy, about 10 minutes. Cool under cold running water then pat dry. Add to the bulghur. Sauté the mushrooms in the butter and add to the bulghur. Add the red pepper, scallion, and parsley, and stir to mix.

3. Place all of the dressing ingredients in a small jar with a tight-fitting lid and shake well. Pour over the bulghur mixture and toss until well coated.

4. Chill at least 2 hours or up to 24 hours. Taste to correct the seasoning before serving. Place 2 lettuce leaves on each of 4 small serving plates and arrange a mound of bulghur in the center.

open-face tomato sandwiches

When the tomatoes are their plumpest and juiciest I can't make enough of these delicacies. They are utterly simple, yet have a superb blending of flavors. Slice some of the best homemade-type bread that you can get (or if you have leftover homemade bread use that) and toast it, then spread it generously with mayonnaise (preferably homemade, p. 269). Take some large, ripe, juicy tomatoes, slice them thick, and place 1 or 2 slices on each toast. Spread a thin layer of mayonnaise on the tomato, then season with freshly ground pepper. Heavenly!

summer fruit salad

A luscious fruit salad that develops a beautiful rosy color as it sits. You can improvise, but I have found this to be the best combination of fruits. It is great for dessert, breakfast, or a light lunch.

serves 6 generously

sauce:
2 cups yogurt (preferably low-fat)
3 tablespoons honey
3/4 teaspoon cinnamon

1/2 pint fresh strawberries,
    hulled and halved

2 ripe bananas (sliced 1/2 inch thick)
1/2 pint blueberries
2 ripe peaches,
    peeled and sliced 1/2 inch thick
1/2 ripe cantaloupe,
    cut into 1/2-inch cubes

1. In a large bowl combine the ingredients for the sauce and mix well.

2. Set aside a few strawberry halves for garnish.

Toss the remaining strawberries and the other fruit with the sauce. Chill for at least 1 hour before serving or up to 24 hours. Serve each portion garnished with a strawberry half.

---

menu eight

cheese and onion boeregs
cacik
cantaloupe with strawberries and lime

The Boeregs are very rich, and the Cacik (yogurt soup) is thick and filling; however, if you'd like to add to this menu, you could serve Tabbouleh (p. 166) with the Boeregs.

cheese and onion boeregs

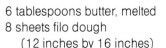

This is a light and flaky Turkish appetizer of filo dough shaped into a triangle and stuffed with a mixture of melted cheese and onion. It is a good choice for entertaining because it can be made in advance and frozen.

makes 12

> 2 medium-size onions, finely diced
> 1 tablespoon olive oil
> 1/2 pound Monterey jack cheese,
>   cut into small cubes (about 2 cups)
>
> 6 tablespoons butter, melted
> 8 sheets filo dough
>   (12 inches by 16 inches)

1. In a medium-size skillet sauté the onions in the olive oil until tender, about 10 minutes. Remove from the heat and transfer to a small bowl. Let cool.

2. Preheat the oven to 400 degrees. Have the onions, cubed cheese, and melted butter in front of you. Place the 8 sheets of filo in front of you, cover them with a sheet of wax paper, then cover the wax paper with a damp towel. (This is essential to prevent the dough from drying out.) Return any remaining filo to the refrigerator well wrapped.

3. Remove 1 sheet of filo from the stack, cover the stack again, and with a pastry brush *lightly* brush the surface of the dough with melted butter. Place a second sheet of filo on top. Brush it lightly with butter, making sure to get the edges. (Always keep the remaining stack of filo covered.) Using the tip of a pointed knife cut the buttered sheets of filo into 3 even lengthwise strips.

4. Place not more than 1 tablespoon each of the cubed cheese and sautéed onion near the corner of 1 strip. Gently fold this corner to make a triangle, covering the filling, and continue to fold the triangle as you would a flag, that is, folding the triangle in half in such a way that the triangular shape is maintained.

5. Lightly brush the top and bottom of the triangle with melted butter and place it on a baking sheet. Repeat this procedure with the 2 remaining strips.

6. Repeat steps 3, 4, and 5 until the 8 sheets of filo have been used. You should have 12 triangles. *May be prepared in advance to this point, covered, and refrigerated up to 8 hours.*

7. Bake for 15 minutes, or until golden all over. To freeze uncooked Boeregs, place them in the freezer uncovered on a platter. When frozen, wrap them in plastic or foil and return to freezer. Do not defrost before cooking.

cacik

Cacik (pronounced *chudge′ chik*) is a cold Turkish soup made with cucumbers and yogurt. It is ideal for a summer meal because no cooking is involved and it is so refreshing and satisfying. It is also wonderful served as a first course to a Middle Eastern meal.

serves 4 as a main course

3 cups yogurt (preferably low-fat)
1/2 cup water
2 medium-size cucumbers
3 tablespoons olive oil
1 tablespoon red wine vinegar
2 cloves garlic, minced
2 tablespoons minced fresh dill,
   or 1 tablespoon dried dill*

1 tablespoon minced fresh parsley
1/2 teaspoon salt
Freshly ground pepper to taste
1/2 cup walnuts, finely chopped

* Dill is one herb that does not dry well; it loses too much of its flavor. Fresh dill is worth going out of your way for.

1. In a large bowl whisk together the yogurt and water.

2. Peel the cucumbers and slice them in half lengthwise. Scrape out all of the seeds with a spoon and discard them. Dice the cucumbers and add to the yogurt.

3. Add all of the remaining ingredients and stir well.

4. Chill for at least 1 hour or up to 48 hours before serving.

cantaloupe with strawberries and lime

serves 4

1 medium-size ripe cantaloupe
12 fresh strawberries
1/2 lime

1. Cut the cantaloupe in half vertically and scoop out the seeds. Cut each half vertically in half again. With a sharp knife cut the fruit away from the skin, keeping it in one piece. Put the fruit back on the skin.

2. Cut the cantaloupe into 1-inch-wide pieces, keeping the fruit still on the skin. Now arrange the pieces of fruit by alternately pushing one piece forward and the next piece back.

3. Place the cantaloupe quarters on individual dessert plates. Slice the lime vertically into 4 wedges. Garnish each cantaloupe top with strawberries and lime wedges.

menu nine

yogurt herb cheese (p. 187)
(french bread)
new potato and dill salad
marinated vegetables with sesame dressing
summer pudding

It is a good idea to spread out your cooking schedule when preparing this menu. Make the yogurt cheese and the Summer Pudding the day before, and prepare the two salads during the morning of the day you are serving this meal. This will allow all the flavors time to develop, and will set a more leisurely pace for you.

new potato and dill salad

New potatoes are not a variety of potato but refer to any tiny, waxy potato that has been freshly dug. I prefer red-skinned for this salad because of their decorative color, although you could substitute any waxy-type potato with successful results.

new potato and dill salad (continued)

serves 6

    3 pounds new potatoes (red-skinned)
        (about 13 small- to medium-size)
    1/4 cup hot Vegetable Stock,
        homemade (p. 267) or store-bought
    3 scallions, thinly sliced

dressing:
1/4 cup red wine vinegar
1 teaspoon Dijon-style mustard
2/3 cup olive oil
1 teaspoon salt
Freshly ground pepper to taste
1 clove garlic, minced
1/4 cup coarsely chopped fresh dill

1. Scrub the potatoes very well with a vegetable brush. Leaving the skin on, cut each one in half. (If some are considerably larger than others, cut them so that the pieces are of equal size.)

2. Bring a large (6-quart) pot of water to a boil. Add the potatoes and cook, covered, for about 25 minutes, or until they are tender—not mushy—when carefully pierced with a knife. Drain in a colander.

3. Cut each potato piece into bite-size pieces and put in a large serving bowl. Pour on the hot vegetable stock and toss gently. Add the sliced scallions and toss again.

4. To make the dressing: Mix all of the ingredients in a medium-size jar with a tight-fitting lid. Shake vigorously. Pour the dressing over the potatoes and toss carefully but thoroughly. Cover and chill for about 30 minutes before serving. Serve cool or at room temperature, but *not* cold.

note:
If you make this dish a day in advance be sure to bring it near room temperature before serving, and taste to adjust the seasonings.

marinated vegetables with sesame dressing

The current popularity and widespread availability of Oriental sesame oil is a great boon for sesame lovers like me. In this salad it has a pronounced, though not overpowering, flavor and provides a welcome change from the more common garlic-herb flavors of many marinated dishes.

serves 6

dressing:
3 tablespoons Chinese rice vinegar
  (or other vinegar)
2 tablespoons tamari soy sauce
2 tablespoons peanut oil
1 tablespoon Oriental sesame oil[G]
1 clove garlic, minced
1/4 teaspoon dried red pepper flakes
1/4 teaspoon sugar

3 medium-size carrots, cut diagonally into
  1/8-inch slices
2 medium-size cucumbers
2 large red bell peppers, seeded and
  cut into 1-inch squares
3 ounces fresh snow peas, strung and
  cut into 1-inch pieces
1 tablespoon sesame seeds
3 scallions, cut diagonally into 1/8-inch slices

1. Put the dressing ingredients in a jar with a tight-fitting lid and shake vigorously.

2. Bring a medium-size pot of water to a boil. Blanch the carrots in boiling water for 4 minutes, or until tender yet still crunchy. Cool under running water, then pat very dry. Put in a medium-large serving bowl.

3. Peel the cucumbers and slice them in half lengthwise. With a small spoon scrape out the seeds and discard them. Cut the cucumbers into slices 1/4 inch thick and add to the serving bowl.

4. Add the red pepper squares and snow peas and toss. Add half the dressing and toss to coat well. Cover and chill at least 2 hours or up to 48 hours. Keep the remaining dressing at room temperature. (Note: If you are going to make this more than 2 hours in advance, don't add the sliced cucumbers until 2 hours before serving.)

5. Meanwhile, toast the sesame seeds in a small saucepan over medium heat until they begin to get fragrant. Stir often and do not let them burn.

6. Before serving add the sliced scallions and the remaining dressing and toss well. Garnish with the sesame seeds. Serve cool, not cold.

----

summer pudding

This English pudding requires only 3 minutes' cooking time—an important consideration on a hot summer day—but it must be chilled for 24 hours before serving so plan ahead. I prefer to make it with thinly sliced whole wheat bread for the added flavor and nutrients it provides, but white bread works well also. Present this on the prettiest platter you have, for its deep blue hue looks stunning when surrounded by vivid red strawberries.

summer pudding (continued)

serves 6

3 cups (1 1/2 pints) blueberries
1 1/2 tablespoons sherry
   (preferably cream sherry)
1/2 cup honey
Dash nutmeg

8 *thin* slices whole wheat bread
   (approximately), crusts removed
6 strawberries for garnish
   (with hulls left on)

1. Combine the blueberries, sherry, honey, and nut-meg in a medium-size saucepan, and bring to a boil. Cook for 2–3 minutes, or until the berries split and the juices are released. Remove from the heat and let cool.

2. Line a 1-quart round mold or round bowl with the bread by laying a slice on the bottom and surrounding it with diagonally cut slices placed around the sides. There should be no spaces showing.

3. Pour the cooled blueberry mixture into the mold and cover the top of it with bread slices. Do not overlap any of the bread. Trim off any excess.

4. Place a small plate on the pudding so that it rests right on the top, covering it completely. Place a 2–3-pound weight on the plate to hold it firmly down. Chill the pudding with the weight for 24 hours.

5. When ready to serve remove the weight and plate, then loosen the edges of the pudding by sliding a knife or rubber spatula around it. Place a serving plate over the mold and invert the pudding onto it. Spoon any accumulated juices back over the pudding. Surround the pudding with the strawberries and serve at room temperature sliced into wedges. This is also delicious served with lightly sweetened whipped cream.

menu ten

chilled summer borscht
wild rice and artichoke salad
(french bread)
strawberries with yogurt

To keep your house cool if you are making this in the summer, try cooking the beets and the rice the night before or in the early morning; this will also give them plenty of time to chill thoroughly before you put together the two dishes.

chilled summer borscht

There seem to be as many versions of borscht as there are species of plants. I like cold borscht to be smooth and spicy and topped with luscious sour cream. My husband looks forward to this soup each summer, and so in our house this recipe serves only two!

serves 4 generously

8 medium-size beets*
1 cup beet cooking liquid
1 1/2 cups tomato purée
Juice of 2 lemons
A few dashes Tabasco
1 small onion, minced
Salt to taste

Freshly ground pepper to taste
1 cup sour cream
Minced fresh parsley for garnish

*Two 1-pound cans of beets can be used instead of fresh beets if it is too hot to cook fresh beets or if you cannot get them. Reserve 1 cup of beet liquid and proceed with step 3.

1. Cut the beet greens off the beets, leaving 1 inch of their stems attached, and leave on the root ends. This ensures that the beets won't bleed profusely and you'll get optimum color. Scrub with a vegetable brush under cold running water to remove all the dirt.

2. If the beets are approximately the same size, then put them in a large pot and cover with water (otherwise cook them in stages, that is, cook the larger ones first and add the smaller ones after a while). Bring to a boil and cook, covered, for about 1 hour, or until tender when carefully pierced with a sharp knife. Drain very well and *reserve the beet liquid.* Let sit until cool enough to handle, then peel them.

3. Chop the beets coarse and put them in a blender or food processor with all of the remaining ingredients except the sour cream and parsley, and blend until smooth. If the soup is too thick add a little more of the reserved beet juice. Pour into a bowl and chill very well. It is a good idea to chill your serving bowls also.

4. When ready to serve, taste to adjust the seasoning. Serve in bowls and top with a spoonful of sour cream and some minced parsley.

note:
If you have fresh-looking beet greens, then serve them as a side dish at another meal. Rinse them very well, steam or sauté them, then stir in some sour cream.

wild rice and artichoke salad

Wild rice, which is technically not a rice at all but a grass, is very expensive so I save it for special occasions and stretch it a bit by cooking it with brown rice. Although this salad does not take a lot of time to prepare, you should begin cooking the rice in the morning or the night before so it can get thoroughly chilled.

serves 4 as a main course

> 3/4 cup wild rice
> 3/4 cup brown rice
> 3 cups water
> 1 tablespoon oil
> 1/2 teaspoon salt
> 6-ounce jar marinated artichoke hearts, drained and halved
> 1 red bell (sweet) pepper, cored and cut into 1/2-inch pieces
> 3 scallions, thinly sliced
> 1 medium-size carrot, very thinly sliced

dressing:
> 2/3 cup olive oil
> 3 tablespoons red wine vinegar
> 1 teaspoon Dijon-style mustard
> 1 clove garlic, minced
> 1/2 teaspoon poultry seasoning
> 1 teaspoon thyme
> 1/4 teaspoon basil
> 1/4 teaspoon oregano
> 1/2 teaspoon salt
> Liberal seasoning freshly ground pepper

> 1 small head leaf lettuce (such as Boston, red or green leaf), washed, dried, and torn into bite-size pieces

1. Rinse the wild rice in a strainer under cold running water. Put in a medium-size bowl and pour on boiling water to cover. Let soak for 30 minutes, then drain thoroughly.

2. Rinse the brown rice in a strainer and put in a medium-size saucepan along with the drained wild rice, 3 cups of water, oil, and salt. Cover and bring to a boil. Reduce the heat to a simmer and cook until all of the liquid is absorbed, about 45 minutes. Do *not* stir the rice at any time. When done put in a large bowl and chill until very cold, about 2 hours.

3. When the rice is cold add the artichoke, pepper, scallions, and carrot, and toss well.

4. To make the marinade combine all of the dressing ingredients in a jar with a tight-fitting lid and shake vigorously. Pour over the salad and toss well. Chill for 2 hours or up to 24 hours. To serve, arrange equal portions of lettuce on 4 large plates and mound on the rice salad.

strawberries with yogurt

serves 4

    1 pint strawberries
    1 1/2 cups plain yogurt
      (preferably low-fat)
    3 tablespoons honey

1. Rinse the strawberries and pat dry with a paper towel. Hull them, then slice each one in half (cut the very large ones in quarters) and place them in a medium-size bowl. Reserve 4 slices for garnish.

2. With a fork mash a few strawberries against the side of the bowl to release their juices and color the sauce. Add the yogurt and honey and stir to blend. Cover and chill for at least 1 hour or up to 8 hours before serving. Serve in decorative goblets or dishes and garnish each serving with a strawberry slice.

breakfast and brunch menus

The line that divides breakfast and brunch is amorphous, although most people have a general idea of what they consider breakfast food and what comprises a suitable brunch. For me, breakfast is usually a simpler affair, in which I serve in some combination: cereal, muffins, scones, yogurt, fruit, pancakes, or perhaps eggs, and breakfast is eaten in the early morning. Brunch is a more festive meal, oftentimes beginning with a fruit-based alcoholic drink, and including a wider variety of foods, which are more elaborately presented, such as quiches, special egg dishes, pastries, baked goods, etc., and frequently ending with a dessert. Brunch, being a combination of breakfast and lunch, is served in the late morning.

Here are some menus that range from the simple to the elaborate, and most of them have suggestions for advance preparation—something that is very important to the breakfast cook, who usually has to handle many dishes requiring attention at the same time.

menu one

orange and grapefruit sections with kiwi
maple pancakes
coffee or tea

Making pancakes for a group of people can turn into a harried affair even if you have an electric pancake griddle. The cook is usually unable to eat with everyone else because he or she must tend to each batch of pancakes that is cooking. A way around this predicament is to heat a cookie sheet in a 300-degree oven, and spread out the cooked pancakes on it as they are completed. This will keep them hot while you cook the remaining batter, and they won't get soggy as they often do when you stack them in the oven.

I think it is a good idea to serve fresh fruit with a pancake breakfast because it offsets the starchiness of the pancakes. This citrus and kiwi mixture is a pleasant combination of sweet and tart flavors.

---

orange and grapefruit sections with kiwi

If you cut the peel off citrus fruit and section it with a knife instead of your hands, it will be infinitely more delicate and colorful. To test the ripeness of kiwis, lightly press your thumb on the skin—they should feel tender, not mushy or hard.

serves 4

   4 large navel oranges
   3 pink grapefruits
   2 ripe kiwis

1. To section the oranges and grapefruits cut a slice off the top and bottom of each fruit to expose the flesh. Stand the fruit upright and cut off the skin from top to bottom. One by one hold a piece of fruit in your hand and with a small sharp knife cut away each section of fruit from its membrane. Do this over a bowl to collect any juice that drips, and let each section fall into the bowl. Squeeze out all of the juice from the remaining membrane into the bowl.

2. Peel the kiwis, cut them into 1/4-inch-thick slices, and add them to the bowl. Serve at room temperature in small bowls or decorative goblets.

maple pancakes

serves 4

2½ cups whole wheat pastry flour
   (or 1¼ cups whole wheat flour and
   1¼ cups unbleached white flour)
1 tablespoon baking powder
1 teaspoon salt
2 eggs, beaten

2 cups milk
2 tablespoons pure maple syrup
6 tablespoons melted butter,
   slightly cooled
Oil
Maple syrup

1. Mix the flour, baking powder, and salt together in a large bowl.

2. Beat the eggs with the milk and maple syrup in a medium-size bowl until well mixed. Add to the dry ingredients along with the melted butter and stir just until blended. It's all right if the batter is lumpy; do not overmix. Let sit for 10 minutes before cooking.

3. Heat a large skillet (or a small one if you prefer to cook 1 medium-size pancake at a time) over medium heat with a little oil to coat the bottom. Test the pan's readiness by adding a drop of batter—it should sizzle immediately. Spoon some batter into the pan to make the pancakes the size you want. Flip them over once the surface is covered with broken bubbles. They should be a nice golden brown. Repeat with the remaining batter.

4. Serve with maple syrup. (If your maple syrup has been chilled, then heat it slightly so it doesn't make your pancakes cold.)

note:
This recipe can be halved successfully if you are serving only 2 people.

menu two

granola (with yogurt or milk)
blueberry muffins
coffee or tea

For a nice change try Granola served with yogurt and a little honey or maple syrup; I think you'll find that it is more delicious that way. These Blueberry Muffins do freeze and reheat well, so if you are going to be pressed for time, or if you have any leftovers, wrap them in foil or plastic once they are thoroughly cooled, then freeze them in a plastic bag. Reheat them unthawed in a 350-degree oven for 15 minutes, or until hot throughout.

---

granola

Some granolas are filled with nutritious ingredients but somehow aren't particularly appetizing. This is the best granola I've tasted. It has a deliciously sweet cinnamon flavor—though not overly sweet—and just the right balance of textures. It is very easy to make, but you must watch it carefully during the second half of cooking, for it burns easily.

makes 3–3 1/2 quarts

1/2 cup oil
1/2 cup honey
6 cups rolled oats (non-instant oatmeal)
2/3 cup bran or wheat germ
2/3 teaspoon salt
1 tablespoon cinnamon

2 cups unsweetened dried coconut
(purchased at health food stores)
1/2 cup sesame seeds
or sunflower seeds
2 cups chopped walnuts
1 1/3 cups raisins

1. Preheat the oven to 350 degrees. Combine the oil and honey in a large pot and heat until blended; do not boil it. Add all of the remaining ingredients except the raisins, and stir until thoroughly mixed.

granola (continued)

2. Bake in 2 or 3 batches. Place one-half or one-third on a jelly roll pan, or any other large shallow pan with sides, for 10 minutes. For the next 5–10 minutes occasionally toss the granola with a spatula to prevent it from burning. Be especially attentive to the sides, where it burns more easily. When ready the granola will be lightly browned but still somewhat soft; it gets crisp when cooled.

3. Remove the pan from the oven and scrape this batch into a large bowl. Add half or a third of the raisins—depending on the size of the batch—toss well, and cool completely before storing in covered jars or tins. Repeat this procedure with the remaining mixture. This granola will keep for 2–3 months in a tightly covered container in the refrigerator.

blueberry muffins

These large, fat muffins are filled with blueberries. The secret to all muffins and other quick breads is to mix just until moistened and no more. This recipe makes eleven instead of a dozen so that each muffin tin can be filled right to the top.

makes 11 muffins

2 cups whole wheat pastry flour
   (or 1 cup whole wheat flour and
   1 cup unbleached white flour)
1/2 cup sugar
2 teaspoons baking powder
1/2 teaspoon salt

2 cups blueberries (unthawed if frozen)
2 eggs
1/3 cup milk
1 teaspoon vanilla extract
4 tablespoons melted butter, slightly cooled
Sugar to sprinkle on top

1. Preheat the oven to 425 degrees. Generously butter 11 cups (medium-size) of a muffin pan (or pans). Make sure also to butter the top surface of the pan because the muffins will spill over during cooking.

2. Combine the flour, sugar, baking powder, and salt in a large bowl and mix well. Add the berries and gently toss to coat them.

3. Beat the eggs, milk, and vanilla together, and carefully mix the liquid into the blueberry mixture just until moistened.

4. Add the melted butter and mix just until blended. Spoon some batter into each muffin cup so that they are filled to the top. Sprinkle some sugar onto the top of each muffin.

5. Bake for 15 minutes, or until a knife inserted in the center of a muffin comes out dry. Let sit on a wire rack for 10 minutes before removing them from the pan. (If you want an extra sparkle, then sprinkle a little sugar on top of your muffins again as soon as they come out of the oven.) Serve hot.

note:
If you cannot serve them right away, then they can be reheated in a 350-degree oven for 10 minutes or so.

menu three

fresh fruit (p. 279)
french toast with orange and brandy
coffee or tea

If you feel that it would be easier to make the French Toast first, as it must be served the minute it is done, serve the Fresh Fruit afterward; you may find the pace more relaxed.

french toast with orange and brandy

Everyone seems to have his or her own idea about which type of bread makes the best French toast. I prefer French bread sliced on the diagonal, but whole wheat bread is a close second. Both are delicious topped with warm maple syrup.

french toast with orange and brandy (continued)

serves 4

5 eggs
2/3 cup milk
1/3 cup sugar
Grated rind of 1 large orange
1/2 teaspoon cinnamon
2 tablespoons brandy,
    or 1 1/2 teaspoons vanilla extract

12–16 slices slightly stale French bread,
    sliced diagonally 3/4 inch thick,
    or 8 slices regular bread
Oil for frying
Warm maple syrup

1. Beat the eggs thoroughly in a large bowl. Add the milk, sugar, orange rind, cinnamon, and brandy, and mix well. Pour into a shallow dish like a pie plate if your bowl doesn't have a good flat bottom.

2. Add a few slices of bread and let soak, turning occasionally, for at least 5 minutes if it's French bread, or 2 minutes if it's regular sliced bread.

3. Put a little oil in a large skillet and heat over medium heat until hot. It should sizzle when a drop of water is flicked on it. Fry the bread on both sides until golden brown and piping hot. Serve immediately or keep warm in the oven (300 degrees) while you prepare the rest. I like to serve these with a pat of butter on each toast and pass the maple syrup at the table.

menu four

(cape codder: vodka and cranberry juice)
egg and pepper croustades
sweet potato home fries
oatmeal scones
homemade prune butter
baked apples with honey and brandy (p. 31)
coffee or tea

This is a full-fledged meal, and one that will need thoughtful planning. I like to serve the scones after the eggs and home fries so they can be enjoyed with coffee or tea, which also allows me to prepare the eggs without any distraction. The baked apple dessert should be prepared and cooked first, then allowed to cool. The scones can be placed on a cookie sheet and chilled, then bake them while you are at the table eating the eggs and home fries. The home fries can be kept warm on the back burner while you cook the eggs and croustades. Got it?

egg and pepper croustades

This is an attractive and unusual way to serve eggs. Crisp, buttery toasted bread squares serve as shells for creamy scrambled eggs. Have everything that you plan to serve with the croustades ready when you begin. You will need about half a loaf of unsliced homemade-type white bread, or you can use French bread.

serves 4

4 slices of white loaf bread 1 inch thick,
   or 8 slices French bread 1 inch thick
1 1/2 tablespoons melted butter
2 tablespoons butter
2 green peppers,
   cored and very finely diced

8 eggs
1/4 cup milk
1/4 teaspoon oregano
Freshly ground pepper to taste

1. Preheat the oven to 300 degrees.

2. Remove the crusts from the bread. Bit by bit tear out the center of each slice, leaving a 3/4-inch wall, or 1/2-inch wall if using French bread. (Save the crusts and centers to make bread crumbs for future use.) Lightly brush the bread all over with the melted butter, and place the slices on a cookie sheet.

3. Bake for 5 minutes, or until lightly golden all over. Turn off the oven and keep the hollowed-out bread warm in it.

4. In a large skillet melt 1 tablespoon of the butter over medium heat and sauté the green peppers until very tender, about 7 minutes.

5. Meanwhile, in a large bowl beat together the eggs, milk, oregano, and pepper just until blended. Don't incorporate too mucn air into the eggs.

6. Reduce the heat under the skillet to low. Add the egg mixture and stir constantly until creamy and just the consistency you like for scrambled eggs. Be sure not to overcook them. Use a tablespoon to stir for the creamiest results.

egg and pepper croustades (continued)

7. Place a croustade on each plate and spoon equal amounts of eggs into the centers, spreading some to the peripheries also. Cut the remaining tablespoon of butter into bits and place on top of the eggs. Serve immediately.

---

sweet potato home fries

These are a nice change from the usual home fries that are made with white potatoes, and the beautiful orange color of the sweet potatoes will brighten up any breakfast (or dinner) plate.

serves 4

4 medium-size sweet potatoes or yams
  (about 1½ pounds), peeled
  and cut about ½ inch thick and
  2 inches long

¼ cup oil
2 large onions, diced (1-inch dice)
Salt to taste
Freshly ground pepper to taste

1. Heat the oil in a large skillet over medium-high heat until it is hot but not smoking. Add the sweet potatoes (they should be in 1 layer so you might have to cook them in 2 batches) and shake the pan to prevent them from sticking. Cook, tossing often, until they are golden all over—about 7 minutes.

2. If you have cooked the potatoes in 2 batches, return the first batch to the pan. Add the onions and cook, tossing often, until the potatoes and onions are tender—about 10 more minutes.

3. Season with salt and pepper and serve immediately, discarding any remaining oil, or keep warm in the oven until needed—no more than 20 minutes.

oatmeal scones

These are my favorite scones; they are light and buttery and have a delightful nubby texture from the oatmeal. You can also serve them for midafternoon tea along with fruit, butter, or jam.

makes 8 large scones

1 cup rolled oats (non-instant oatmeal)
1/2 cup buttermilk or yogurt
1/2 cup whole wheat flour
1/2 cup unbleached white flour
2 tablespoons firmly packed
   light brown sugar

1 1/2 teaspoons baking powder
1/2 teaspoon baking soda
1/4 teaspoon salt
4 tablespoons chilled butter
2 eggs

1. Preheat the oven to 400 degrees. Butter a baking sheet. Combine the oats and buttermilk or yogurt in a large bowl and let soak for 15 minutes.

2. In a separate bowl mix the flours, sugar, baking powder, baking soda, and salt until well blended. Cut the butter into the mixture with a pastry blender until the mixture resembles coarse meal yet still shows little chunks of butter.

3. Beat 1 egg lightly and add to the oatmeal mixture; blend well. Stir in the flour mixture and mix just until evenly moistened, then gather into a ball. If it is too dry add a little more buttermilk or yogurt. Turn the mixture onto a lightly floured board and knead 5 times. Form into a circle about 3/4 inch thick, and with a knife that has been dipped into flour cut the circle into 8 wedges. Place them a few inches apart on the baking sheet.

4. For an attractive glazed look beat the remaining egg with a teaspoon of water and brush some of this egg wash on each scone, if desired. Bake for 15–17 minutes, or until evenly golden. Serve immediately with fruit preserves and/or butter, or eat plain.

homemade prune butter

This Czechoslovakian specialty is my favorite topping for scones, muffins, and toast. It is sweet and richly flavored, and so a little goes a long way. This makes a nice gift when given in an attractive jar.

makes about 4 cups

3/4 pound pitted prunes
2 cups water
1/2 cup orange juice

Juice of 1 lemon
2 cups sugar
Dash salt

1. Combine everything in a heavy-bottomed medium-size saucepan and bring to a boil. Reduce to a simmer and cook for 30 minutes.

2. In batches purée the prune mixture in the blender or food processor and return it to the pot. Simmer another 20 minutes, or until the mixture is thick and smooth. To test whether or not it is thick enough, remove the pan from the heat, then drop a spoonful of the prune butter on a small plate. Chill it for 5 minutes. Remove and check to see if a rim of water has separated from around the prune butter. If so, it is too watery and should cook an additional 10 minutes. Test again. If no water has separated then it is done.

3. Let cool to lukewarm, then spoon into glass jars or containers with tight-fitting lids. Chill until ready to use. Prune butter will keep, refrigerated, for a few months.

menu five

orange lassi
samosa
bombay-style curried eggs
brown rice pilaf (p. 266)
brandied fruit compote (p. 127)

Here is an unusual brunch that is spicy yet not over-powering. It is a good idea to make the filling for the Samosa, the Brown Rice Pilaf, and the fruit compote the day before, so you will have more time the next morning for the remaining tasks. Keep the Samosa and rice hot in the oven while you prepare the eggs, so you can devote your full attention to them.

---

orange lassi

Lassi is the popular milkshake drink of India, made with buttermilk or yogurt and thinned with ice. It is served either sweetened, salted, or plain. Here is an interesting sweetened version that is made with orange juice and is served with crushed ice, Indian style.

serves 4

Juice of 2 large oranges
(about ½ cup)
2 cups buttermilk or yogurt
(preferably low-fat yogurt)
2 tablespoons honey

In batches place all of the ingredients in the blender with some ice and blend until the ice is crushed. Pour into tall glasses and serve immediately.

samosa

These Indian deep-fried turnovers are stuffed with a spicy potato filling and have a light crisp exterior. They are wonderful for entertaining because they can be prepared in advance, although they must be cooked just before serving, like most Indian breads.

makes 16

filling:
1 large potato, peeled
1 tablespoon Ghee (p. 272), oil, or butter
1 large onion, finely diced
1 teaspoon minced gingerroot
1/4 teaspoon turmeric
1/2 teaspoon ground cumin
1/2 teaspoon ground coriander
1/4 teaspoon cayenne pepper
1/2 teaspoon salt
2/3 cup frozen peas, thawed

dough:
1 cup whole wheat flour
1/2 teaspoon salt
2 tablespoons melted Ghee
   or melted butter, cooled
3–4 tablespoons water
2 cups oil for deep frying

1. Cut the potato into quarters and boil just until cooked through. Drain very well and cut into 1/4-inch dice.

2. Heat the ghee in a medium-size skillet over medium heat. Add the onion and sauté for 7–8 minutes, or until it is clear and limp.

3. Add all of the spices and stir to blend. Cook 1 minute.

4. Add the peas and diced potato, and cook for 2 minutes more, stirring often. Set aside to cool.

5. To make the dough: Put the flour and salt in a medium-size bowl. Add the ghee or cooled melted butter, and with your fingertips blend it into the flour until it is evenly incorporated. Sprinkle on 3 tablespoons of water and stir to blend. Gather the dough into a ball (if it is too crumbly add another table-spoon of water) and knead it for 5–7 minutes, or until it is smooth and elastic. Cover with a damp towel and let the dough rest for 15 minutes.

6. Divide the dough in half and roll each half into a log shape. Cut each log into 8 pieces and roll each piece into a ball. Cover the balls with a damp towel while you proceed with the next step.

7. Lightly flour your work surface and roll each ball of dough into a circle 3 1/2 inches in diameter. Keep the circles of dough covered with a damp towel. (You can let them sit for 4–5 hours.)

8. Put a small bowl of water in front of you. Divide the filling into 16 portions. With your finger lightly dampen the edge of a circle and spoon a portion onto the center of the circle. Pick up the turnover and keep it in one hand. With the other hand fold the turnover in half and pinch the edges together to completely

encase the filling. Repeat with the remaining dough and filling. *May be prepared to this point up to 3 hours in advance. Cover with foil or plastic and chill.*

9. Heat the oil in a medium-size saucepan. When it is hot but not smoking fry 2 or 3 samosas at a time, turning them to make them evenly golden. Cook only about 30 seconds; they should be light in color. Keep them warm in a 350-degree oven as you proceed with the remaining samosas. Serve and enjoy.

bombay-style curried eggs

This bright-colored Indian dish is excellent served as a breakfast, lunch, or dinner course, and it takes only minutes to make. It is creamy and spicy, and if it weren't for my concern about too much cholesterol, I could easily eat half of this recipe myself.

serves 4

8 eggs
¼ cup milk
½ teaspoon salt
Liberal seasoning freshly ground pepper
2 tablespoons Ghee (p. 272) or butter
¾ cup finely chopped mushrooms
6 scallions, thinly sliced
½ red or green chili G
    (seeds removed), minced, or
    ⅛ teaspoon cayenne pepper
1 teaspoon minced gingerroot
1 tomato, seeded and finely diced
    (fresh or canned)
¼ teaspoon turmeric
½ teaspoon ground cumin
Fresh coriander or parsley sprigs
    for garnish

G See Glossary of Ingredients about handling chilies.

1. Beat the eggs, milk, salt, and pepper together in a large bowl until well blended but not airy.

2. Heat the ghee or butter in a large skillet over medium heat, and when hot add the mushrooms, scallions, chili or cayenne pepper, and gingerroot. Sauté, tossing often, until the mushrooms are tender, about 10 minutes.

3. Add the tomato, turmeric, and cumin, and cook 3 minutes more, or until the tomato is heated through and tender. Reduce the heat to medium-low.

4. Pour in the egg mixture and cook, stirring constantly with a large spoon, until the eggs are set yet still very creamy; do not let them dry out. Serve immediately, garnished with coriander or parsley sprigs.

menu six

(fresh strawberries and sliced mango, if in season)
or winter fruit salad with apple cider glaze (p. 44)
irish soda bread
mushroom quiche
home-fried potatoes and onions
coffee or tea

If you make the Irish Soda Bread and the pie crust the day before, it will give you a lot more time to organize yourself on the day of this dinner. Be sure to plan so that you serve the quiche warm, not hot, and if you want to include a dessert, try Blueberry Streusel Cake (p. 6).

irish soda bread

When I was in Ireland I was served soda bread in every bed-and-breakfast house I stayed in (some ten to fifteen of them), and each one was different from the last. This is my favorite version, and one that is always eaten all up in one day in our house.

makes 1 loaf

2 cups unbleached white flour
1/2 cup whole wheat flour
1/2 cup bran
1/2 cup sugar
3/4 teaspoon salt
2 teaspoons baking soda

4 tablespoons butter, cut into bits
1 cup raisins
2 tablespoons caraway seeds
1–1 1/4 cups buttermilk or yogurt
   (preferably low-fat)
Milk

1. Preheat the oven to 350 degrees. Butter a round 1 1/2-quart baking dish and set aside. (If your dish is glass, then set the oven at 325 degrees.)

2. In a large bowl combine the 2 flours, bran, sugar, salt, and baking soda. Mix well.

3. Add the cut-up butter and toss. With your fingertips rub the butter into the flour mixture until it resembles coarse meal. Add the raisins and caraway seeds and mix well.

4. Add the buttermilk or yogurt and stir until the dough is evenly moistened, but don't overwork it. If the dough is too dry add a little more buttermilk or yogurt until it is the right consistency for kneading.

5. Turn the dough onto a lightly floured board and knead for 1 minute, or just until it is pliable; it will be sticky. Put it in the prepared baking dish and cut an X on top. (The easiest way to do this is to snip the dough with large scissors.) Brush the top of the dough with milk.

6. Bake for 55–60 minutes, or until golden brown. Remove the bread from the baking dish and let cool on a wire rack. Cool thoroughly before slicing.

note:
To avoid a crust that is too hard I put Irish Soda Bread in a plastic bag for the last half of the cooling time. I find it slices more easily when the crust is tender.

---

mushroom quiche

Many people have become indifferent to quiche because restaurants so often serve soggy versions of it. But a well-made creamy quiche can be a superlative dish, and is equally good for brunch, lunch, or dinner. The secret of a good quiche is the crust; it must be crisp and flaky. If it is undercooked it will be soft and soggy, so be sure to precook it as directed. It would be better to have it slightly overcooked than undercooked.

serves 4–6

1 recipe Pâte Brisée
   with Whole Wheat Flour (p. 275)
1 1/2 tablespoons butter
2 cups (6 ounces) thinly sliced
   mushrooms
1 medium-size onion, diced
4 eggs

1 cup heavy or whipping cream
1/2 cup milk
Dash nutmeg
Dash cayenne pepper
1/2 teaspoon salt
1 cup (4 ounces) grated cheese, either
   Swiss, Gruyère, or Monterey jack

1. Make the pâte brisée and prebake as directed — 13 minutes total. Let cool on a wire rack, and reduce the oven heat to 375 degrees.

mushroom quiche (continued)

2. Melt 1 tablespoon of the butter in a large skillet. Add the mushrooms and onion, and cook until the mushrooms are brown, about 7 minutes. Remove the pan from the heat.

3. Beat the eggs in a large bowl and add the cream, milk, nutmeg, cayenne, and salt. Mix until well blended. Add the mushrooms and mix again.

4. Cover the bottom of the pie crust with the grated cheese. Carefully pour the custard into the pie shell and shake gently to distribute it (see Note). Cut the remaining 1/2 tablespoon of butter into bits and top the quiche with it.

5. Bake for 20–25 minutes, or until it is golden on top and a knife inserted in the center comes out clean. Do not overcook the quiche or it will either become too dry or will separate and become watery. Cool on a wire rack for 15 minutes before serving. Quiche has a better flavor and consistency if served warm rather than hot.

note:
When you fill the pie shell don't overfill it with the custard. If there is any leftover custard, bake it in a small buttered dish until set.

home-fried potatoes and onions

serves 4–6

> 6 medium-size waxy boiling potatoes,
>   peeled and halved
> 3 tablespoons oil
> 2 medium-size onions, diced
> 1 teaspoon paprika
> Salt to taste
> Freshly ground pepper to taste

1. Fill a medium-size saucepan halfway with water and add the potatoes. Bring to a boil, then reduce the heat to a simmer, and cook, uncovered, for about 20 minutes, or until the potatoes are tender when gently pierced with a knife. Drain well. *May be prepared to this point up to 24 hours in advance, covered, and chilled.*

2. Cut the potatoes into 1-inch pieces and chill until they are cold, about 30 minutes (if they haven't already been chilled in advance).

3. Heat the oil in a large skillet over medium heat until hot. Add the onions and sauté for 5 minutes.

4. Add the cold potatoes and toss well. Cook, tossing often, until the potatoes begin to get brown, about 10 minutes.

5. Add the paprika, salt, and pepper, and toss well. Cook another 5 minutes, or until the potatoes are nicely browned. Serve immediately or keep hot in the oven (350 degrees) until you are ready, no longer than 20 minutes.

soups and breads

Since soup and bread are two of the most complementary and satisfying of foods, I thought they deserved a chapter of their own. Occasionally I will serve a small cup of soup as a first course, but I prefer it to be light and simple, that is, not a full-bodied soup that can stand on its own. A well-seasoned, robust soup is something to relish in its own right, and can therefore be the main course of a hearty meal, served with freshly baked bread and sweet butter or cheese. A meal based on piping hot soup and homemade bread can be suitable for a lunch, informal party, or dinner, and almost any type of salad will enhance the menu.

One of the great benefits of preparing home-made soup is that you can easily double the recipe and freeze a portion of it, or store the soup in the refrigerator for up to one week, in most cases. (Cream-based soups don't last quite as long as non-cream soups.) This is a smart thing to do if you wish to have a trouble-free meal readily at hand. An added bonus is that the flavor of soup improves with time. If mealtimes are hectic for you during the week, then plan ahead and prepare a pot of soup on the weekend. You'll thank yourself for your foresight.

cauliflower and pasta soup

A thick, luscious soup that doesn't demand much time to prepare. This soup is an exception to the soup rule in that it should not be prepared well in advance because the cauliflower and macaroni risk being overcooked and becoming mushy. Serve with a good whole-grain bread to add more protein to your meal.

serves 6 as a main course

4 tablespoons butter
1/4 cup olive oil
6 cloves garlic, minced
2 medium-size onions, diced
2 tablespoons tomato paste
10 cups Vegetable Stock,
    homemade (p. 267) or store-bought
1 tablespoon tamari soy sauce
1 bay leaf
1/4 teaspoon oregano

1/4 teaspoon basil
1/4 teaspoon thyme
1 1/2 teaspoons salt
Liberal seasoning freshly ground pepper
1 medium-size cauliflower (2 pounds)
1 cup macaroni
2 eggs, well beaten
1/4 cup minced fresh parsley
Grated Parmesan cheese

1. In a large stockpot over medium heat melt the butter with the olive oil. Add the garlic and onions, and cook for 10 minutes, stirring often.

2. Add the tomato paste and cook for 1 minute. Add the vegetable stock, soy sauce, herbs, salt, and pepper, and bring to a boil. *May be prepared to this point up to 48 hours in advance. Bring to a boil before proceeding with the next step.*

3. Cut the cauliflower into bite-size pieces. When the soup is boiling add the cauliflower and macaroni. Bring the soup to a boil again, reduce the heat, and cook for 20 minutes, or until the cauliflower and macaroni are tender, not mushy. Stir occasionally or the macaroni will stick to the bottom.

4. Raise the heat and bring the soup to a rolling boil and add the beaten eggs. Keep stirring until fine shreds form, about 30 seconds. Stir in the parsley. Serve in soup bowls with a liberal amount of grated cheese on each serving.

pumpkin bisque

This is a perfectly smooth soup with a delicate pumpkin flavor that is reminiscent of winter squash. Pumpkins intended for cooking should be small (preferably not over 5 pounds) to ensure a sweet flavor and smooth texture. For this soup be sure to use a good-flavored vegetable stock and include a few dashes of cayenne pepper for a hint of spiciness.

serves 4 as a main course

1 small sugar or eating pumpkin
    (about 2 1/2 pounds)
2 tablespoons butter
1 medium-size carrot, grated
2 medium-size onions, diced
2 cloves garlic, minced
1/2 teaspoon salt

5 cups Vegetable Stock,
    homemade (p. 267) or store-bought
A few dashes cayenne pepper
1 medium-size tomato
1/2 cup sour cream
Additional butter

1. Slice off the top and bottom of the pumpkin and set it upright. From top to bottom cut off the skin as you would cut off the peel of an orange. Cut the pumpkin in half and scoop out the seeds. Discard them. Cut the pumpkin into 1 1/2-inch chunks.

2. In a medium-size saucepan melt the butter, then add the carrot, onions, and garlic, and cook for 10 minutes over medium heat.

3. Add the pumpkin, salt, vegetable stock, and cayenne pepper, cover the pan, and bring to a boil. Drop the whole tomato in for 30 seconds, then remove with a slotted spoon. Peel off the skin and discard it. Cut the tomato in half horizontally, then squeeze out the seeds and discard them. Mince the tomato and add to the soup. Reduce the heat to a simmer and cook, uncovered, for 30 minutes, or until the pumpkin is very tender.

4. Purée the soup in batches in a blender or food processor until it is very smooth. Return the soup to the pot and whisk in the sour cream. Taste to adjust the seasoning. Serve in bowls with a pat of butter on each serving.

curried red lentil soup

This soup is quick and easy to prepare and is one of my favorites. The red lentils (actually tiny orange lentils) turn a golden color when cooked and have a rich, buttery flavor. If you have the red lentils and spices on hand, this is a fine soup to prepare on a moment's notice.

serves 4 as a main course

1 1/2 cups red lentils*
4 cups water
1 tablespoon oil
1/2 teaspoon salt
2 medium-size potatoes,
    peeled and diced (1/2-inch dice)
4 tablespoons butter
1 medium onion, diced

2 cloves garlic, minced
1 teaspoon turmeric
1 1/2 teaspoons ground cumin
1 1/2 teaspoons ground coriander
1/8 teaspoon cayenne pepper
Additional butter

*Red lentils are available at health food and Indian food shops.

1. Rinse the lentils in a strainer under cold running water. Pick them over and discard any stones, etc. Put them in a medium-size saucepan along with the water, oil, and salt. Bring to a boil and cook, uncovered, for 20 minutes over medium heat. Stir occasionally. (If a lot of foam rises to the surface, scoop it off with a spoon.)

2. Add the diced potatoes and stir to blend.

3. In a small skillet melt the butter. Add the onion, garlic, and all of the spices. Cook for 3 minutes, or until the onions begin to get tender.

4. Add to the soup, stir, and cook until the potatoes are tender, about 20 more minutes. If the soup is too thick thin with a little water.

5. Taste to correct the seasoning. Serve with a small pat of butter on each serving.

note:
Although this soup is delicious if served immediately, it is more flavorful if prepared at least an hour before serving, then reheated.

cream of fennel soup

This is a smooth and creamy soup with a mild anise flavor. The fennel that is usually available in this country is the variety known as finocchio, or Florence fennel. It has a large bulbous root with long stalks and feathery leaves. It can be eaten raw (in salads, for example), but has a much sweeter and more delicate flavor when cooked.

serves 3–4 as a main course

3 large fennel bulbs (about 3 pounds
   with stalks, about 8–9 cups diced)
5 tablespoons butter
1 medium-size onion, diced
1 large potato, peeled and diced

3 cups Vegetable Stock,
   homemade (p. 267) or store-bought
1/2 teaspoon salt
Freshly ground pepper to taste
1/2 cup milk
1 cup sour cream

1. Cut the tops off the fennel and reserve a few sprigs of the feathery part as a garnish for each serving. Cut the root end off the bulb, then cut each bulb into quarters. Slice the quarters into pieces 1/2 inch thick. You should have 8–9 cups.

2. In a large stockpot melt 3 tablespoons of butter over medium heat. Add the onion and sauté for 5 minutes. Add the fennel and potato and sauté for 5 more minutes, stirring often.

3. Add the vegetable stock, salt, and pepper, and bring the soup to a boil. Cover the pot, reduce the heat to a simmer, and cook for 20–30 minutes, or until the vegetables are very tender.

4. Purée the soup in a blender or food processor or put through a food mill, then pour it into a medium-size saucepan. If you purée it in the blender or food processor pour it through a medium-mesh sieve when transferring it to the pot.

5. Stir in 2 tablespoons butter, and after it has blended stir in the milk. Whisk in the sour cream until blended. Taste to adjust the seasoning. Serve piping hot, with the reserved sprigs of fennel for garnish.

kale and vegetable soup

This meatless version of the traditional Portuguese soup is both distinctive and substantial. Kale gives the soup a wonderful flavor and texture, and along with the kidney beans provides a good source of iron.

serves 6 as a main course

1 cup dried kidney beans
1/2 cup olive oil
3 large onions, diced
4 cloves garlic, minced
2 bay leaves
10 cups Vegetable Stock,
    homemade (p. 267) or store-bought
1 cup chopped peeled tomatoes
    with their juice
    (imported canned tomatoes)
1 1/2 teaspoons paprika

1/8 teaspoon cayenne pepper
1 1/2 teaspoons salt
Liberal seasoning freshly ground pepper
1 pound fresh kale
    (total weight with stems)*
3 medium-size potatoes,
    unpeeled and diced
2 tablespoons butter

*Extra kale can be served another time in Sautéed Greens with Garlic (p. 51).

1. Pick over the kidney beans and remove any stones, etc. Rinse them in a strainer under cold running water. Soak them overnight in water to cover. Or use the quick-soak method: Cover with water, bring to a boil in a covered pot, and cook 2 minutes, then let sit covered for 1 hour. Drain the beans.

2. In a large stockpot heat the olive oil over medium heat. Add the onions, garlic, and bay leaves, and cook for 10 minutes, stirring often.

3. Add the vegetable stock, tomatoes, paprika, cayenne pepper, salt, pepper, and kidney beans, and bring to a boil. Reduce the heat to a lively simmer and cook for 45 minutes, stirring occasionally.

4. Meanwhile clean the kale by dunking it in a bowl of cold water. Pour out the water, and repeat several times until the water is clean. Cut the stems off and discard. If there are any coarse ribs on the leaves, then rip the leaves off and discard the ribs. Roughly chop the kale. You should have 8–10 cups.

5. Add the kale and potatoes to the soup and cook an additional 30 minutes, or until the beans and potatoes are tender. If the soup is too thick add additional stock.

6. Remove the bay leaves and discard. To give the soup a wonderful creamy consistency remove about 2 cups of it and purée it in the blender. Return it to the pot.

7. Before serving add the 2 tablespoons of butter and stir to melt.

peasant cabbage soup

A thick, flavorful soup that is easy to prepare and would satisfy any appetite. It is served over a slice of toasted French bread and melted Swiss cheese, and finally topped with grated Parmesan cheese.

serves 6 as a main course

1/2 cup olive oil
4 medium-size onions, diced
4 cloves garlic, minced
2 bay leaves
3 cups (8 ounces) sliced mushrooms
1 small cabbage (1 1/2 pounds)
    shredded (7–8 cups shredded)
2 medium-size potatoes,
    diced, unpeeled
12 cups Vegetable Stock,
    homemade (p. 267) or store-bought

2 teaspoons tamari soy sauce
4 tablespoons butter
1/2 teaspoon thyme
1 teaspoon salt
Liberal seasoning freshly ground pepper
12 slices French bread (1 inch thick)
1 garlic clove, cut in half
3 cups (about 12 ounces) grated Swiss
    cheese (preferably Gruyère)
Freshly grated Parmesan cheese

1. In a large stockpot heat the olive oil over medium heat. Add the onions, garlic, and bay leaves, and cook for 10 minutes, stirring often. Add the mushrooms and cook for 10 more minutes.

2. Add all of the remaining ingredients up to the French bread. Bring to a boil, then reduce the heat to a simmer. Cook, stirring occasionally, for about 1 hour, or until the vegetables are tender.

3. Meanwhile rub the slices of the French bread with the garlic halves. Toast them under the broiler on both sides until golden. Be careful not to burn them. You can let them sit at room temperature to harden.

4. When the soup is ready to be served, taste it and adjust the seasoning. Place a slice of French bread in each serving bowl. Top with a generous amount of Swiss cheese, then ladle the soup over it. Sprinkle on some grated Parmesan cheese. Serve additional Parmesan cheese at the table. (Remember—don't eat the bay leaves.)

note:
For best results prepare the soup a few hours before serving to develop the flavor. If you have individual soup crocks, you can serve this as you would French onion soup. Ladle the soup into each crock, top with a slice of French bread, then Swiss cheese. Broil until melted.

curried chickpea and ginger stew

serves 4 as a main course

3/4 cup dried chickpeas
   (2 cups cooked chickpeas)*
1/4 cup oil
2 medium-size onions, diced
3 cloves garlic, minced
2 tablespoons minced gingerroot
2 teaspoons ground coriander
1/4 teaspoon ground cardamom
1/8 teaspoon cayenne pepper
16-ounce can imported plum tomatoes
   minced, with their juice (2 cups)

1 medium-size carrot, diced
1 medium-size potato, diced
1 teaspoon salt
4 cups water
3 tablespoons butter
Lemon wedges (1 per serving)
Yogurt (optional)

*If you are using canned chickpeas for this then rinse them in a strainer under cold running water. Proceed with step 3.

1. Pick through the chickpeas and remove any stones, etc. Put in a large (6-quart) stockpot and cover with water. Soak overnight. (Alternatively, boil the chickpeas for 2 minutes, and let sit covered for 1 hour.) Drain.

2. Fill the pot halfway with water and bring to a boil. Cook the chickpeas for 1 1/2 hours, or until tender. Drain in a colander.

3. In the same pot heat the oil with the onions, garlic, gingerroot, coriander, cardamom, and cayenne pepper. Sauté, stirring frequently, for about 7 minutes, or until the onions are tender.

4. Add the cooked chickpeas, tomatoes, carrot, potato, salt, and water, and bring to a boil. Cook for 30 minutes, stirring often, or until the vegetables are tender.

5. Swirl in the butter, and taste for seasoning.

6. Spoon into bowls and serve with a lemon wedge on the side. This dish is especially delicious with yogurt; serve a bowlful so each person can add his own if desired.

cream of broccoli soup

In my vegetable cooking classes we prepare almost every vegetable available, both the common and the exotic. But, if I had to choose *one* that has all the qualities that make a vegetable great, it would have to be broccoli. It is extremely delicious, nicely textured, very attractive, easy to prepare, relatively inexpensive, and highly nutritious—packed with vitamins A and C, iron, and calcium. Broccoli is wonderful in soups, salads, pasta dishes, quiches, stir-fried dishes, and simply steamed and topped with butter. It is not surprising, then, that cream of broccoli is one of my favorite soups. It *is* rich and high in calories, so I don't make it often, but when I do, I like it thick and creamy, and with chunks of broccoli throughout. Serve this soup with a salad beforehand and crusty French bread alongside it, and you'll have a luscious, satisfying meal.

serves 4 as a main course

2 heads broccoli
2 cups Vegetable Stock,
    homemade (p. 267) or store-bought
6 tablespoons butter
6 tablespoons unbleached white flour

3 1/2 cups milk
1/2 teaspoon salt
Freshly ground pepper to taste
1 cup sour cream

1. Cut the florets off the broccoli, then dice the stalk. Cook, in a medium-size saucepan, in the vegetable stock until tender yet still bright green. Remove the broccoli with a slotted spoon and reserve the stock. Set aside about 1 1/2 cups of the florets.

2. Melt the butter in a medium-size (3-quart) saucepan, then whisk in the flour. Cook this roux over medium-low heat for 2 minutes, whisking constantly. Whisk in the reserved vegetable stock, milk, salt, and pepper, and cook, whisking often, until it thickens and begins to boil, about 10 minutes.

3. Add the broccoli (not the reserved florets) and stir. Purée in batches in a blender or food processor until smooth. Return it to the pot and whisk in the sour cream. Add the reserved florets and taste to adjust the seasoning. If the soup is too thick, add a little more milk. Serve piping hot.

note:
If you are using powdered vegetable stock, add a little extra for a full flavor. You could turn this soup into a delicious cream of cauliflower soup by substituting one large head of cauliflower for the broccoli and proceeding in the same manner.

lentil soup

A popular vegetarian soup that is high in protein and iron and low in fat. Like many soups it improves with age, so try making it the day before you plan to serve it.

serves 6–8 as a main course

3 tablespoons oil
2 large onions, finely diced
4 cloves garlic, minced
2 green peppers, finely diced
10 cups Vegetable Stock,
  homemade (p. 267) or store-bought
2 carrots, thinly sliced
1½ cups lentils, picked over and rinsed
½ teaspoon thyme

Liberal seasoning freshly ground pepper
1 teaspoon salt
28-ounce can imported plum tomatoes
  with their juice, finely chopped
10-ounce bag fresh spinach or 1 pound
  loose fresh spinach (stems removed),
  finely chopped; or 10-ounce package
  frozen chopped spinach, thawed
2 tablespoons butter

1. Heat the oil in a large stockpot over medium heat. Add the onions, garlic, and green peppers, and sauté for 10 minutes.

2. Add all of the remaining ingredients except the spinach and butter, and bring to a boil. Reduce the heat to a simmer and cook, stirring occasionally, for 45 minutes, or until the lentils are tender.

3. Add the chopped spinach and cook for 5 more minutes, or until it has wilted and become tender. Taste to adjust the seasoning and add the butter just before serving. Stir until melted.

elegant yam soup

This sherry-scented soup is quick to make and very tasty. It is smooth and rich and most satisfying if served as a simple meal along with a salad and some homemade bread, such as Oatmeal Bread (p. 253) or Limpa Bread (p. 256).

serves 4

3 cups Vegetable Stock,
   homemade (p. 267) or store-bought
5 large yams (about 2 pounds), peeled
   and diced
3/4 cup heavy or whipping cream
3 tablespoons butter

1/4 cup dry sherry
A few dashes cayenne pepper
Salt to taste
Freshly ground pepper to taste
Additional butter

1. Combine the vegetable stock and yams in a medium-size saucepan, bring to a boil, and cook until very tender, about 20 minutes.

2. In batches purée the mixture in a blender or food processor until smooth, and return it to the saucepan. Stir in the remaining ingredients and heat through. Serve piping hot with a pat of butter on each serving.

making bread

Nothing delights the senses more than a kitchen that is fragrant with the aroma of home-baked bread. It is probably the *one* food that everyone loves and eagerly awaits. Unfortunately, many people imagine bread making to be an all-day affair, and that is clearly not the case. After approximately 30 minutes of preparing the dough, most of the other time involved is in waiting, and we're all good at that. You should allow 4 1/2–5 hours from start to finish, with most of that time available to do other things.

If for some reason you are interrupted and cannot complete making the bread, then wrap the dough in a plastic bag and chill it for up to 2 days. Knead it lightly each day to release carbon dioxide, then return it to the refrigerator. When you are ready to resume making it, continue where you left off, but it will take longer than usual to rise because the dough is cold.

If you want to freeze the dough, let it begin to rise, about 30 minutes, then punch it down and flatten it into a disk. Place it in a plastic bag and freeze up to 3 weeks. When you are ready to bake it, let it thaw at room temperature, and continue with rising where you left off.

Here are some things to keep in mind to ensure successful results:

• Have all of your ingredients at room temperature when you begin. If the flour has been refrigerated, put it in a bowl and slightly warm it in the oven. (Read about flour in the Glossary of Ingredients.)

• Yeast dissolves best in liquid that is about 90 degrees; it dies at 120 degrees. At 90 degrees the liquid will feel lukewarm — not at all hot. Many people kill the yeast by dissolving it in water that is too warm. Dissolved yeast will only bubble on the top when a sweetener is present. In these bread recipes I use packaged dry active yeast. One package is equivalent to 1 cake of compressed yeast or 1 tablespoon dry active yeast that is sold in bulk in health food stores.

• The more you knead the dough the lighter the bread will be. You want to develop the gluten in the flour, which will trap carbon dioxide generated by the yeast and give the bread elasticity. Knead with the heels of your hands and push the dough away from you, then fold the dough in half toward you, turn the dough 90 degrees and repeat. The dough should feel very smooth and elastic when it is ready, and it will spring back when two fingers are gently pressed on it.

• Bread rises best at 80–90 degrees. Cover the bowl that contains the dough with a newspaper (it's good insulation) or a damp towel to prevent a crust from forming on the dough. Set it in a warm place — an oven with a pilot light is ideal — or if you have an electric oven you can slightly warm it for a few minutes before placing the dough in it. Dough should take 1–1½ hours to double in bulk. If it rises too quickly, or if too much yeast was used, there will be large air bubbles baked in the bread. To test if the dough has risen enough, press two fingers ½ inch into the dough; the indentation should remain. The bread will have a finer texture the more times it is allowed to rise. I usually allow 3 risings to get a very fine crumb.

• If the bread is browning too fast when baking, cover it loosely with aluminum foil to prevent further browning. To test for doneness, first check the color of the crust; it should be a rich golden brown. Then remove the loaf from its pan and tap the bottom; it should sound hollow. When the bread is done it should be removed from its pan and cooled on a wire rack. If it cools in the pan the sides will get soggy.

• If wrapped well in foil, then placed in a plastic bag, bread can be frozen for 3–4 months without too much loss in freshness.

whole wheat bread

For superb flavor, texture, and quickness you can't beat a well-made loaf of whole wheat bread. If you are just learning how to make bread, then this is a good recipe to begin with; the dough is easy to handle and the results are impressive. The actual time of your labor will be only 25 minutes or so; the rest is waiting.

makes 2 loaves

3 cups warm water
1/2 cup honey
2 packages dry active yeast
1/4 cup oil

1 tablespoon salt
7–8 cups whole wheat flour
(preferably stone-ground)

1. Combine the warm water, honey, and yeast in a large bowl and let sit for 5 minutes, or until bubbles form on the surface of the mixture.

2. Add the oil, salt, and 5 cups of the flour, and beat vigorously with a wooden spoon about 100 strokes. This ensures lightness in the bread.

3. Add the remaining flour in stages, stirring until the dough becomes too stiff to handle. Turn onto a floured board and knead the dough diligently, adding more flour as necessary, for at least 10 minutes; it should be smooth and elastic.

4. Place in a greased bowl, pat down, then turn greased side up. Cover the top of the bowl with newspaper and allow the dough to rise in a warm place (85 degrees) until double in bulk, about 1 1/2 hours. (An oven with a pilot light is a good place.)

5. When double in bulk, punch down the dough to its original size, cover again with the newspaper, return to the warm spot, and allow to rise again until double in size, about 45 minutes.

6. Punch down again to its original size, and divide the dough in two. Butter two 1 1/2-quart loaf pans, shape the dough into loaves, and place in the pans.

7. Return the pans, again covered with the newspaper, to the warm spot and allow to rise until the dough reaches the top of the pans. Preheat the oven to 350 degrees about 10 minutes before the completion of this rising.

8. Bake for 50–60 minutes, or until the bread is golden brown and there is a hollow sound when the bottom of a loaf is tapped. Remove the loaves from the pans and cool on a wire rack before slicing.

oatmeal bread

A delicate-flavored all-purpose bread made with cooked and raw oatmeal for optimum flavor and texture. It is delicious served with soup, used for sandwiches, or eaten as a nutritious snack.

makes 2 loaves

2 cups rolled oats (non-instant oatmeal)
2 cups milk
1/3 cup honey
1/4 cup oil
2 teaspoons salt
2 packages dry active yeast
1/2 cup warm water
2 1/2 cups whole wheat flour
2 cups unbleached white flour
Milk for coating
1 tablespoon rolled oats (approximately)
    for coating

1. In a medium-size saucepan combine 1 1/2 cups of the rolled oats and the milk, and cook over medium heat until it is thick and begins to tear away from the sides of the pan, about 7 minutes. Stir often.

2. Scrape into a large bowl and add the honey, oil, and salt. Mix well and cool to tepid.

3. In a small cup mix the yeast and warm water together until the yeast is thoroughly dissolved. Add it to the oatmeal mixture and mix well. Let sit for 5 minutes.

4. Add the remaining 1/2 cup of oats, 2 cups of the whole wheat flour, and the unbleached white flour, and beat well with a wooden spoon until incorporated. (It will be difficult to mix but keep working on it.)

5. Turn onto a lightly floured surface and knead for 7 minutes (no less), adding the remaining 1/2 cup whole wheat flour as needed to prevent sticking.

6. Lightly oil a large bowl (ceramic is best), place the dough in it, then flip the dough over so the oiled side is up. Cover with a newspaper (for insulation) and keep in a warm place until double in size, about 1 1/2 hours. (An oven with a pilot light is good.)

7. Punch down, cover with the newspaper again, and return to the warm place until again double in size, about 30 minutes.

8. Punch down again and remove the dough from the bowl. Divide in two and shape into loaves. Butter two 1 1/2-quart bread pans and place a loaf in each. Cover the pans with the newspaper and let the dough rise until it just about reaches the tops of the pans, about 30 minutes.

9. Preheat the oven to 375 degrees. For an attractive coating, brush the tops of each loaf with some milk and sprinkle on some raw oats. Press on lightly with your hands to help them adhere well.

10. Bake for 45 minutes, or until golden brown. Test for doneness by removing a loaf and tapping its bottom; it should sound hollow.

11. Remove the loaves from the pans and cool on a wire rack until thoroughly cooled. If you are going to freeze a loaf, wrap it well in foil, then place it in a plastic bag and freeze.

four-grain bread

This is a highly nutritious and flavorful bread with a chewy, nubby texture—great for sandwiches, toast, or just as is. This gets my vote for a favorite all-time bread.

makes 2 loaves

    1 cup bulghur
    2 cups warm water
    3/4 cup honey
    2 packages dry active yeast

    1/4 cup oil
    6 cups whole wheat flour
    1 tablespoon salt
    1/2 cup cornmeal
    1 cup rolled oats (non-instant oatmeal)
    Oil

1. Make sure all of the ingredients are at room temperature. Put the bulghur in a small bowl, cover with boiling water, and let soak for 30 minutes.

2. Meanwhile put the warm water in a large bowl and stir in the honey and yeast. Let sit for 5 minutes or so, or until bubbles form on the surface of the mixture.

3. Add the oil, 5 cups of the whole wheat flour, and salt. Beat vigorously with a wooden spoon 100 strokes—not 1 less. This ensures lightness in the bread.

4. In 2 batches put the bulghur into a strainer and press out all of the liquid, then add the bulghur to the dough along with the cornmeal, rolled oats, and the remaining cup of whole wheat flour. Beat in these ingredients until well mixed. The dough will become difficult to handle.

5. Turn the dough onto a floured board or work surface and knead diligently for 10 minutes—no less. Keep flouring the work surface as the dough becomes too sticky to handle. You will probably use about 1 cup additional flour.

6. Place in a greased bowl, pat down, then turn greased side up. Cover the top of the bowl with a newspaper and allow to rise in a warm place (85 degrees) until double in bulk, about 1 1/2 hours. (An oven with a pilot light is a good place.)

7. When double in bulk punch down the dough to its original size, cover with the newspaper, and return to the warm spot. Let rise again until double in bulk.

8. Punch down again to its original size and divide the dough in two. Butter two 1 1/2-quart bread pans, shape the dough into 2 loaves, and place in the pans.

9. Return the pans to the warm spot, cover with the newspaper, and allow the dough to rise until it reaches the top of the pans, about 30 minutes.

10. Preheat the oven to 350 degrees. Brush the top of each loaf with a light coating of oil. Bake for 50 minutes, or until the loaves are nicely browned. After the bread is half cooked (25 minutes) brush again with oil—this ensures a tender crust. To double-check for doneness, remove a loaf from its pan and tap the bottom—it should sound hollow.

11. Remove the loaves from the pans, brush again with a light coating of oil, and cool on a wire rack. To freeze a loaf, allow it to cool thoroughly, then wrap in aluminum foil, and place in a plastic bag.

onion board

This delicious German bread is somewhat like a cross between a quiche and a pizza. It is about one inch thick and fits into a jelly roll pan, and is topped with a thick layer of onions in a light custard. It is easy to make and goes especially well with a large salad or soup to make a complete meal. I love to eat onion board any of three different ways—plain, with cumin seeds, and with caraway seeds. Because I find it difficult to decide which way I prefer it, I have come up with a clever solution—I make half of it plain, one-quarter of it topped with cumin seeds, and the remaining quarter topped with caraway seeds. One teaspoon of seeds will cover the entire bread, so decide which way you'd prefer it and measure the seeds accordingly. If you want to time it so that the onion board is ready at a certain hour, then allow yourself 3 hours and 15 minutes from start to finish (including cooling time).

makes 12 servings

1/4 cup warm water
1 tablespoon honey
1 package dry active yeast
1 teaspoon salt
1 tablespoon oil
3/4 cup milk, at room temperature
   or slightly warm
2 1/2 cups unbleached white flour

topping:
2 tablespoons butter
8 medium-size onions (2 pounds),
   halved vertically and very thinly sliced
2 eggs
1/2 cup sour cream
1 tablespoon unbleached white flour
1/2 teaspoon salt
Freshly ground pepper to taste
1 teaspoon caraway or cumin seeds
   (or a portion of each)
Paprika

1. Combine the water and honey in a large bowl. Mix in the yeast, and let sit for 5 minutes.

2. Stir in the salt, oil, milk, and flour, and beat until blended. Turn onto a lightly floured board and knead for at least 5 minutes, or until the dough is smooth and elastic. Flour your work surface as necessary.

3. Lightly oil a large bowl and place the dough in it. Cover the bowl with a newspaper or damp towel and put it in a warm place (an oven with a pilot light is ideal). Let rise until double in bulk, about 1 1/2 hours.

4. Meanwhile make the topping. Melt the butter in a large skillet over medium heat and sauté the onions until they are clear and tender, but not yet brown, about 5 minutes. Set aside to cool.

5. Beat the eggs in a medium-size bowl, then beat in the sour cream, flour, salt, and pepper. Stir in the onions, cover, and chill until ready to use.

6. When the dough is ready, punch it down and knead a few times, then let it rest for 10 minutes. Butter a 10 1/2-by-15 1/2-inch jelly roll pan, then roll

onion board (continued)

the dough out to fit and place it in the pan. Let rise for 10 minutes. Meanwhile preheat the oven to 375 degrees.

7. Spoon the topping onto the bread, leaving a 1/2-inch edge all around. Sprinkle on the seeds as desired, then lightly sprinkle paprika over the entire surface.

8. Bake for 30 minutes, or until the crust is golden. (Use a spatula to lift a corner of the onion board and peek underneath it.) Let cool for 20–30 minutes before serving, since it should be served warm, not hot. I find that it is easier to cut if I slide the entire onion board onto my work surface and then cut it into 12 squares. Serve them nicely arranged on a platter. Cover and refrigerate any leftover onion board.

note:
Onion board reheats very well. Place leftover slices on a pan or sheet of aluminum foil and heat in a 350-degree oven for 10 minutes, or until warm throughout.

limpa bread

This is a Swedish rye bread that is redolent of orange and fennel. Its slightly sweet character goes well with a spicy curried soup, and it is also delicious as a snack spread with a generous amount of natural peanut butter.

makes 2 round loaves

> 1 1/2 cups beer
> 1/4 cup (4 tablespoons) butter
> 1/4 cup honey
> 1/3 cup molasses
> 1 teaspoon salt
> 1/2 cup warm water
> 2 packages dry active yeast

> Grated rind of 2 large oranges
> 1 tablespoon fennel seeds, crushed
> 2 cups rye flour
> 2 cups whole wheat flour
> 2 cups unbleached white flour
> Oil or beer for coating

1. Combine the beer, butter, honey, molasses, and salt in a medium-size saucepan, and heat just until the butter is melted. Remove from the heat and let cool to lukewarm.

2. Combine the warm water and yeast in a large bowl and stir to blend. Let sit for 5 minutes.

3. When the beer mixture is lukewarm, add it to the yeast mixture. Stir in all of the remaining ingredients (except the oil or beer) with a wooden spoon until blended.

4. Turn the dough onto a floured surface and knead for 10 minutes (don't cheat), adding more flour as necessary. The dough should be smooth and elastic.

5. Oil a large bowl, then put the dough in and turn it so that the oiled side is up. Cover with a newspaper (the newspaper retains the heat) and keep it in a warm place until double in bulk, about 1 1/2 hours. (An oven with a pilot light is good.)

6. Punch down the bread, then cover and let rise again until double in bulk.

7. Punch down again and divide the dough in two.

Form each into a ball, then press down to flatten the bottoms slightly. Place on a buttered baking sheet and cover with the newspaper again. Let rise again until nearly double.

8. Preheat the oven to 350 degrees. Brush the loaves with oil or beer. Bake for about 50 minutes, or until golden brown. There should be a hollow sound when the bottoms of the loaves are tapped with your finger.

9. Brush again with oil or beer and cool on a wire rack. To ensure a soft, pliable crust you should place the loaves, when they are slightly warm, in a plastic bag for 1/2 hour or so, or until the crusts feel tender.

---

unyeasted gruel bread

This unusual and delicious bread is a modified version of Gruel Bread found in the *Tassajara Bread Book*. It is undoubtedly one of the easiest and most flavorful of breads to make, and it is similar in texture to the thin-sliced German bread that is sold in square packages in delis. Save leftover grains and vege-

tables and freeze them until you have enough to make the gruel, or make this bread in conjunction with Vegetable Stock (p. 267). I think it is best sliced very thin and spread with chilled sweet butter, and I've found that it becomes more flavorful with each passing day.

makes 1 large loaf

    6 cups leftover cooked grains,
       vegetables, beans, soup,*
       and/or salad (approximately)
    1/4 cup oil
    5 cups whole wheat flour
    1 teaspoon salt

* If you do use soup, then hold back some of the liquid and purée the vegetables, adding just enough of the soup's liquid to give you a thick, gruel-like consistency.

1. Combine the grains, vegetables, etc., with the oil in a blender or food processor, and purée until smooth. The purée should be the consistency of a very thick cream soup. You need 4 cups of it.

2. Scrape it into a large bowl and add the flour and salt. Beat with a wooden spoon until well mixed. Turn it onto a floured surface and knead for 10 minutes — not 1 minute less! If the dough is too moist, keep

unyeasted gruel bread (continued)

adding more flour until it is a workable consistency.

3. Grease a 1½-quart loaf pan with oil, then shape the dough into a loaf and place it in the pan. Cut 3 diagonal slits into the top of the dough with scissors or a sharp-pointed knife, and brush the top of the loaf with oil. It is best to let the dough sit overnight at room temperature, covered with a damp towel, but you can cook it immediately if you prefer. It becomes slightly lighter from sitting.

4. Preheat the oven to 375 degrees. Bake for 1¼ hours. To test for doneness remove the loaf from the pan and tap the bottom—if it sounds hollow it's done.

5. Remove the loaf from the pan and cool completely on a wire rack before slicing, at least 2 hours. Because one loaf goes a long way, I have found that it is a good idea to wrap half of it in foil, then place in a plastic bag and freeze. To serve, slice very thin with a serrated knife.

---

quick cottage cheese dill bread

Here is a bread that takes only 10 minutes to prepare, and the result is an impressive whole-grain loaf with a pronounced dill flavor, which tastes as though it had demanded the time and attention of a yeast bread. Its high protein content makes it an ideal companion to a large salad or soup to comprise a full meal.

makes 1 loaf

2½ cups whole wheat pastry flour
   (or 1¼ cups whole wheat flour and
   1¼ cups unbleached white flour)
2 teaspoons baking powder
½ teaspoon baking soda
¾ teaspoon salt

2 heaping tablespoons minced fresh dill
¼ cup oil
¼ cup honey
¾ cup milk
1 egg, well beaten
1 cup cottage cheese

1. Preheat the oven to 375 degrees. Butter and flour a 1½-quart loaf pan.

2. In a large bowl mix the flour, baking powder, baking soda, salt, and dill.

3. In a small saucepan combine the oil and honey, and heat just until blended. Remove from the heat and stir in the milk, beaten egg, and cottage cheese.

4. Pour this mixture into the flour mixture and mix

just until combined. Do not overbeat. Scrape into the prepared pan and press down the batter with a rubber spatula to prevent any air pockets from developing. Smooth over the top, then give the pan a good thump on your counter.

5. Bake for 45–50 minutes, or until golden on top. You can also test for doneness by inserting a knife in the center—it should come out clean. Cool for 10 minutes on a wire rack before removing it from the pan, and let cool at least 1 hour before slicing it.

note:
One tablespoon of dried dill weed could be substituted for the fresh dill but the flavor will not be as distinct.

cornbread

makes one 8-by-8 inch shallow loaf

1 1/4 cups cornmeal
1 cup unbleached white flour
 or whole wheat flour
4 teaspoons baking powder
1/2 teaspoon salt

1/3 cup honey
3 tablespoons butter
1 egg
1 1/4 cups milk

1. Preheat the oven to 400 degrees. Butter an 8-by-8-inch pan. (If the pan is glass then set the oven at 375 degrees.)

2. In a large bowl combine the cornmeal, flour, baking powder, and salt. Mix very well.

3. In a small saucepan melt the honey and butter together just until melted.

4. In a medium-size bowl beat the egg. Beat in the milk and the honey mixture. Add to the cornmeal mixture and stir just until blended.

5. Scrape into the prepared pan and bake for 25 minutes, or until a knife inserted in the center comes out clean. The cornbread should be golden on top. Serve immediately.

quick buttermilk herb and onion bread

A very light bread with a pronounced herb flavor.

makes 1 loaf

> 2 1/2 cups whole wheat pastry flour
>   (or 1 1/4 cups whole wheat flour and
>   1 1/4 cups unbleached white flour)
> 1/2 teaspoon baking soda
> 2 teaspoons baking powder
> 1/2 teaspoon salt
> 1 teaspoon basil
> 1/2 teaspoon oregano
> 1/4 teaspoon thyme
> 1/4 teaspoon tarragon, crumbled
> 3 tablespoons minced onion
> 1/4 cup oil
> 1/4 cup honey
> 1 egg, beaten
> 1 cup buttermilk

1. Preheat the oven to 375 degrees. Butter and flour a 1 1/2-quart loaf pan.

2. In a large bowl combine the flour, baking soda, baking powder, salt, herbs, and onion. Mix well.

3. In a small saucepan combine the oil and honey, and heat just until they are blended. Remove from the heat and add the beaten egg and buttermilk. Mix well.

4. Add to the flour mixture and stir just until evenly moistened. Do not overbeat. Scrape into the prepared pan and smooth over the top.

5. Bake for 30–35 minutes, or until it is golden brown and a knife inserted in the center comes out clean. Cool for 10 minutes on a wire rack before removing it from the pan. Let cool at least 30 more minutes before slicing it with a serrated knife.

---

sweet potato biscuits

Crisp on the outside, flaky and moist within, these buttery biscuits are a wonderful accompaniment to soup, or a delightful addition to a multicourse meal.

Actually, yams are preferred for their bright color but other sweet potatoes will work well also.

makes ten–twelve 2-inch biscuits

$3/4$ cup cooked,
    mashed yams or sweet potatoes
    (1 medium-large potato), cooled
$2/3$ cup milk
$1/2$ cup whole wheat flour

$3/4$ cup unbleached white flour
$2 1/2$ teaspoons baking powder
1 teaspoon sugar
$1/2$ teaspoon salt
4 tablespoons butter

1. Preheat the oven to 400 degrees. Butter a cookie sheet.

2. In a medium-size bowl combine the yams and milk. Stir until well mixed.

3. In a large bowl combine the flours, baking powder, sugar, and salt. Mix well until blended.

4. Cut the butter into the flour mixture until it resembles coarse meal. Stir in the wet ingredients just until blended. Do not overmix.

5. Turn the dough onto a floured surface and knead for just a few seconds. If the dough is too wet, add just enough white flour to make it manageable.

6. Pat it out a $1/2$ inch thick. With a 2-inch floured biscuit cutter or drinking glass cut out 10–12 biscuits, keeping the cutter floured so the dough doesn't stick. Place them on the cookie sheet, and then chill the sheet of biscuits for 30 minutes or up to 4 hours. (Cover with plastic if longer than 30 minutes.)

7. Bake for 12 minutes, or until evenly puffed and golden. Serve immediately. If you want to serve them in a bread basket don't cover them with a napkin or else they will lose their crispness.

note:
To reheat leftover biscuits, place them in a preheated 350-degree oven for 5–10 minutes, or until hot and slightly crisp.

whole wheat biscuits

My husband, Ed, who tries hard to stick to a low-fat, high-fiber diet, created these delicious biscuits, and they have proven to be a family favorite. We love to eat them with soups and salads, and for breakfast. They take no more than 10 minutes to prepare and should be served hot from the oven.

whole wheat biscuits (continued)

makes 9 biscuits

2 cups whole wheat flour
2 teaspoons baking powder
1/2 teaspoon salt

1 teaspoon oil
1 cup low-fat milk

1. Preheat the oven to 400 degrees. Lightly butter a cookie sheet.

2. Mix the flour, baking powder, and salt in a large bowl. Add the oil and milk and stir to blend. Stir into the dry ingredients and mix thoroughly. Turn the dough onto a lightly floured board and knead for about 30 seconds.

3. Pat out about a 1/2 inch thick, or just thick enough to make 9 biscuits. (Make slight impressions on the dough with a 2-inch cutter to see that you get 9 biscuits.) With a floured 2-inch biscuit cutter or drinking glass cut out 9 biscuits.

4. Place on the cookie sheet and brush lightly with milk. Bake for about 15 minutes, or until golden all over. Serve immediately.

---

sunflower buttermilk biscuits

If you like to serve homemade bread with soup or another type of meal and you don't have time for a yeast bread, then try these biscuits. They are so satisfying yet take only a few minutes to prepare. The sunflower seeds add a good flavor as well as texture.

makes 10–12 biscuits

1/4 cup sunflower seeds
1 1/2 cups unbleached white flour
1/2 cup whole wheat flour
2 teaspoons baking powder
1 teaspoon baking soda
1/2 teaspoon salt
4 tablespoons butter
7/8 cup buttermilk

1. Preheat the oven to 450 degrees. Butter and flour a baking sheet and set aside.

2. Toast the sunflower seeds in a shallow dish in the oven until they are golden and fragrant, about 5 minutes. Set aside.

3. In a large bowl combine the flours, baking powder, baking soda, and salt, and mix very well.

4. Cut the butter into the flour mixture until it resembles coarse meal. Add the sunflower seeds and toss well.

5. Stir in the buttermilk just until evenly moistened. Do not overwork the dough.

6. Turn the dough out onto a lightly floured work surface and knead it 5 or 6 times, or just enough to make it pliable. Pat it out a 1/2 inch thick.

7. With a 2-inch biscuit cutter or drinking glass cut out 10–12 biscuits. Lightly flour the cutter as necessary. Place the biscuits on the cookie sheet and chill for at least 15 minutes or up to 4 hours.

8. Bake for 12 minutes or until evenly golden. Serve immediately.

---

golden fruitcake

This is my most cherished recipe. I have worked on it for years to produce a rich, luxurious fruitcake that slices well and has a dense, yet delicate texture. It doesn't contain any citron or candied or glacéed fruit, but rather dried apricots, dates, raisins, and almonds. Candied fruit, which has been bleached, dyed, artificially flavored and preserved, is more like plastic than fruit, and I don't understand how people can make a cake filled with it. I think it has given a bad name to fruitcake for those who have never tasted other versions, and I hope this recipe will gain many converts.

I make this fruitcake each Christmas season and divide the batter into 10 baby loaf pans (I use disposable aluminum ones), and give them as gifts. You can make them up to a month in advance, chill them, and occasionally brush the tops with rum, sherry, or brandy for added moistness and flavor, or you can freeze them for up to 3 months. The cake is exceptionally good if served *thinly* sliced with a few orange or pear slices and either freshly ground coffee or a pot of special tea, such as Earl Grey. It is equally good for breakfast, tea, or dessert time.

To simplify the procedure for making the loaves, I like to cut up the fruit and dredge it in a little flour (to prevent it from sticking) the night before, and the next day I subtract that amount of flour from the recipe when I begin to put the batter together.

golden fruitcake (continued)

makes 10 small loaves (5 by 3 by 2 inches)

4 cups unbleached white flour
2 teaspoons baking powder
1/2 teaspoon salt
1/2 teaspoon allspice
1 teaspoon cinnamon
2 cups (10 ounces) finely chopped
   pitted dates*
4 cups (1 1/2 pounds) finely diced
   dried apricots, snipped with scissors
1 1/2 cups (6 ounces) seedless raisins
3 cups (12 ounces) finely chopped
   (not ground) almonds

1 pound butter, softened
1 pound dark brown sugar
1 cup honey
10 eggs
1 cup apple cider, or apricot nectar,
   or orange juice
2 tablespoons lemon juice
1/2 cup heavy or whipping cream
1/3 cup rum, sherry, or brandy

*For added convenience you can purchase dates already chopped.

1. Oil and flour ten 5-by-3-by-2-inch baby loaf pans. Preheat the oven to 250 degrees. In a large bowl combine the flour, baking powder, salt, allspice, and cinnamon.

2. In another large bowl combine the dates, apricots, raisins, and almonds. Mix in about one-quarter of the dry ingredients to evenly coat the fruit.

3. In a large bowl cream the butter with the sugar and honey until smooth and fluffy. Add the eggs and beat until well mixed.

4. Add the dry ingredients and mix until blended, then pour in the cider (or other juice), lemon juice, and cream, and mix again.

5. Stir in the dried fruit mixture by hand until it is well blended. Spoon the batter into the prepared pans and smooth over the tops.

6. Bake for 1 hour and 45 minutes, or until a knife inserted in the center of a fruitcake comes out clean. Cool on a wire rack for 10 minutes, then run a knife around each loaf and invert. Remove the pans, turn the loaves upright, then, using a pastry brush, brush the top of each fruitcake with some of the rum, sherry, or brandy. Cool completely before wrapping in foil, about 2 hours. Place the wrapped loaves in plastic bags and refrigerate up to 1 month, or freeze for up to 3 months. (It is a good idea occasionally to unwrap them and brush the tops with some rum, sherry, or brandy.) Although these fruitcakes are delicious on the first day, they develop a fuller flavor if they are allowed to age somewhat before serving. To serve, thinly slice with a serrated knife.

the basics

Every cook needs a collection of reliable recipes for basic techniques that are used repeatedly in cooking. A flaky, tender pie crust; a garlicky vinaigrette with just the right balance of vinegar and oil; fluffy brown rice; and a fragrant, rich marinara sauce are just a few examples of staple recipes that you should be able to depend on.

Here are my favorite versions of "the basics." I've worked them out so they are delicious, foolproof, and easy to make.

perfect brown rice

Brown rice, if cooked properly, should be light and fluffy. Follow these rules to avoid gummy rice: *Never* stir brown rice while it is cooking; do not overcook the rice or the starch will escape from the grains and the rice will be gummy; use long-grain brown rice for extra lightness; use the proper size pan in propor-tion to the amount of rice cooked; and add a little oil and salt to prevent foam from rising during cooking.

A clue to dishes using cooked brown rice: To ensure lightness use *cold* cooked rice when making any stir-fried rice dish or cold rice salad.

makes 2¹/2–3 cups cooked rice
serves 4

1 cup long-grain brown rice
2 cups water or Vegetable Stock,
    homemade (p. 267) or store-bought

¹/2 teaspoon salt
1 tablespoon oil

1. Put the rice in a strainer and rinse under cold running water. Turn it into a 1¹/2-quart saucepan along with the remaining ingredients.

2. Cover the pan and bring to a boil. Reduce the heat to a simmer and cook undisturbed for about 45 minutes, or until all of the liquid is absorbed. There are a few ways to make sure it is all absorbed: Look to see that there is no bubbling liquid; use a knife tip to carefully make a small separation in the rice to see that the liquid is absorbed; and finally listen to hear if the rice has begun to stick to the pan—if it hasn't, then there is still more liquid to be absorbed. You should taste the rice to make sure it is tender. If by chance it needs further cooking then add a little boiling water (do *not* stir), cover the pan, and simmer until it is all absorbed.

3. Serve immediately, or put into a covered baking dish and keep warm in the oven (350 degrees).

perfect brown rice with peas:

Cook the rice in vegetable stock as directed. About 5 minutes before the rice is done sprinkle ¹/2 tea-spoon basil and 1 cup cooked fresh peas or thawed frozen peas on top of the rice. Do not mix. When all of the water is absorbed remove the pan from the heat. Gently toss the rice and peas and add 1 table-spoon of butter cut into bits. Cover the pan and let sit for 5 minutes. Serve.

perfect brown rice pilaf:

Melt 2 tablespoons of butter in the saucepan. Add 1 large minced onion and sauté for 5 minutes. Add the uncooked brown rice and toss well. Cook 2 min-utes. Add the vegetable stock, salt, and oil, and cook as directed in the basic recipe.

vegetable stock

Here is a recipe for vegetable stock for those who want to or need to make it fresh. It would be dishonest of me to say that I make my own stock because I don't. Personally, I prefer to use vegetable powder or cubes from the health food store. They are extremely flavorful, have no preservatives or artificial ingredients, aren't overly salted, and allow you to spend your precious time elsewhere.

When you make homemade vegetable stock you have to use a lot of vegetables to get a concentrated flavor, and you must cook them a long time. After the stock is strained you are left with overcooked, under-colored vegetables that aren't suitable for serving. (However, if you have a garden, making vegetable stock can be a clever way to use oversized and imperfect vegetables that might otherwise go to waste.) But, if you prefer to make your own stock, there is really no need for those cooked vegetables to be discarded. You can use them in Unyeasted Gruel Bread (p. 257). If homemade stock greatly appeals to you, try this recipe; it is delicious and unfailingly easy.

makes 7 cups

8 cups water
1/4 cup tamari soy sauce
3 carrots, washed, unpeeled, and diced
3 celery ribs (leaves included), diced
4 cups chopped cabbage
1/2 bunch parsley (with stems),
    chopped

3 onions, diced, or 2 large leeks,
    thoroughly washed and sliced
    (green tops included)
6 cloves garlic, coarsely chopped
2 bay leaves
10 grindings black pepper
Dash nutmeg

1. Put everything in a large stockpot and bring to a boil. Reduce to a simmer and cook for 1 hour, stirring occasionally.

2. Remove the bay leaves and discard. Strain the stock and reserve the vegetables for Unyeasted Gruel Bread (p. 257).

3. Let the stock cool. Store in a tightly covered jar in the refrigerator, or pour into ice cube trays and freeze.

When frozen, put the ice cubes in a plastic bag and use the cubes as needed. The stock will stay fresh in the refrigerator for 7 days. After 1 week bring the stock to a boil, then simmer for 10 minutes. The stock will keep fresh for 1 more week.

note:
You can let the vegetables cool, then freeze them in a plastic bag until you are ready to make the bread.

vinaigrette

makes about 1 cup

3 tablespoons red wine vinegar
1 teaspoon Dijon-style mustard
2 cloves garlic, minced
3/4 cup olive oil
Salt to taste
Freshly ground pepper to taste

Put all of the ingredients into a jar with a screw top and shake well.

note:
This will make enough salad dressing for a salad to serve about 6 people.

---

creamy dill dressing

In produce stands now fresh dill is nearly as common-place as fresh parsley. This is fortunate because dill loses much of its flavor when dried. I love to use it in salads, breads, dips, marinades, and spreads, and so I try always to have some on hand. The most convenient way to do this, I have found, is to wash it and gently pat it very dry (or spin dry), then tear the feathery part from its stem (discard the stems), and keep it chilled in a covered container until ready to use. It will last 5–7 days this way.

makes 1 cup

1/2 cup yogurt (preferably low-fat)
1/2 cup Mayonnaise, homemade (next recipe)
   or store-bought
1 teaspoon red wine vinegar

2 teaspoons olive oil
1 clove garlic, minced
1 tablespoon minced fresh dill
Freshly ground pepper to taste

Mix all of the ingredients together in a medium-size bowl until well blended. Chill until ready to use.

note:
Can be prepared up to 3 days in advance, covered, and refrigerated.

mayonnaise

Many people have relegated homemade mayonnaise to the category of "untouchables," along with such culinary wonders as soufflés, pie crusts, breads, and home canning. As with these other feats, mayonnaise can be mastered with a little effort and a good dose of knowledge. If you have never made homemade mayonnaise, now is the time to face the challenge. That rich, fresh flavor will surely win you over from its sugary competitor.

There are two methods to making mayonnaise: either beating it by hand, or making it in the blender or food processor. The hand-beaten method produces a smoother, glossier mayonnaise. Machine-made mayonnaise (made with a whole egg rather than with just an egg yolk) is quicker to make, has more volume, and will last longer because the ingredients are more finely bound together. I prefer to make it by machine because it is so quick. Follow the guidelines below and your first batch of mayonnaise will be a glowing success.

• Make sure your ingredients and the container of the blender or food processor are slightly warmer than room temperature, otherwise the mayonnaise will separate. (If the oil, egg, and lemon juice are too cold, place each in a separate bowl or dish and warm them over a larger bowl containing hot water. Also, rinse your utensils in hot water to warm them.)

• Use a vegetable oil for a delicately flavored mayonnaise; or use a combination of vegetable oil and a light olive oil for a more flavorful version.

• After thoroughly beating the egg (this helps it absorb the oil), add the oil no more than a teaspoonful at a time, and thoroughly incorporate it before you add the next teaspoonful. If you add the oil too quickly the mayonnaise will separate.

• All is not lost if your mayonnaise separates. You can reconstitute it by adding one of the following to a clean bowl—an egg yolk, a tablespoon of very cold water, or a tablespoon of vinegar—and beating in a teaspoon of broken mayonnaise. Once it is blended add a little more mayonnaise, beat, then slowly beat in the remaining mayonnaise until it is well blended.

• Always cover and refrigerate mayonnaise promptly, for it can be a haven for toxic bacteria without showing signs of spoilage.

• Some say it is best to postpone making mayonnaise if a thunderstorm is predicted or is in progress because it will probably prevent it from binding. I have never had any problems, but I'm not sure if it was luck or a weak storm. Try it and see.

makes 1 cup

> 1 whole egg
> 1/2 teaspoon ground (dry) mustard
> 1/2 teaspoon salt
> Dash cayenne pepper
>
> 1 cup oil (preferably 1/2 cup olive oil
>   and 1/2 cup vegetable oil)
> 2 tablespoons lemon juice

1. Have all of the utensils warm or at room temperature. Put the egg, mustard, salt, and cayenne pepper into the blender and blend for 30 seconds. Or, if you are using a food processor, combine them in the bowl of the processor and set the metal blade in place. Process for 60 seconds.

mayonnaise (continued)

2. If using the blender remove the cover. While the machine (either the blender or the food processor) is still running add 1 teaspoon of the oil. Wait until it is incorporated, then add another teaspoon. Keep adding the oil at this slow pace until you have used 1/2 cup of the oil.

3. Add the lemon juice and blend. Add the remaining 1/2 cup of oil, continuing with a slow pace, though it may be increased a bit. You will probably have to stop the blender or processor and scrape down the sides occasionally as the mayonnaise thickens. Store in a covered container in the refrigerator for up to 6 days.

pesto

This Italian basil and garlic sauce is one of the greatest delicacies of all time. It is usually used as a sauce for pasta, but my favorite way to savor it is to spread it on lightly toasted French bread and eat it as an appetizer (p. 90). Traditionally it is pounded in a mortar, but this blender method works just as well and it is a lot quicker. Many contemporary recipes call for the addition of pine nuts, but I find them superfluous and indistinguishable in pesto.

makes 1 1/3 cups

> 2 cups moderately well-packed fresh
>   basil leaves (about 1 bunch basil)

> 2/3 cup olive oil
> 4 cloves garlic
> 1/2 cup grated Parmesan cheese
> 2 tablespoons butter, softened

1. Wash the basil very well to rid it of *all* of its dirt. It is best to do this by dunking it repeatedly in a large pot of cold water. Remove the basil leaves from their stems and pat very dry on a towel. Discard the stems. Measure 2 cups of packed leaves.

2. Put the basil, olive oil, and garlic in the container of a blender or food processor and purée until smooth. Turn off the machine and scrape down the sides as necessary.

3. Pour this mixture into a container and stir in the cheese. Stir in the soft butter and chill until ready to use. (Note: The secret of a smooth pesto is to stir in the cheese and butter by hand—not machine.) If you are going to use the pesto on pasta, then thin the pesto with a few tablespoons of boiling pasta water just before saucing the pasta. Pesto will keep for 1 month if covered with 1/4 inch of olive oil and stored in the refrigerator.

note:
To prepare pesto for freezing don't add the cheese or butter. Freeze the basil, olive oil, and garlic purée in a tightly covered container for up to 6 months. When ready to use, thoroughly defrost, then stir in the cheese and butter.

winter pesto

In the midst of winter many people regret not having had the foresight to freeze batches of pesto when fresh basil was in season; others self-indulgently used up their supply much faster than they expected. In either case, here is a recipe that will satisfy pesto addicts anywhere, and can be made in any season.

makes 2 cups

3 cups tightly packed fresh spinach,
   stems removed, rinsed,
   and patted dry
1 tablespoon dried basil
4 cloves garlic, peeled and halved

$1/4$ cup walnuts (optional)
$2/3$ cup olive oil
$2/3$ cup grated Parmesan cheese
3 tablespoons butter, softened
$1/4$ teaspoon salt

1. Make sure the spinach is patted dry. Put the spinach, basil, garlic, walnuts, and olive oil into the container of the blender. Blend until smooth, turning off the motor and scraping down the sides as necessary.

2. Pour the pesto into a container with a tight-fitting lid, and stir in the cheese by hand until blended. Stir in the softened butter and salt by hand until blended.

3. If the pesto is to be used as a sauce for pasta, add a few tablespoons of the boiling pasta water to the pesto to thin it out before tossing it on the pasta.

note:
This pesto keeps well refrigerated for 2 weeks with a tablespoon of oil poured on the surface to prevent dryness. For freezing, omit the cheese and butter and freeze in an airtight container. Thoroughly defrost before using, and add the cheese and butter after it is defrosted.

---

crème fraîche

This homemade version of crème fraîche is similar to the kind you can purchase in France. The culture in the buttermilk thickens the cream and causes it to develop a tart flavor. It is so simple to prepare and is a wonderful addition to desserts, sauces, soups, or whatever.

crème fraîche (continued)

1 cup heavy or whipping cream

1 tablespoon buttermilk

1. Put the cream and buttermilk into a small jar with a screw top. Shake a few seconds to blend.

2. Let sit at room temperature for at least 8 hours if your room is warm, or up to 24 hours if it is cool. Shake again to mix. It is ready when the cream is thick like sour cream. Chill until ready to serve.

note:
If you are in a hurry for the crème fraîche and your room is cool, you can *slightly* warm your oven for a few seconds, then turn the oven off and keep the crème fraîche in there to thicken for 8 hours. Crème fraîche can be stored in the refrigerator up to 2 weeks. It will become increasingly tart with age.

---

ghee

Ghee is a butter oil that is used by Indians because of its excellent keeping qualities. The milk solids and moisture, which promote rancidity in butter, are removed, thereby ensuring the ghee a longer life, and also allowing it to withstand higher temperatures than butter without burning. In addition, ghee has a distinctive nutlike flavor produced by slow cooking before straining; this distinguishes it from clarified butter.

makes about 1 1/2 cups

1 pound unsalted butter

1. In a heavy medium-size saucepan heat the butter over medium heat until melted. Be careful not to let it burn.

2. Increase the heat to high and bring the butter to a boil, then immediately reduce the heat to the lowest possible point. Skim off the foam that has risen and discard. Repeat this process once more.

3. Keeping the heat at the lowest possible point, simmer the ghee, uncovered, for 45 minutes. The milk solids on the bottom will turn a golden brown.

4. Remove the pan from the heat and strain the ghee through 2 layers of dampened cheesecloth into a storage container with a tight-fitting lid. (Note: If there are *any* solids left in the ghee, strain it again to prevent it from later becoming rancid. The ghee must be perfectly clear.)

5. Store it in the refrigerator or at room temperature until ready to use. Ghee will solidify when chilled. It will keep safely at room temperature for 2–3 months. If chilled it will keep indefinitely.

marinara sauce

This is my favorite tomato sauce, very garlicky and flavorful.

makes about 3 cups

1/4 cup olive oil
4 cloves garlic, minced
28-ounce can tomato purée
2 tablespoons red wine
2 teaspoons oregano
1 teaspoon basil
1/2 teaspoon thyme
1/2 teaspoon salt
Liberal seasoning freshly ground pepper

1. In a medium-size saucepan over medium-low heat heat the olive oil and garlic. Cook for 3 minutes, or until the garlic is lightly golden. Stir often and be careful not to burn the garlic.

2. Add all of the remaining ingredients and bring to a boil. Simmer the sauce for 20 minutes. Stir occasionally.

---

raspberry vinegar

makes 2 cups

2 cups white wine vinegar or
   distilled white vinegar
1 cup raspberries

1. In a medium-size saucepan combine the vinegar and raspberries and bring to a boil. Turn off the heat and let sit until cool.

2. Strain through a fine-mesh strainer into a bowl. Strain again through double thicknesses of cheesecloth into a jar with a plastic screw top. Store in a cool, dark place. It lasts indefinitely.

pâte brisée
(sweet or savory)

After much experimentation I have found that it is best to roll the dough right after mixing it; the traditional method of chilling the dough beforehand makes it unnecessarily hard to handle. Work quickly, though, to keep the butter cold.

makes one 9–10-inch crust

    3–4 tablespoons ice water
    1 1/4 cups unbleached white flour

    2 teaspoons sugar, or 1/4 teaspoon salt
    5 tablespoons chilled butter, cut into bits
    2 tablespoons oil

1. Put some ice in a glass of water and set aside.

2. In a large bowl combine the flour and either the sugar *or* salt (depending upon whether or not you want a sweet or savory crust). Add the bits of butter and toss to coat with the flour.

3. With a pastry cutter, or 2 knives, or the tips of your fingers work the butter into the flour until it resembles coarse meal.

4. Sprinkle on the oil and toss, then sprinkle on 3 tablespoons of ice water and toss again. Gather the dough into a ball (if you need more water add 1 more tablespoon) and knead 3 or 4 times to help distribute the moisture. Gather into a ball again and flatten into a disk. (To make the dough with a food processor combine the flour, sugar or salt, and butter in the bowl of a food processor. Set the metal blade in place and process for about 8 seconds, or just until *coarse* meal is formed. With the processor still running pour in the ice water [try 3 tablespoons; if more is needed add a little more bit by bit], then stop the machine as soon as the dough begins to form a ball. There should be bits of butter visible in the dough; you don't want it to be perfectly smooth. Gather the dough into a ball, then flatten into a disk.)

5. Lightly flour your work surface, your rolling pin, and the top of the dough. Roll it into a circle to fit your tart or pie plate. Make sure to keep turning the dough as you roll to keep it a perfect circle, and lightly flour underneath whenever it begins to stick. If it breaks at all pinch the edges together until mended.

6. Place the rolling pin on the center of the dough and fold one half of the pastry over it. Carry the pastry this way to your pie plate and unfold it over the plate. Press it in thoroughly and flute the edges. If you are using a tart pan then roll the rolling pin over the top of the pan to cut off any excess dough. Chill for at least 30 minutes, or cover and chill for up to 24 hours, or cover well and freeze. Proceed with your recipe. If you need to prebake the crust, then follow step 7.

7. To prebake: Prick the pastry bottom all over and spread a sheet of foil over it. Press the foil into the sides, then fill with dried beans or aluminum pastry pellets to weight it down. Bake in a preheated 400-degree oven for 10 minutes. Remove the foil and beans (save the beans for future crusts), and prick again. Bake an additional 5 minutes. Remove from the oven and proceed with your recipe.

pâte brisée with whole wheat flour

makes 1 crust

3–5 tablespoons ice water
1 1/3 cups whole wheat pastry flour,
   or 2/3 cup whole wheat flour and
   2/3 cup unbleached white flour

1/4 teaspoon salt
5 tablespoons chilled butter
2 tablespoons oil

1. Put 1 or 2 ice cubes in a glass with about 1/4 cup cold water and set aside.

2. Put the flour and salt into a large bowl, or mound it on a board or good work surface. Cut the butter into small pieces and add to the flour. Toss with the flour, then with a pastry cutter or the tips of your fingers work the butter into the flour until it resembles coarse meal. There should still be bits of butter visible, though.

3. Continue with steps 4–7 in the preceding recipe.

pâte sucrée
(sweet pie crust)

makes one 9–10-inch crust

1⅓ cups unbleached white flour
¼ cup sugar
½ cup (1 stick) chilled butter
1 egg, lightly beaten

1 egg yolk
1 teaspoon vanilla extract
1 egg white

1. Put the flour and sugar in a large bowl. Cut the butter into small bits, add, and toss with the flour.

2. Cut the butter into the flour with a pastry cutter or 2 knives until it resembles coarse meal. Alternatively, pinch the flour and butter between your fingertips until it is evenly distributed and forms a coarse meal texture.

3. Beat the egg, egg yolk, and vanilla together and stir it in with a fork until well mixed. Gather the dough into a ball and knead it 3 or 4 times to evenly moisten the dough. Gather into a ball again, then flatten into a disk.
(To make the dough in a food processor combine the flour, sugar, and butter in the bowl of a food processor. Beat the egg, egg yolk, and vanilla together and keep nearby. Set the metal blade in place and process for about 8 seconds, or just until coarse meal is formed. With the processor still running pour in the egg mixture, then stop the machine as soon as the dough begins to form a ball. There should be bits of butter visible in the dough; you don't want it perfectly smooth. Gather the dough into a ball, then flatten into a disk.)

4. Preheat the oven to 400 degrees. Lightly flour a work surface and the top of the dough. Roll out the pastry slightly larger than the pie pan into which it will fit. To keep the pastry round, turn it regularly while rolling, and lightly flour beneath it if necessary.

5. Drape the pastry over the rolling pin, carry it to the pie plate, and unfold it over the plate. Press it into the sides of the plate and flute the edges. If you are using a tart pan or quiche dish, then roll over the top of the pan with a rolling pin to trim the edges. Prick the crust a few times with a fork. Chill at least 30 minutes, or cover and chill for 24 hours, or cover well and freeze.

6. To bake blind (without a filling) line the pastry with aluminum foil, then fill it with dried beans or aluminum pastry pellets to cover the surface. This must be done when prebaking a crust or else it will shrink too much. Bake for 10 minutes.

7. Remove the crust from the oven, and remove the foil and beans or pellets. (Save the beans for future use.) Lightly brush the crust with some of the egg white to coat it—this will seal the crust and prevent sogginess. Prick the crust again, then return it to the oven and bake for 10–12 minutes more, or until golden all over and crisp looking.

8. Cool on a wire rack until ready to use.

note:
A crust baked like this is completely cooked and is used when the filling for the pie does not have to be baked.

almond nut crust

makes 1 crust

6 tablespoons butter, softened
1/2 cup sugar
1 egg yolk
1/2 teaspoon almond extract

2/3 cup unbleached white flour
2/3 cup (about 3 ounces) finely
    ground almonds

1. Lightly butter a tart pan and set aside. In a large bowl cream the butter and sugar with an electric beater until well blended. Add the egg yolk and almond extract and blend.

2. Add the flour and almonds and beat just until the mixture blends; do not overwork the dough.

3. Spoon the crumbled dough into the tart pan. Dust your fingers lightly with flour and press the dough firmly into the pan. Be sure to press it evenly into the sides. Chill for 1/2 hour. Proceed with your recipe.

orange almond crust:
Substitute the grated rind of 1 large orange for the almond extract.

wheat tortillas

Wheat tortillas are made from wheat flour, which distinguishes them from corn tortillas. They are light and delicate, and are popular in northern Mexico. Store-bought versions are often called "flour tortillas." It's a good idea to make these someday when you have extra time, and then freeze them, because they are much more tender than store-bought wheat tortillas. You'll be glad to have them on hand when you need them.

wheat tortillas (continued)

makes twelve 8-inch tortillas

2 cups unbleached white flour
1 teaspoon salt

1 tablespoon corn oil
3/4 cup warm water

1. Mix the flour and salt together in a medium-size bowl. Sprinkle on the oil and rub it into the flour with your fingertips until it is evenly blended.

2. Make a well in the center and pour in the warm water. With a spoon stir the water into the flour mixture until blended. Turn the dough onto a lightly floured board or work surface and knead for 5 minutes. Let the dough sit covered with a towel for 30 minutes (or wrap in plastic and chill overnight, bringing to room temperature before using).

3. Divide the dough in half. Roll each half into a cylinder and cut each cylinder into 6 pieces. Take a piece of dough and roll it into a ball in your hands, then flatten it into a disk. With a rolling pin roll the disk into an 8-inch circle, turning the dough as necessary to keep the circle evenly round. Lightly flour your work surface as necessary. (You should stack the tortillas unevenly as you finish them, so you can separate them easily.)

4. Heat a large skillet over medium heat until a drop of water sizzles when dropped on it. One at a time cook the tortillas about 1 minute on each side, or until light brown flecks appear. Turn with a spatula. Stack them on your work surface as you proceed. *You can use the tortillas immediately, or wrap them in plastic wrap and refrigerate them up to 4 days, or wrap them in foil, then plastic, and freeze them for a few months. Defrost before using.*

whole wheat bread crumbs

I always have these on hand in the freezer. They are very quick to make and can be made with stale bread or fresh bread.

1. Save ends from whole wheat bread and freeze them until you have enough to make bread crumbs, or use regular slices of whole wheat bread. Toast the slices in the toaster (if you only have a few), or lay them on a cookie sheet and broil on both sides until golden brown. Be careful not to burn them.

2. Let the toast sit at room temperature until it is cool and dry. Turn the slices over occasionally so no moisture collects underneath from their heat.

3. Tear a few slices into small pieces and put in a blender or food processor. Blend until fine crumbs are formed. Pour into a plastic bag. Repeat with the remaining slices.

4. Freeze in the plastic bag and use them as needed. As you collect more crusts keep making bread crumbs and add to this bag, so that you always have some on hand.

fresh fruit

Perfectly ripe, flavorful fresh fruit can make a light and satisfying dessert with little fuss. Rather than present a bowl of fruit at dessert time, I think it is infinitely more appealing to artfully arrange sliced fresh fruit (at room temperature) on a platter or on individual serving plates. You can serve the fruit as is, or macerate it beforehand in a liqueur such as Grand Marnier or Framboise, or add rum, sherry, or brandy with or without some sugar or honey mixed in. You can serve a scoop of sherbet with the fruit, and perhaps make a sauce of honey mixed with sherry or rum to serve on the side. Sweetened whipped cream or crème fraîche is also luscious served with fruit, especially berries.

Many people enjoy fruit and cheese for dessert, although I must admit that I don't care for cheese at the end of a meal; I much prefer it as an appetizer, or for breakfast with toast, or at teatime. If you want to serve cheese, then arrange it on the fruit platter with some crackers, and perhaps some seedless green and red grapes.

Children can be finicky about eating fruit, especially if you serve it for dessert. They somehow feel cheated. I have found, though, that most children can't resist dipping their fingers into a fruit platter, particularly at breakfast time. Aim for a striking color combination—easy with fruits, which are naturally so decorative—and you'll discover that most people will find it irresistible.

glossary of ingredients, etc.

Beans,

in their dried form, are a very important food for vegetarians and non-vegetarians alike because they provide generous amounts of protein and iron, and a moderate amount of calcium, while being low in fat. All dried beans, except lentils and split peas (which are technically legumes), should be soaked before cooking to cut back considerably on their cooking time. Pick them over to remove stones, etc., and rinse them in a strainer, then put them in a bowl, cover with plenty of water, and soak them overnight. Or you can put them in a pot with water to cover plus 2 inches, and boil them for 2 minutes. Cover the pot and let soak for 1 hour. Whether you soak them overnight or use the quick-soak method, you should drain them well, then cover again with fresh water and cook until tender. Do not add baking soda, for although it tenderizes the beans it also kills B vitamins. One cup of dried beans yields approximately 2½ cups cooked beans. It is always a good idea to cook extra beans because they can enhance so many vegetable dishes, or can be added to salads for extra protein. I oftentimes toss them with some vinaigrette and herbs, and keep them chilled to eat as a snack or appetizer. Canned beans, although slightly poorer in nutrients, can be substituted for dried beans, but you should rinse them well in a strainer before using them because the liquid in the can is unappetizing and usually contains a preservative.

Brown rice

is rice that has had only its hull removed. It contains fiber, B vitamins, minerals, and some protein. White rice has had the bran layer and germ removed and has been polished. It then has almost no nutritive value and so it must be enriched. Converted rice is considerably more nutritious than regular white rice because the rice is partially cooked (before the bran and germ are removed) in such a way that the nutri-

ents are forced into the core of each kernel, then the bran and germ are removed so that the rice is white. Brown rice has a nuttier flavor and chewier texture than white rice, and takes about twice as long to cook. For fluffy results try Perfect Brown Rice (p. 266).

Buckwheat noodles (Soba)

These are made from buckwheat flour, which is a good source of protein (p. 284), iron, and B vitamins. They can be purchased at health food stores and some specialty food shops. Because they have a strong taste, they seem to be more compatible with Oriental flavors than with traditional pasta sauces.

Bulghur

is made from crushed wheat berries that were cooked beforehand. This precooking imparts a nutty flavor and reduces the cooking time of the bulghur. Contrary to popular belief bulghur and cracked wheat are not identical. Cracked wheat is not precooked and therefore has a faintly raw taste to it. Bulghur comes in different colors depending on the type of wheat used. A reddish-brown color indicates hard American winter wheat; a golden color indicates Middle Eastern soft wheat. It is available in different gradations from fine to coarse. I prefer the coarse variety for its nubby texture. Bulghur is an excellent source of protein and a good source of iron.

Butter

Most professional cooks prefer sweet (unsalted) butter for its fresh, delicate flavor. If you must be very careful about your cholesterol count, then you can substitute margarine for butter in all of these recipes. I find that a change in flavor is most noticeable in baking, especially cookies, cakes, and pie crusts, but they will still be delicious. Margarine is usually quite salty, so cut back on the amount of salt in each recipe it is used in, or buy the unsalted variety. Salted butter (usually marked "lightly salted") is generally not as fresh as sweet butter because salt masks the flavor of rancidity if it develops, and therefore stores can get away with prolonging its shelf life. Rancidity would be very noticeable in sweet butter.

Buttermilk

is so named because originally it was the by-product of the butter-making process. Today buttermilk is made by adding a lactic acid bacteria culture to pasteurized skim milk to produce a milk that is thick and tart. It actually contains no butterfat and has the same caloric content as skim milk. (Be sure to read the label because some brands add whole milk or cream.) As with yogurt, the friendly bacteria that are introduced help destroy harmful bacteria in the intestines, and aid in the production of B vitamins. Buttermilk is an excellent low-fat source of calcium, and makes a wonderful snack food because it is filling yet low in calories.

Calcium

Recently there has been a lot of attention given to the need for more calcium in most people's diet, especially that of women. Osteoporosis—weak bones that lead to debilitating fractures—has reached epidemic proportions in the U.S., and white women over the age of sixty are the largest target group. It develops slowly, beginning at an early age, so people of all ages should be mindful of their calcium intake. Experts in bone disease recommend 1,000–1,200 milligrams of calcium a day, the equivalent of a quart of milk. But there are other excellent sources of calcium that are also low in fat, such as low-fat yogurt, buttermilk, skim milk, collard greens, kale, and broccoli; and tofu is a moderately good source. Spinach, Swiss chard, beet greens, and sorrel are also rich in calcium, but they contain oxalic acid, which binds with calcium, making it inaccessible to the body.

Chilies

come in various shapes, colors, and sizes, and there are estimated to be between 300 and 1,500 varieties,

ranging from sweet to fiery hot. The mild chilies called for in some of the recipes in this book can be purchased in 4-ounce cans. They impart a distinct flavor to dishes without any of the hotness associated with chilies. Never touch hot chilies with your hands, because if you inadvertently touch your face or eyes afterward, you will experience an unbearable burning. If this happens, flush your skin with plenty of water. Handle hot chilies, whether fresh, canned, or pickled, with rubber gloves, or when cutting them, use two small knives as though you were dissecting them. The seeds are the hottest part of the chili and are removed by most people except extreme chili aficionados. Chilies—even the most fiery varieties—aid digestion and don't irritate the stomach, as many people suspect. Your tolerance for them will greatly increase if you eat them regularly, and the *flavor* of the chili will be more pronounced as your taste buds adjust.

Cloud ears

These dark-brown dried fungi are sometimes called tree or wood ears, and when they are soaked they become crinkly and gelatinous, resembling floppy ears. They have a smoky taste and somewhat crunchy texture. Stored in a covered container in a cool, dark place, they will last indefinitely. They can be purchased in Chinese food shops and in some supermarkets, health food stores, and specialty food shops.

Coconut

I use unsweetened dried coconut, which is sold in health food stores, to make coconut milk and to add to various dishes. Supermarkets tend to sell only a highly sweetened variety. To make coconut milk put about 3 cups hot water and 2¼ cups unsweetened dried coconut in a blender and blend for 1 minute. Put it through a strainer over a bowl and press out all of the liquid in the pulp; you will get about 2½ cups coconut milk. Discard the pulp. Store it in a tightly covered jar in the refrigerator for up to 4 days. It will eventually separate, and the thick, creamy film that rises to the top will be coconut cream. (If you want to use the cream for something like piña coladas, then spoon it off the top.) When you are ready to use the coconut milk, shake the jar to blend. If you want to make coconut milk out of fresh coconut, pierce the eyes of a coconut with an ice pick or skewer and drain out and discard the coconut water. Preheat the oven to 400 degrees, and bake the coconut for 15 minutes. Wrap a towel around it, then bang it with a hammer until it cracks open. Remove the meat from the shell with the tip of a strong knife and peel away the brown membrane with a vegetable peeler. Cut the flesh into small pieces, place in the blender with hot water, and proceed as you would with dried coconut. If you want grated coconut instead of coconut milk, grate the flesh in a food processor.

Eggplant

I have singled out this vegetable because much has been written about the need to salt eggplant before cooking in order to remove the bitterness and/or cut down on its absorption of oil. I have experimented with various methods and have discovered that salting is unnecessary; fresh eggplant is not bitter, and the "sweating" that takes place when an eggplant is salted will not affect the amount of oil it absorbs. Eggplant does drink up a lot of oil, but you must be as stubborn as it is and just keep tossing it in the pan without adding more oil. Eggplant should be firm and shiny when purchased, and free of brown bruises.

Flour

I prefer to use Unbleached White Flour over bleached all-purpose flour because it is not treated with chemicals. Wheat flour is an excellent source of protein. It is milled from a mixture of hard wheat and soft wheat, and has slightly more gluten than all-purpose white flour. Gluten is the protein component of wheat, which imparts elasticity to dough when mixed with water. Breads require a lot of gluten to achieve a chewy consistency; pastries require little or no gluten for flaky, tender results. Whole Wheat Flour is made from the entire kernel of wheat (wheat berry). I prefer stone-ground whole wheat flour because otherwise the flour is ground with steel rollers, which produce heat and consequently kill B vitamins and vitamin E.

Whole wheat flour is an excellent source of fiber and B vitamins, as well as protein, and should be stored in a cool, dry place (preferably in the refrigerator) to prevent rancidity. Whole Wheat Pastry Flour is a whole-grain flour that is made from a soft spring wheat that contains little or no gluten; this makes it ideal for pastries and quick breads. Whole wheat pastry flour can be found in most health food stores, and should be stored in a cool, dry place, preferably the refrigerator. If you cannot get this flour, then you can substitute half whole wheat flour and half unbleached white flour for similar results.

Garlic

The popularity of garlic has waxed and waned throughout history, and it has been said to cure everything from leprosy to the common cold. Luckily it is fully appreciated now, for its potential as a flavor enhancer is unequaled. Garlic is known to lower high blood pressure; in fact, you can purchase garlic oil capsules for this purpose. It is certainly worth getting into the habit of always using fresh garlic in cooking because dried garlic is a poor substitute. To make peeling easier remove a garlic clove from a head of garlic and cut off the tip that was attached. Place the blade of a large knife on its side on the clove and give it a thump with your fist. Peel away the skin, then mince the garlic. Some garlic has purplish skin and some has white skin. What determines its potency is not its variety but the temperature during its growing season. Coldness tends to increase its assertiveness. But, once picked, garlic should be kept in a cool, dark, well-ventilated spot, not the refrigerator.

Gingerroot

Choose firm, plump roots with shiny skins and avoid gingerroot that is wrinkled and light in weight for its size. The skin is edible, but I prefer to peel it off because I don't like its texture. Store leftover gingerroot—either whole or chopped—in a tightly covered jar containing enough vinegar, sherry, or vodka to completely cover it, and refrigerate it for up to 6 months. You can freeze gingerroot wrapped in foil or plastic, but I find that its texture gets too spongy and it becomes difficult to grate or mince. You can make a delicious and potent ginger tea by chopping or thinly slicing about 2 tablespoons gingerroot and simmering it in 1 1/2 cups water for 20 minutes or so. Strain it, then sweeten it with some honey. It is the best remedy to relieve the congestion of a cold, or the aches and pains from flu. To mince peeled gingerroot, slice it very thin, then stack the slices and cut into very fine strips. Cut these strips crosswise into very fine pieces.

Honey

It might surprise you to discover that honey is not indigenous to the U.S.; honey bees were brought to this country by the colonists. Maple syrup is the sweetener that the Indians used. From a nutritional standpoint the value of honey lies in the fact that it is unrefined and untreated. Sugar has been bleached, and is devoid of all nutrients. Honey, if it is uncooked and unfiltered, has some vitamins and minerals, but not much to boast of. If taken in large amounts honey will act in the body the same way sugar does, though it is absorbed into the bloodstream a little more slowly. Mild-flavored honeys include clover, alfalfa, orange blossom, thistle, and tupelo. If you want to substitute honey for sugar in baking, use 3/4 cup honey for every cup of sugar, reduce the liquid in the recipe by a few tablespoons, and add a bit of baking soda (about 1/2 teaspoon) to counteract the acid in the honey. Some honey producers pasteurize their honey to increase its shelf life (which is ridiculous because honey is naturally bacteria-resistant), and also dilute it with other sweeteners such as corn syrup; so buy uncooked, unfiltered honey, if possible. If honey crystallizes in the jar, then stand the jar in a bowl of warm water until it liquefies again; crystallization is not a sign of spoilage.

Hot spicy or chili oil

This Chinese oil comes under many names; all of them indicate what it is, a fiery hot oil made with chili extract. It is reddish in color, and is used in many Szechuan and Hunan recipes. You could substitute Tabasco sauce, but it won't coat the food the way chili oil does. It can be purchased in Oriental food stores and in many health food stores and supermarkets, and will last indefinitely. If you have acquired a taste for hot food, then you'll probably enjoy chili oil sprinkled on vegetables, added to sauces and to many Chinese dishes.

Iron

Vegetarians as well as non-vegetarian women should be particularly careful to get enough iron. There are many non-meat sources that can provide an adequate amount, and one should strive to get his/her intake from a variety of sources. Dried beans (including tofu and tempeh), bulghur, bran, seeds, almonds, molasses, dried apricots, and dried prunes are all excellent sources of iron. Cooking in a cast-iron skillet also adds iron to one's diet. Greens such as spinach, Swiss chard, and beet greens are rich in iron but they also contain oxalic acid, which prevents the iron from being assimilated and causes it to pass through the system. Vitamin C helps the body absorb iron, so it is wise to eat foods that are plentiful in vitamin C—such as citrus fruit, bell peppers, and tomatoes—in combination with iron-rich foods. Remember, though, they must be eaten during the same meal. Women need about 18 milligrams of iron a day (about 10 milligrams after menopause); men need a little less. Iron is partially destroyed in cooking, and you should be aware that canned beans have slightly less iron than dried beans you prepare yourself.

Kasha

is ground buckwheat kernels that are cooked like rice and bulghur. It is sold in packages in supermarkets, and either in packages or in bulk in health food stores, and is available in fine, medium, and coarse granulation (I prefer medium). It is an excellent source of protein and a good source of iron.

Maple syrup

This is the sweetener, indigenous to North America, that was discovered by the Indians. Maple syrup is simply sap from sugar maple trees that has been boiled down to nearly one-fortieth of its original volume. Although the finest grade (Grade A) carries a heftier price, I prefer the medium grade (Grade B) for its darker color and stronger flavor. In this book I use the term "pure maple syrup" to distinguish it from "pancake syrup" or "maple-flavored syrup," both of which are diluted with cheaper sweeteners, such as corn syrup. Although maple syrup is natural, that is, untreated, it is about 65 percent sucrose, and therefore acts like sugar in the body when eaten in large amounts. Once opened, maple syrup should be refrigerated. For pancakes or French toast it should be heated and served warm.

Miso

This highly nutritious Japanese concentrate is a naturally fermented soybean and grain purée that is replete with friendly bacteria and digestion-aiding enzymes. It comes in various colors (the darker the color the stronger the flavor) and strengths, and is aged anywhere from 1 month to 3 years. It is sometimes used as a spread either alone or mixed with other ingredients, such as tahini, but its primary use is to make a delicious-flavored stock. It must first be diluted with a small amount of water before being added to soups, etc., or else the miso will remain in clumps. Miso is filled with protein, minerals, and vitamins, and is a good source of vitamin B-12. Store it in the refrigerator and it will last indefinitely; the high concentration of salt acts as a preservative.

Oil

In this book, when a recipe calls for "oil" any flavorless or mild-flavored oil will do, such as corn, safflower, or vegetable oil. When either peanut or olive oil will enhance a dish, then that oil is specified.

Olive oil

There is a startling degree of variation in the quality and flavor of the numerous olive oils on the market. The key to the difference lies in the number of pressings and filterings the oil is subject to. "Extra virgin" olive oil is a full-bodied "first pressing" oil that has a robust, fruity flavor and a dark-green color. It is pressed without heat and is the most expensive of olive oils. "Virgin" olive oil is also an oil from the first pressing, but the flavor is more subtle because of additional filtering, and the color ranges from light green to golden. Herein lies the confusion. Olive oil that is bottled in this country is not subject to the strict labeling regulations that foreign bottled olive oil is. If the oil is made from further pressings of the remaining flesh and pits (which sometimes produces an unpleasant aftertaste), it can still be labeled "virgin" in this country, whereas it would be mandatory to label it "100% olive oil" in other countries. Therefore, make sure your olive oil is bottled in the country in which it is made—France, Italy, or Greece—and is marked "extra virgin," "virgin," or "first pressing" if you want a fruity olive oil. If you want a mild-flavored oil, then other types will suffice. Taste before using them to make sure they aren't bitter. Store olive oil in a cool, dark place, but not in the refrigerator. Olive oil can become rancid if exposed to hot weather for too long a period.

Oriental sesame oil

is a dark, strong-flavored oil made from toasted sesame seeds. It can be found in Oriental food stores and sometimes in specialty food shops and large supermarkets. It is not the same thing as cold-pressed sesame oil (purchased in health food stores), which is lighter in color and milder in flavor. Toasting the sesame seeds before pressing out the oil makes the taste of Oriental sesame oil stronger, so only a small amount is needed to flavor a dish. It is added at the end of cooking to impart its distinct flavor, rather than used as an oil for stir-frying.

Protein

One often hears about "protein complementarity" with regard to non-meat sources of protein. It is a good idea to simplify the theory that Frances Moore Lappé detailed in *Diet for a Small Planet* so that it can become more useful in daily living. Except for soybeans, plant-based protein does not have all of the eight essential amino acids necessary to make it a complete protein. If some of these amino acids are missing, even partially, the use of all of the other amino acids for protein synthesis in the body is reduced proportionately. So one must match foods in order to make them "complete." Whole grains are complemented by dairy products, whole grains complement legumes, and seeds complement legumes. Complementarity exists between other food groups but not as well. It is important to remember that the combining of foods must be done during the same meal in order for it to be effective.

Sesame seed paste

This is a dark Oriental paste that is made from ground roasted sesame seeds, and it has a much stronger flavor than tahini (Middle Eastern sesame butter). If you cannot get sesame seed paste, then peanut butter is a better substitute than tahini. Because the oil separates from the paste, I find that it is best to put it in a large bowl and whisk it until it is emulsified, then measure what is needed and return the remainder to the jar. You can store it in the refrigerator indefinitely. It can be purchased in Oriental food stores, and some specialty food shops, health food stores, and supermarkets.

Sunflower seeds

are an excellent source of protein, iron, calcium, and potassium. They can be purchased, already hulled, in health food stores. Their flavor is heightened, like that of most seeds and nuts, if they are toasted before being used in cooking or eaten as a snack. Avoid buying those little snack packets of toasted sunflower seeds because they are always greasy, overly salted, and overpriced.

Tahini,

a smooth Middle Eastern butter made from hulled sesame seeds, is an exceptionally good source of calcium and is rich in protein and iron. Like peanut butter it is rather high in calories, but it is very nutritious. In addition to using it in Middle Eastern dishes such as hummus, I like to sweeten it with honey and use it as a spread on toast or rice cakes. It

is a good idea to put the entire contents of the can or jar in a large bowl and whisk until blended because the oil separates from tahini. Measure the amount needed, then return the remainder to the container. Store it in the refrigerator after it is opened. It can be purchased in health food stores, specialty food shops, and some supermarkets. Read about sesame seed paste (above) to distinguish it from tahini.

Tamari

is a soy sauce that is aged in wooden vats for at least 2 years to develop a full-bodied flavor and color. Commercial soy sauce is not aged, and it is artificially colored and treated with a preservative. Stored in the refrigerator tamari lasts indefinitely. In addition to using it in Oriental dishes, I like to put it in some Western-style soups and sauces for an added dimension in flavor. Tamari can be purchased in health food stores. If you cannot get any, then commercial soy sauce can be substituted for it. Some soy sauce is labeled "shoyu" tamari or just "shoyu." This means that it is made from wheat as well as soybeans, but its flavor is almost identical to regular tamari.

Tempeh

is a mixture of ground soybeans and a rhizopus culture (mold), which has fermented and been formed into a cake. This Indonesian staple, like most soybean products, is packed with nutrients — complete protein, iron, and vitamin B-12 — and is very low in fat. It is usually cut into cubes and either steamed, sautéed, or fried, and then can be seasoned in myriad ways. When it is fresh, there are, oftentimes, black spots on it; don't worry about it — that's natural to tempeh. When it is spoiled it could have an ammonia smell, be slimy, or have blue, green, pink, or yellow mold on it. Check the expiration date on the package when you buy it. Tempeh freezes very well, so it is a good idea always to have a package or two in the freezer. It can be purchased at health food stores.

Tiger lily buds

These are dried elongated lily buds about 2–3 inches long, which are used as a vegetable in Chinese cooking. They must be soaked beforehand, and any hard stems should be cut off after soaking. Stored in a covered container in a cool, dark place, they will last indefinitely. They can be purchased in Chinese food shops, and in some health food stores, specialty food shops, and supermarkets.

Tofu,

also called bean curd, is a type of soybean "cheese" that is made through a process which is similar to cottage cheese making. Soybeans are cooked and mashed, then their liquid (soy milk) is pressed out of them and mixed with a coagulant to separate the curds from the whey. The curds are then pressed into cakes to form tofu. It is an excellent source of complete protein and iron, and a good source of calcium. It is very low in fat and easy to digest. Store it in the refrigerator, in water, in a covered container, and change the water every other day (unless it is purchased in a sealed container). It will keep about a week this way. It is spoiled when it shows signs of sliminess and tastes and smells sour. If you purchase it in a store that keeps it in open containers, and therefore exposes it to bacteria, before using it you can boil the individual cakes for 1 minute to kill germs, then pat them dry with paper towels. The change in texture will be negligible. You can freeze tofu by draining it and wrapping it in foil or plastic. The texture will change as a result; it will be crumbly and chewy, and therefore not suitable for dishes in which it should be cubed.

Tomatoes

Oftentimes in the winter months the only fresh tomatoes available are the hothouse varieties or the ones shipped from far distances. These flavorless atrocities are picked unripe and green for easy shipment, and are exposed to ethylene gas to cause them to turn red. The skin is like leather, and they will never turn truly red, no matter how ripe they get. When these are the only tomatoes at the market, I substitute canned Italian plum tomatoes, the best brand I can get. (This is one product in which the generic brand is always unacceptable.) They are picked at their

peak, and are infinitely more flavorful, tender, and colorful than their "fresh" distant cousins—hothouse tomatoes. Never leave leftover canned tomatoes in their can because the lead that seals the can will seep into food once the lead is exposed to air. To peel and seed a fresh tomato drop the whole tomato into a pot of boiling water and leave for 10–60 seconds, depending on its ripeness. (Summer garden tomatoes need be blanched only a few seconds.) Remove with a slotted spoon, and place under cold running water until it is cool enough to handle. With a sharp knife mark a very shallow X on the top of the tomato, then peel off the skin and discard. Cut the core out of the tomato, then cut the tomato in half *horizontally,* and very gently squeeze each half over a bowl until the seeds fall out. Discard the seeds.

Tomato paste

Most recipes call for a small amount of tomato paste, which means that if you purchased it in a small can, you will have quite a bit left over. Rather than letting it get moldy in the back of your refrigerator, try scraping it into a small jar with a tight-fitting lid and freezing it. When you need some, just spoon out what you need and return the remainder to the freezer. It will keep, frozen, for 4–6 months.

Vegetables

It is good to learn about the proper purchasing, storing, and cooking of vegetables because many nutrients are easily destroyed through careless handling. It is always better, of course, to choose vegetables that are in season. They should be firm, glossy, and free of bruises. Leafy green vegetables should be crisp—not wilted—free of yellow spots, and not excessively dirty. Never wash vegetables before storing them in the refrigerator, because too much moisture will encourage bacteria and decay. Keep all vegetables —except potatoes and onions—in plastic bags with a few holes punched in them so air can circulate. Store them in the crisper drawers in your refrigerator, because that is the coldest area and contains the most moisture. There is an increasing loss of nutrients as days pass, so use your vegetables as soon as possible. The easiest way to wash greens is to dunk them in a large pot of cold water, and let their dirt fall to the bottom. Remove the greens, drain out the dirty water, and repeat until the water is clean. The general rule for vitamin retention when cooking vegetables is to cook them as quickly as possible in the least amount of water, and eat them immediately thereafter. Vitamins B and C are the most perishable because they are water soluble and are easily destroyed in water, especially boiling water. Vitamins A and D are fat soluble, and are relatively resistant to destruction. Steaming, stir-frying, and sautéing are the cooking methods that preserve the most nutrients.

Yogurt

is made by adding two live cultures—lactobacillus bulgaricus and streptococcus thermophilus—to warm milk and letting the cultures grow to thicken the milk and make it acidic. The cultures are known as "friendly bacteria," and one of the greatest benefits of yogurt is that these bacteria help clean the colon by destroying harmful bacteria that are present. Yogurt is also an excellent source of protein and easily assimilated calcium. It helps the body manufacture B vitamins, aids digestion, and can be enjoyed by people with milk allergies, because the milk sugar is partially digested by the friendly bacteria. I prefer low-fat yogurt because it is just as delicious as whole-milk yogurt, yet is significantly lower in fat. The yogurt called for in these recipes is always *plain* yogurt, unsweetened and unflavored. Read the label on the yogurt container; it should list just milk and yogurt culture as the ingredients. If it includes anything else, such as gelatin or modified food starch, find another brand.

index

alfalfa sprouts in mixed green salad, 21
almond(s)
    bulghur pilaf, 25–6
    butter cookies, 104
    in golden fruitcake, 263–4
    nut crust, 277
    nut crust with pear tart, 176
    orange crust, 277
    orange crust with prune tart, 152
    peach torte, 196
    raspberry torte, 172–3
    rice, and cardamom pudding
        (kheer), 158
    in stuffed peaches with fresh cherries,
        26
appetizers
    asparagus vinaigrette, 79–80
    avocado and bathed bread
        vinaigrette, 10
    baked stuffed artichokes with
        pine nuts and lemon herb sauce,
        116–17
    cheese and crackers, 73
    cheese and onion boeregs, 213
    crudités with creamy garlic tofu dip,
        7
    crudités with yogurt herb dip, 76
    deep-fried cheese-filled polenta balls,
        177–8
    guacamole, 174
    homemade yogurt herb cheese,
        187–8
    hummus, 165
    indian eggplant dip, 109–10
    pâté de légumes, 136–7
    pesto on toasted french bread, 90
    ricotta basil spread, 13
    salsa picante with hot pita triangles,
        70
    samosa, 234–5
    stuffed mushrooms with blue cheese,
        185

appetizers (cont.)
    stuffed mushrooms with feta and dill,
        42
    stuffed red pepper strips with ricotta
        basil spread, 27
    three-layered vegetable pâté with herb
        mayonnaise, 159–61
    tzadziki with pita bread, 194
apple(s)
    baked with honey and brandy, 31
    in brandied fruit compote, 127
    and cashews in curried rice salad,
        195
    crisp, 58
    in fresh fruit with yogurt lime sauce,
        72
    in fruited rice curry, 33
    maple-glazed, baked and stuffed with
        crème fraîche, 148
    and red cabbage, braised, 190–91
    sautéed, with maple syrup topped
        with yogurt, 15
    in winter fruit salad, 44
apple cider glaze with winter fruit
    salad, 44
apricot(s)
    in brandied fruit compote, 127
    dried, in fruited rice curry, 33
    in golden fruitcake, 263–4
    orange mousse, 9
    and pear crisp, 41
    sauce with honey bread pudding,
        88–9
artichoke(s)
    baked, stuffed with pine nuts and
        lemon herb sauce, 116–17
    hearts with tofu francese,
        178–9
    and wild rice salad, 220–21
arugula
    and boston lettuce salad, 84
    in mixed green salad, 21

asparagus
    cooking of, 79
    in crudités, 7
    tofu, and red pepper stir-fried,
        55
    vinaigrette, 79–80
avocado(s)
    and bathed bread vinaigrette, 10
    in chalupas, 92
    in guacamole, 174
    and mango salad with raspberry
        vinaigrette, 149–50

bamboo shoots in spicy buddha's
    delight, 123–4
banana(s)
    in brandied fruit compote, 127
    in fresh fruit with honey zabaglione
        sauce, 108
    fried, 112
    in fruited rice curry, 33
    in ginger syrup, 29
    raita, 97
    rum roll cake, 168–9
    stuffed with rum cream and cashews,
        48
    in summer fruit salad, 212
    in winter fruit salad, 44
barley pilaf, 133
basil
    fresh and uncooked, sauce on pasta,
        197–8
    ricotta spread, 13
    ricotta spread with stuffed red pepper
        strips, 27
    shredded, with skillet bulghur and
        vegetables, 11
    zucchini, and tomato frittata,
        24–5

bean curd (tofu)
cucumber, and radish salad, marinated, 205–06
and vegetables, szechuan braised, 60–61
see tofu *for additional recipes*
beans (dried)
about, 280
baked mexican-style with sour cream and chilies, 50–51
black
and cream cheese enchiladas, 174–5
cuban, and rice, 113–14
kidney
in tamale pie, 57
in vegetarian chili, 77
lima
baked basque-style, 94–5
in vegetable stew with corn dumplings, 62–3
pinto, in baked mexican-style with sour cream and chilies, 50–51
tostadas, 17
white, and pesto in chilled stuffed tomatoes, 209–10
see also chickpeas *and* lentils
beans (green)
in bulghur salad with tarragon and vegetables, 211
in pâté de légumes, 136–7
provençale, 121
with sesame sauce, chilled, 147
in szechuan braised bean curd and vegetables, 60–61
beans, shell, and zucchini salad, marinated, 99–100
beets
in chilled summer borscht, 219
grated, and beet greens, sautéed, 101
berries with honey zabaglione sauce, 108
biscuits
sunflower buttermilk, 262–3
sweet potato, 260–61
whole wheat, 261–2

black bean(s)
and cream cheese enchiladas, 174–5
cuban, and rice, 113–14
blueberry/ies
in fresh fruit with yogurt lime sauce, 72
muffins, 226–7
streusel cake, 6
in summer fruit salad, 212
in summer fruit tart, 204
in summer pudding, 217–18
blue cheese stuffed mushrooms, 185
bombay-style curried eggs, 235
breads
about, 250–1
blueberry muffins, 226–7
cornbread, 259
four-grain bread, 254
golden fruitcake, 263–4
irish soda bread, 236–7
limpa bread, 256–7
oatmeal bread, 253
oatmeal scones, 231
onion board, 255–6
puris, 154
quick buttermilk herb and onion bread, 260
quick cottage cheese dill bread, 258–9
sunflower buttermilk biscuits, 262–3
sweet potato biscuits, 260–61
unyeasted gruel bread, 257–8
wheat tortillas, 277–8
whole wheat biscuits, 261–2
whole wheat bread, 252
whole wheat bread crumbs, 278
breakfast and brunch dishes
bombay-style curried eggs, 235
egg and pepper croustades, 229–30
french toast with orange and brandy, 227–8
granola, 225
maple pancakes, 224
mushroom quiche, 237–8
broccoli
braised with wine and garlic, 107
butter sauce with spaghetti squash, 126

broccoli *(cont.)*
and cashews with cold sesame noodles, 206–07
and cottage cheese pie, crustless, 30
in crudités, 7
florets in spicy buddha's delight, 123–4
sesame, 129
soup, cream of, 247
stalks julienne, lemon-glazed, 30–31
in stir-fried noodles and vegetables with sesame seeds, 74
broccoli di rapa with farfalle, 22
brownies, chocolate-chip fudge, 52–3
brown rice
about, 280
and cuban black beans, 113–14
curried with tofu and vegetables, 96–7
perfect, 266
with peas, 266
pilaf, 266
risotto of, with mushrooms, 106–07
see also rice
brussels sprouts with lemon soy glaze, 162
buckwheat noodles (soba)
about, 280
and tofu, 37
buddha's delight, spicy, 123–4
bulghur
about, 280
almond pilaf, 26
in four-grain bread, 254
pilaf, 25–6
salad with tarragon and vegetables, 211
in tabbouleh, 166
and vegetables in skillet with shredded basil, 11
in vegetarian chili, 77
burgundy sauce with walnut loaf, 188–9
butter
about, 280–81
homemade prune, 232
see also ghee
buttermilk
about, 281
herb and onion bread, quick, 260

buttermilk *(cont.)*
  herb and onion tart, 128–9
  sunflower biscuits, 262–3
butternut squash in mixed vegetable
    slaw, 93–4

cabbage
  bok choy, in spicy buddha's delight,
    123–4
  napa, in spicy buddha's delight,
    123–4
  red, braised, with apples, 190–91
  sautéed with fennel seed, 40
  soup, peasant, 245
  in vegetable slaw, mixed, 93–4
cacik, 214
cake(s)
  banana rum roll, 168–9
  blueberry streusel, 6
  carrot, with cream cheese icing, 66
  gingerbread, 12
  glazed pear, 122
  golden fruitcake, 263–4
  hot fudge pudding, 18
  susanne's spice, 75
calcium, about, 281
cantaloupe
  with strawberries and lime, 214–15
  in summer fruit salad, 212
cardamom, rice, and almond pudding
    (kheer), 158
carrot(s)
  cake with cream cheese icing, 66
  in crudités, 7
  grated, and cucumber salad in
    creamy dill dressing, 16
  in marinated vegetables with sesame
    dressing, 216
  in mixed vegetable slaw, 93–4
  and sugar snap peas, honey-glazed,
    168
  in three-layered vegetable pâté, 159–61
  in vegetable kofta, 155–6
  in vegetable stew with corn
    dumplings, 62–3

cashew(s)
  and apples in curried rice salad, 195
  and broccoli with cold sesame
    noodles, 206–07
  and cauliflower croquettes,
    119–20
  nut curry, 110–11
  and rum cream in stuffed bananas,
    48
  in spicy buddha's delight, 123–4
cauliflower
  and cashew croquettes, 119–20
  in crudités, 7
  and jalapeño peppers baked with
    cheese and macaroni, 85
  and pasta soup, 240
  and peas, curried, 111
celery, braised, 184
celery root au gratin, 86–7
chalupas, 92
cheddar cheese
  in celery root au gratin, 86–7
  in collards mornay, 131–2
  and macaroni baked with cauliflower
    and jalapeño peppers, 85
cheese
  and crackers, 73
  filled polenta balls, deep-fried,
    177–8
  and macaroni baked with cauliflower
    and jalapeño peppers, 85
  and onion boeregs, 213
  yogurt herb, 187–8
  see also under blue, cheddar, cottage,
    cream, feta, gruyère, monterey
    jack, mozzarella, muenster,
    parmesan, ricotta
cherries in stuffed peaches with
    almonds, 26
chestnut(s)
  extracting flesh from, 190
  purée, 189–90
chickpea(s)
  baked provençale, 103–04
  eggplant, and tomatoes baked,
    80–81
  and ginger stew, curried, 246
  in hummus, 165

chilies
  about, 281
  and sour cream with baked mexican-
    style beans, 50–51
chili, vegetarian, 77
chocolate
  chocolate-chip cookies, 38
  dipped strawberries, 207
  oatmeal bars, 23
chocolate-chip
  chocolate cookies, 38
  fudge brownies, 52
  oatmeal cookies (cowboy), 98
  walnut squares, 130
chutney, raisin, 157
cloud ears
  about, 281
  in moo shoo vegetables with
    mandarin pancakes, 144–6
cobbler, rhubarb, 118
coconut
  about, 281–2
  macaroons, 125
  milk with indonesian curried vegetable
    stew, 47
collards
  in greens sautéed with garlic, 51
  mornay, 131–2
  in rolled stuffed lasagne in a tomato
    cream sauce, 140–41
cookies
  almond butter, 104
  chocolate-chip fudge brownies, 52
  chocolate chocolate-chip, 38
  chocolate oatmeal bars, 23
  cowboy (chocolate-chip oatmeal),
    98
  ginger, 134
  walnut chocolate-chip squares, 130
cornbread, 259
corn dumplings with fragrant vegetable
    stew, 62–3
cornmeal in four-grain bread, 254
cottage cheese
  and broccoli pie, crustless, 30
  dill bread, quick, 258–9
  in spanakopita (spinach and cheese
    pie), 166–7

cowboy cookies (chocolate-chip
    oatmeal), 98
crackers and cheese, 73
cranberry fruit tart, 192
cream cheese
    and black bean enchiladas, 174–5
    icing on carrot cake, 66
crème fraîche, 271–2
    with maple-glazed baked stuffed
        apples, 148
crisp
    apple, 58
    pear and apricot, 41
croquettes, cashew and cauliflower,
    119–20
croutons, making of, 202
crudités
    with creamy garlic tofu dressing or
        dip, 7
    with yogurt herb dip, 76
cuban black beans and rice, 113–14
cucumber(s)
    bean curd, and radish salad,
        marinated, 205–06
    in cacik, 214
    in gazpacho, 202
    and grated carrot salad in creamy dill
        dressing, 16
    in marinated vegetables with sesame
        dressing, 216
    salad, spicy, 34
    and watercress soup, cold, 208–09
curry/ied
    braised eggplant, 32–3
    cashew nut, 110–11
    cauliflower and peas, 111
    chickpea and ginger stew, 246
    eggs, bombay-style, 235
    fruited rice, 33
    indonesian vegetable stew with
        coconut milk, 47
    red lentil soup, 242
    rice salad with apples and cashews,
        195
    tempeh in yogurt sauce, 19
    tofu, rice, and vegetables, 96–7
    vegetables in baked stuffed eggplant,
        67–8

custard
    ginger, on poached honey pears,
        180–81
    maple, with maple pecan sauce, 139

dall, red lentil, 156
dates in golden fruitcake, 263–4
desserts
    almond butter cookies, 104
    apple crisp, 58
    apricot orange mousse, 9
    baked apples with honey and brandy,
        31
    banana rum roll cake, 168–9
    bananas in ginger syrup, 29
    blueberry streusel cake, 6
    brandied fruit compote, 127
    cantaloupe with strawberries and
        lime, 214–15
    carrot cake with cream cheese icing,
        66
    chilled zabaglione with honey, 95
    chocolate-chip fudge brownies, 52
    chocolate-chip walnut squares, 130
    chocolate chocolate-chip cookies, 38
    chocolate-dipped strawberries, 207
    chocolate oatmeal bars, 23
    coconut macaroons, 125
    cowboy cookies, 98
    cranberry fruit tart, 192
    fresh fruit, 279
    fresh fruit with honey zabaglione
        sauce, 108
    fresh fruit with yogurt lime sauce, 72
    fresh peaches with honey rum sauce,
        201
    gingerbread, 12
    ginger cookies, 134
    glazed pear cake, 122
    honey bread pudding with apricot
        sauce, 88–9
    hot fudge pudding cake, 18
    ice cream sprinkled with espresso,
        112
    indian pudding, 20

kheer, 158
desserts (cont.)
    linzertorte, 142–3
    maple custard with maple pecan
        sauce, 139
    maple-glazed baked stuffed apples
        with crème fraîche, 148
    maple pecan pie, 63–4
    marinated oranges in grand marnier
        sauce, 114–15
    mocha walnut torte, 163–4
    peach almond torte, 196
    peaches marsala, 210
    pear and apricot crisp, 41
    pear tart with almond nut crust, 176
    poached honey pears topped with
        ginger custard, 180–81
    poached pears with red wine and
        raisins, 78
    prune tart with orange almond crust,
        152
    raspberry almond torte, 172–3
    raspberry pie, 198
    rhubarb cobbler, 118
    rhubarb tart, 56
    sautéed apples and maple syrup
        topped with yogurt, 15
    strawberries and wine, 69
    strawberries with yogurt, 221
    stuffed bananas with rum cream and
        cashews, 48
    stuffed peaches with fresh cherries
        and almonds, 26
    summer fruit tart, 204
    summer pudding, 217–18
    susanne's spice cake, 75
    sweet potato pie, 83
    winter fruit salad with apple cider
        glaze, 44
dill
    cottage cheese bread, quick,
        258–9
    dressing, creamy, 268
        with cucumber and grated carrot
            salad, 16
        with spinach salad, 62
    and feta stuffed mushrooms, 42
    and new potato salad, 215–16

dips
  creamy garlic tofu, 7
  guacamole, 174
  indian eggplant, 109–10
  salsa picante, 70
  tzadziki, 194
  yogurt herb, 76
dressings
  creamy dill, 268
  creamy garlic tofu, 7
  lemon soy, 60
  sesame ginger, 36
  spicy peanut, 46
  sweet mustard, 49
  vinaigrette, 268
    raspberry, 149
drinks
  orange lassi, 233
  sangria, 52

egg(s)
  curried, bombay-style, 235
  and pepper croustades, 229–30
eggplant
  about, 282
    cooking of, 80
  baked, stuffed with curried vegetables, 67–8
  braised, curried, 32–3
  chickpeas, and tomatoes baked, 80–81
  dip, indian, 109–10
  sauce with penne, 8
  in szechuan braised bean curd and vegetables, 60
enchiladas, black bean and cream cheese, 174–5
endive
  belgian, in mixed green salad, 21
  in crudités, 7
entrées
  baked chickpeas provençale, 103–04
  baked eggplant, chickpeas, and tomatoes, 80–81
  baked lima beans basque-style, 94–5

entrées (cont.)
  baked macaroni and cheese with cauliflower and jalapeño peppers, 85
  baked mexican-style beans with sour cream and chilies, 50
  baked stuffed eggplant with curried vegetables, 67–8
  bean tostadas, 17
  black bean and cream cheese enchiladas, 174–5
  bombay-style curried eggs, 235
  braised tempeh napoletano, 4–5
  braised tofu and vegetables with white wine and tarragon, 82
  buckwheat noodles (soba) and tofu, 37
  buttermilk herb and onion tart, 128–9
  cashew nut curry, 110–11
  cauliflower and cashew croquettes, 119–20
  chalupas, 92
  chilled tomatoes stuffed with white beans and pesto, 209
  cold sesame noodles with broccoli and cashews, 206–07
  crustless broccoli and cottage cheese pie, 30
  cuban black beans and rice, 113–14
  curried rice, tofu, and vegetables, 96–7
  farfalle with broccoli di rapa, 22
  fragrant vegetable stew with corn dumplings, 62–3
  indonesian curried vegetable stew with coconut milk, 47
  kasha topped with mushrooms in sour cream sauce, 39–40
  leek timbales with white wine sauce, 185–6
  mexican-style stuffed summer squash, 70–71
  moo shoo vegetables with mandarin pancakes, 144–7
  mushroom quiche, 237–8
  neapolitan pizza, 65
  noodle timbales with pesto cream sauce, 170–71

entrées (cont.)
  pasta with swiss chard and garlic, 28
  pasta with uncooked tomato and fresh basil sauce, 197–8
  penne with eggplant sauce, 8
  polenta and pesto soufflé, 100–01
  polenta puttanesca, 14
  rolled stuffed lasagne with kale in a tomato cream sauce, 140–41
  sautéed tofu in french sweet butter and vinegar sauce, 138
  skillet bulghur and vegetables with shredded basil, 11
  skillet tofu and vegetables in brandy cream sauce, 161–2
  spaghettini with garlic and hot peppers, 43
  spaghetti squash with broccoli butter sauce, 126
  spanakopita, 166–7
  spicy buddha's delight, 123–4
  spinach custard ring with tomato cream sauce, 150–51
  stir-fried asparagus, tofu, and red pepper, 55
  stir-fried noodles and vegetables with sesame seeds, 74
  stir-fried tempeh with hot pepper sauce, 35
  szechuan braised bean curd and vegetables, 60–61
  tamale pie, 57
  tempeh in curried yogurt sauce, 19
  tofu fra diavolo with spinach fettuccine, 90–91
  tofu francese with artichoke hearts, 178–9
  vegetable kofta, 155–6
  vegetarian b'stilla, 182–3
  vegetarian chili, 77
  walnut loaf with burgundy sauce, 188–9
  zucchini, tomato, and basil frittata, 24
escarole in greens sautéed with garlic, 51
espresso sprinkled on ice cream, 112

farfalle with broccoli di rapa, 22
fennel
    seed with sautéed cabbage, 40
    soup, cream of, 243
feta
    cheese in spanakopita (spinach and
        cheese pie), 166-7
    and dill stuffed mushrooms, 42
fettuccine and spinach with tofu fra
        diavolo, 90-91
filo
    in cheese and onion boeregs, 213
    in spanakopita (spinach and cheese
        pie), 166-7
    in vegetarian b'stilla, 182-3
flour
    unbleached white, 282
    whole wheat pastry flour, 282
four-grain bread, 254
framboise with fresh fruit, 279
french toast with orange and brandy,
        227-8
frittata, zucchini, tomato, and basil, 24
fruit
    compote, brandied, 127
    fresh
        about, 279
        with honey zabaglione sauce, 108
        with yogurt lime sauce, 72
    salad, summer, 212
    salad, winter, with apple cider glaze,
        44
    tart, summer, 204
fruitcake, golden, 263-4
fruited rice curry, 33
fudge
    chocolate-chip brownies, 52
    pudding cake, hot, 18

garden salad with creamy garlic tofu
        dressing, 102
garlic
    about, 282
    with pasta and swiss chard, 28
    sauce with fine egg noodles, 5

garlic (cont.)
    sautéed with greens, 51
    with spaghettini and hot pepper, 43
    tofu dressing or dip, creamy, 7
    and wine with braised broccoli, 107
gazpacho, 202
ghee (butter oil), 272
ginger
    and chickpea stew, curried, 246
    cookies, 134
    sesame dressing with salad, 36
    syrup with bananas, 29
gingerbread, 12
gingerroot, about, 282-3
golden fruitcake, 263-4
grand marnier
    with fresh fruit, 279
    sauce, oranges marinated in, 114-15
granola, 225-6
grapefruit and orange sections with kiwi,
        223
greens sautéed with garlic, 51
gruel bread, unyeasted, 257-8
gruyère cheese in celery root au gratin,
        86-7
guacamole, 174

herb
    buttermilk and onion tart, 128-9
    lemon sauce with baked stuffed
        artichokes with pine nuts, 116-17
    mayonnaise with three-layered
        vegetable pâté, 160
    onion buttermilk bread, quick, 260
    yogurt cheese, 187-8
    yogurt dip, 76
honey
    about, 283
    and brandy with baked apples, 31
    bread pudding with apricot sauce,
        88-9
    glazed sugar snap peas with carrots,
        168
    pears, poached, topped with ginger
        custard, 180-81

honey (cont.)
    rum sauce with fresh peaches, 201
    with zabaglione, chilled, 95
    zabaglione sauce with fresh fruit,
        108
hummus, 165

ice cream
    sprinkled with espresso, 112
    vanilla, with bananas in ginger syrup,
        29
indian
    eggplant dip, 109-10
    pudding, 20
indonesian
    curried vegetable stew with coconut
        milk, 47
    salad with spicy peanut dressing, 46
irish soda bread, 236-7
iron, about, 283

jalapeño peppers
    in black bean and cream cheese
        enchiladas, 174-5
    and cauliflower baked with macaroni
        and cheese, 85
    in chalupas, 92
    in guacamole, 174
jerusalem artichoke and watercress
        salad with sweet mustard
        dressing, 49-50

kale
    in greens sautéed with garlic,
        51
    mornay, 131-2
    with rolled stuffed lasagne in a tomato
        cream sauce, 140-41
    and vegetable soup, 244

kasha
  about, 283
  pilaf, 88
  topped with mushrooms in sour
    cream sauce, 39–40
kheer (rice, almond, and cardamom
    pudding), 158
kidney beans
  in baked mexican-style beans with
    sour cream and chilies, 50–51
  in tamale pie, 57
  in vegetarian chili, 77
kiwi(s)
  in fresh fruit with yogurt lime sauce, 72
  with honey zabaglione sauce, 108
  with orange and grapefruit sections,
    223
  in winter fruit salad, 44

Lappé, Frances Moore: Diet for a Small
    Planet, 284
lasagne, rolled, stuffed with kale in a
    tomato cream sauce, 140–41
leek(s)
  in three-layered vegetable pâté,
    159–61
  timbales with white wine sauce,
    185–6
lemon
  glazed broccoli stalks julienne, 30–31
  herb sauce with baked stuffed
    artichokes with pine nuts, 116–17
lemon soy
  dressing, 60
  dressing with simple salad, 59
  glaze with brussels sprouts, 162
lentil(s)
  in pâté de legumes, 136–7
  red, curried soup, 242
  red, dal, 156
  soup, 248
lima beans
  baked basque-style, 94–5
  in vegetable stew with corn
    dumplings, 62–3

lime
  with cantaloupe and strawberries,
    214–15
  yogurt sauce with fresh fruit, 72
limpa bread (swedish rye), 256–7
linguine in pasta with uncooked tomato
    and fresh basil sauce, 197–8
linzertorte, 142–3

macaroni and cheese baked with
    cauliflower and jalapeño
    peppers, 85
macaroons, coconut, 125
mandarin pancakes with moo shoo
    vegetables, 146–7
mango(s)
  and avocado salad with raspberry
    vinaigrette, 149–50
  in fresh fruit with yogurt lime sauce,
    72
  with honey zabaglione sauce, 108
maple
  custard with maple pecan sauce, 139
  glazed baked stuffed apples with
    crème fraîche, 148
  pancakes, 224
  pecan pie, 63–4
maple syrup
  about, 283–4
  and sautéed apples topped with
    yogurt, 15
marinara sauce, 273
marsala
  peaches, 210
  wine in chilled zabaglione with honey,
    95
Marshall, Lydie, 138
mayonnaise, 269–70
  blender, 269–70
  hand, 269
  herb, with three-layered vegetable
    pâté, 160
melon
  in fresh fruit with yogurt lime sauce, 72
  with honey zabaglione sauce, 108

mexican-style
  baked beans with chilies and sour
    cream, 50
  stuffed summer squash, 70–71
miso
  about, 284
  soup, 144
mocha walnut torte, 163–4
monterey jack cheese
  in baked macaroni and cheese with
    cauliflower and jalapeño peppers,
    85
  in bean tostadas, 17
  in black bean and cream cheese
    enchiladas, 174–5
  in chalupas, 92
  in cheese and onion boeregs, 213
  in mexican-style baked beans, 50–51
  in tamale pie, 57
moo shoo vegetables with mandarin
    pancakes, 144–6
moroccan tomato and roasted pepper
    salad, 182
mousse, orange apricot, 9
mozzarella cheese
  in neapolitan pizza, 65
  roasted pepper, and black olive salad,
    105–06
  in rolled stuffed lasagne with kale,
    140–41
muenster cheese in neapolitan pizza,
    65
muffins, blueberry, 226
mushroom(s)
  in baked eggplant stuffed with curried
    vegetables, 68
  in barley pilaf, 133
  in braised tofu and vegetables with
    white wine and tarragon, 82
  and brown rice risotto, 106–07
  in bulghur salad with tarragon and
    vegetables, 211
  in curried rice, tofu, and vegetables,
    96–7
  on kasha with sour cream sauce,
    39–40
  in marinated pasta and vegetable
    salad, 203

mushroom(s) *(cont.)*
  in moo shoo vegetables with
    mandarin pancakes, 144–6
  in neapolitan pizza, 65
  quiche, 237–8
  in sautéed tofu in french sweet butter
    and vinegar sauce, 138
  in skillet tofu with brandy cream
    sauce, 161–2
  in spicy buddha's delight, 123–4
  stuffed with blue cheese, 185
  stuffed with feta and dill, 42
  in szechuan braised bean curd and
    vegetables, 60
  in tempeh with curried yogurt sauce,
    19
  in vegetarian b'stilla, 182–3
mustard dressing, sweet, on watercress
  and jerusalem artichoke salad,
  49–50
mustard greens
  in greens sautéed with garlic, 51
  in rolled stuffed lasagne in a tomato
    cream sauce, 140–41

neapolitan pizza, 65
noodle(s)
  buckwheat (soba) and tofu, 37
  fine egg, with light garlic sauce, 5
  sesame, cold, with broccoli and
    cashews, 206–07
  timbales with pesto cream sauce,
    170–71
  and vegetables stir-fried with sesame
    seeds, 74

oatmeal
  bread, 253
  chocolate bars, 23
  chocolate-chip cookies (cowboy), 98
  scones, 231
oats, rolled, in four-grain bread, 254

oil
  about, 284
  hot spicy or chili, 283
  olive, 284
olive(s)
  black, mozzarella and roasted pepper
    salad, 105–06
  kalamata, 105
olive oil, about, 284
onion(s)
  board, 255–6
  in braised tofu and vegetables with
    white wine and tarragon, 82
  buttermilk and herb tart, 128–9
  and cheese boeregs, 213
  herb buttermilk bread, quick, 260
  and potatoes, home-fried, 238
  in vegetable stew with corn
    dumplings, 62–3
orange(s)
  almond crust with prune tart, 152
  apricot mousse, 9
  and brandy with french toast, 227–8
  in fresh fruit with yogurt lime sauce,
    72
  and grapefruit sections with kiwi,
    223
  with honey zabaglione sauce, 108
  lassi, 233
  marinated in grand marnier sauce,
    114–15
  raita, 157
  in winter fruit salad, 44

pancakes
  mandarin with moo shoo vegetables,
    144–7
  maple, 224
papaya in fresh fruit with yogurt lime
  sauce, 72
parmesan cheese
  in deep-fried cheese-filled polenta
    balls, 177–8
  in noodle timbales with pesto cream
    sauce, 170–71

parmesan cheese *(cont.)*
  in pasta with uncooked tomato and
    fresh basil sauce, 197
  in pesto, 270
  in rolled stuffed lasagne with kale,
    140–41
  in spinach custard ring with tomato
    cream sauce, 150–51
  in winter pesto, 271
parsnips in vegetable stew with
  dumplings, 62–3
pasta
  buckwheat noodles (soba) and tofu,
    37
  and cauliflower soup, 240
  cold sesame noodles with broccoli
    and cashews, 206–07
  farfalle with broccoli di rapa, 22
  macaroni and cheese with cauliflower
    baked with jalapeño peppers, 85
  noodles, fine egg, with light garlic
    sauce, 5
  noodle timbales with pesto cream
    sauce, 170–71
  penne with eggplant sauce, 8
  rolled stuffed lasagne with kale in
    tomato cream sauce, 140–41
  spaghettini with garlic and hot pepper,
    43
  spinach fettuccine with tofu fra
    diavolo, 90–91
  stir-fried noodles and vegetables with
    sesame seeds, 74
  with swiss chard and garlic, 28
  with uncooked tomato and fresh basil
    sauce, 197–8
  and vegetable salad, marinated, 203
pâté
  de légumes, 136–7
  vegetable, three-layered, with herb
    mayonnaise, 159–61
pâte brisée (sweet or savory), 274
  with whole wheat flour, 275
pâte sucrée (sweet pie crust), 276
pea(s)
  in baked eggplant stuffed with curried
    vegetables, 67–8
  and cauliflower, curried, 111

pea(s) (cont.)
in curried rice, tofu, and vegetables, 96–7
fresh, salad rémoulade, 54
in marinated pasta and vegetable salad, 203
with perfect brown rice, 266
sugar snap, and carrots, honey-glazed, 168
see also snow peas
peach(es)
almond torte, 196
fresh, with honey rum sauce, 201
with honey zabaglione sauce, 108
marsala, 210
stuffed, with fresh cherries and almonds, 26
in summer fruit salad, 212
in summer fruit tart, 204
peanut dressing, spicy, with indonesian salad, 46
pear(s)
and apricot crisp, 41
cake, glazed, 122
in fresh fruit with yogurt lime sauce, 72
with honey zabaglione sauce, 108
poached with honey, topped with ginger custard, 180–81
poached in red wine with raisins, 78
tart with almond nut crust, 176
in winter fruit salad, 44
pecan
maple pie, 63–4
maple sauce on maple custard, 139
penne with eggplant sauce, 8
pepper(s)
chili(es)
about, 281
and sour cream with baked mexican-style beans, 50
and egg croustades, 229–30
green
in gazpacho, 202
in mixed vegetable slaw, 93–4
hot, with spaghettini and garlic, 43
jalapeño. See jalapeño

pepper(s) (cont.)
red (bell)
asparagus, and tofu, stir-fried, 55
in crudités, 7
in marinated vegetables with sesame dressing, 216
in spicy buddha's delight, 123–4
strips, stuffed with ricotta basil spread, 27
zucchini, and snow pea sauté, 171–2
roasted, mozzarella and black olive salad, 105–06
roasted, and tomato salad, moroccan, 182
pepper sauce, hot, with stir-fried tempeh, 35
perfect brown rice, 266
with peas, 266
pilaf, 266
pesto, 270
cream sauce with noodle timbales, 170–71
and polenta soufflé, 100–01
on toasted french bread, 90
and white beans in chilled stuffed tomatoes, 209
winter, 271
pie crusts
almond nut, 277
pâte brisée, 274
pâte brisée with whole wheat flour, 275
pâte sucrée, 276
orange almond, 277
pies
crustless broccoli and cottage cheese, 30
maple pecan, 63–4
raspberry, 198
spanakopita (spinach cheese), 166–7
sweet potato, 83
tamale, 57
pilaf
barley, 133
bulghur, 25
kasha, 88
perfect brown rice, 266

pineapples
in fresh fruit with yogurt lime sauce, 72
with honey zabaglione sauce, 108
pine nuts in baked stuffed artichokes with lemon herb sauce, 116–17
pinto beans in baked mexican-style beans with sour cream and chilies, 50–51
pizza, neapolitan, 65
plum(s)
with honey zabaglione sauce, 108
soup, iced, 199–200
in summer fruit tart, 204
polenta
balls, cheese-filled, deep-fried, 177–8
and pesto soufflé, 100–01
puttanesca, 14
potato(es)
new, and dill salad, 215–16
and onions, home-fried, 238
roasted with rosemary, 191
in vegetable kofta, 155–6
in vegetable stew with corn dumplings, 62–3
see also sweet potato and yam
protein, about, 284–5
prune(s)
in brandied fruit compote, 127
butter, homemade, 232
tart with orange almond crust, 152
pudding
cake, hot fudge, 18
honey bread, with apricot sauce, 88–9
indian, 20
kheer (rice, almond, and cardamom), 158
summer, 217–18
pumpkin bisque, 241
purée, chestnut, 189–90
puris (deep-fried puffed bread), 154
puttanesca sauce with polenta, 14

quiche, mushroom, 237–8

radicchio in mixed green salad, 21
radish, bean curd, and cucumber salad, marinated, 205–06
raisin(s)
    chutney, 157–8
    golden, in brandied fruit compote, 127
    in golden fruitcake, 263–4
    in mixed vegetable slaw, 93–4
    with pears poached in red wine, 78
raita
    banana, 97
    orange, 157
raspberry
    almond torte, 172–3
    pie, 198
    preserves in linzertorte, 142–3
    vinaigrette with mango and avocado salad, 149–50
    vinegar, 273
red lentil
    curried soup, 242
    dal, 156
red pepper(s)
    asparagus, and tofu stir-fried, 55
    in crudités, 7
    in marinated vegetables with sesame dressing, 216
    in spicy buddha's delight, 123–4
    strips, stuffed with ricotta basil spread, 27
    zucchini, and snow pea sauté, 171–2
rhubarb
    cobbler, 118
    tart, 56
rice
    almond and cardamom pudding (kheer), 158
    brown
        about, 280
        and cuban black beans, 113–14
        curried with tofu and vegetables, 96–7
        perfect, with peas, 266
        perfect, pilaf, 266
        risotto of, with mushrooms, 106–07
    see also wild rice

ricotta
    basil spread, 13
    basil spread with stuffed red pepper strips, 27
    in rolled stuffed lasagne with kale, 140–41
    risotto of brown rice and mushrooms, 106–07
romaine in mixed green salad, 21
rosemary with roasted potatoes, 191
rotini in marinated pasta and vegetable salad, 203
rum
    banana roll cake, 168–9
    cream and cashews in stuffed bananas, 48
    with fresh fruit, 279
    honey sauce with fresh peaches, 201
rutabaga (yellow turnip) gratin, 179–80

salads
    arugula and boston lettuce, 84
    bulghur, with tarragon and vegetables, 211
    cucumber and grated carrot in creamy dill dressing, 16
    curried rice, with apples and cashews, 195
    fresh pea, rémoulade, 54
    garden, with creamy garlic tofu dressing, 102
    indonesian, with spicy peanut dressing, 46
    mango and avocado, with raspberry vinaigrette, 149–50
    marinated bean curd, cucumber, and radish, 205–06
    marinated pasta and vegetable, 203
    marinated shell bean and zucchini, 99–100
    marinated vegetables with sesame dressing, 216–17
    mixed green, 21
    mixed vegetable slaw, 93–4

salads (cont.)
    moroccan tomato and roasted pepper, 182
    mozzarella, roasted pepper, and black olive, 105–06
    new potato and dill, 215–16
    orange and grapefruit sections with kiwi, 223
    with sesame ginger dressing, 36
    simple, with lemon soy dressing, 59
    spicy cucumber, 34
    spinach, with creamy dill dressing, 62
    summer fruit, 212
    tabbouleh, 166
    tempeh salade niçoise, 200
    watercress and jerusalem artichoke, with sweet mustard dressing, 49–50
    wild rice and artichoke, 220–21
    winter fruit with apple cider glaze, 44
salsa picante, 70
salsa picante with bean tostadas, 17
samosa, 234–5
sandwiches, open-face tomato, 211
sangria, 52
sauces
    burgundy, 188–9
    lemon herb, 116
    marinara, 273
    mayonnaise, 269–70
    pesto, 270
    puttanesca, 14
    salsa picante, 70
    tomato cream, 141
    winter pesto, 271
    yogurt lime, 72
scones, oatmeal, 231
sesame
    broccoli, 129
    dressing with marinated vegetables, 216
    ginger dressing with salad, 36
    noodles, cold, with broccoli and cashews, 206–07
    sauce with chilled green beans, 147
sesame oil, oriental, about, 284
sesame seed paste, about, 285

sesame seeds with stir-fried noodles and vegetables, 74
shell bean and zucchini salad, marinated, 99–100
sherry with fresh fruit, 279
side dishes
  banana raita, 97
  barley pilaf, 133
  braised broccoli in wine and garlic, 107
  braised celery, 184
  braised curried eggplant, 32–3
  braised red cabbage with apples, 190–91
  brussels sprouts with lemon soy glaze, 162
  bulghur pilaf, 25
  celery root au gratin, 86–7
  chestnut purée, 189–90
  chilled green beans with sesame sauce, 147
  collards mornay, 131–2
  curried cauliflower and peas, 111
  fine egg noodles with light garlic sauce, 5
  fried bananas, 112
  fruited rice curry, 33
  green beans provençale, 121
  home-fried potatoes and onions, 238
  honey-glazed sugar snap peas with carrots, 168
  kasha pilaf, 88
  lemon-glazed broccoli stalks julienne, 30–31
  open-face tomato sandwiches, 211
  orange raita, 157
  perfect brown rice, 266
  raisin chutney, 157–8
  risotto of brown rice and mushrooms, 106
  roasted potatoes with rosemary, 191
  rutabaga gratin, 179–80
  sautéed cabbage and fennel, 40
  sautéed greens with garlic, 51
  sesame broccoli, 129
  sweet potato home fries, 230
  zucchini, red pepper, and snow pea sauté, 171–2

skillet
  bulghur and vegetables with shredded basil, 11
  tofu and vegetables in brandy cream sauce, 161–2
slaw, mixed vegetable, 93–4
snow pea(s)
  and carrots, honey-glazed, 168
  in marinated vegetables with sesame dressing, 216
  in spicy buddha's delight, 123–4
  zucchini, and red pepper sauté, 171–2
soufflé, polenta and pesto, 100–01
soups and stews
  cacik, 214
  cauliflower and pasta, 240
  chilled summer borscht, 219
  cold cucumber and watercress, 208–09
  cream of broccoli, 247
  cream of fennel, 243
  curried chickpea and ginger, 246
  curried red lentil, 242
  elegant yam, 249
  fragrant vegetable, with corn dumplings, 62–3
  gazpacho, 202
  iced plum soup, 199–200
  indonesian curried vegetable, with coconut milk, 47
  kale and vegetable, 244
  lentil, 248
  miso, 144
  peasant cabbage, 245
  pumpkin bisque, 241
  vegetarian chili, 77
sour cream
  and chilies with baked mexican-style beans, 50
  sauce on kasha topped with mushrooms, 39–40
spaghetti in pasta with uncooked tomato and fresh basil sauce, 197
spaghetti squash with broccoli butter sauce, 126
spaghettini with garlic and hot pepper, 43

spanakopita (spinach cheese pie), 166–7
spice cake, susanne's, 75
spinach
  custard ring with tomato cream sauce, 150–51
  fettuccine with tofu fra diavolo, 90–91
  in greens sautéed with garlic, 51
  in mixed green salad, 21
  in rolled stuffed lasagne in a tomato cream sauce, 140–41
  salad with creamy dill dressing, 62
  in spanakopita (spinach cheese pie), 166–7
  in vegetable kofta, 155–6
  in winter pesto, 271
spread, ricotta basil, 13
squash
  butternut, in mixed vegetable slaw, 93–4
  hubbard, in mixed vegetable slaw, 93–4
  spaghetti, with broccoli butter sauce, 126
  summer, stuffed mexican-style, 70–71
  zucchini. See zucchini
stew
  curried chickpea and ginger, 246
  fragrant vegetable, with corn dumplings, 62–3
  indonesian, curried, vegetable with coconut milk, 47
stock, vegetable, 267
strawberries
  chocolate-dipped, 207
  in fresh fruit with yogurt lime sauce, 72
  in summer fruit salad, 212
  and wine, 69
  and wine with cantaloupe, 214–15
  with yogurt, 221
  in zabaglione, chilled, with honey, 95
streusel blueberry cake, 6
summer
  fruit salad, 212
  fruit tart, 204
  pudding, 217–18

sunflower buttermilk biscuits, 262–3
sunflower seeds
    about, 285
    in stuffed mushrooms with blue
        cheese, 185
sweet potato
    biscuits, 260–61
    home fries, 230
    pie, 83
swiss chard with pasta and garlic, 28
swiss cheese in peasant cabbage soup,
    245
szechuan braised bean curd and
    vegetables, 60–61

tabbouleh (bulghur wheat salad), 166
tahini
    about, 285
    in hummus, 165
tamale pie, 57
tamari, about, 285
tarragon
    and vegetables in bulghur salad,
        211
    and white wine with braised tofu and
        vegetables, 82
tarts
    buttermilk herb and onion, 128–9
    cranberry fruit, 192
    pear with almond nut crust, 176
    prune with orange almond crust,
        152
    rhubarb, 56
    summer fruit, 204
Tassajara Bread Book, 257
tempeh
    about, 285
    braised napoletano, 4–5
    in curried yogurt sauce, 19
    salade niçoise, 200
    stir-fried with hot pepper sauce,
        35
thanksgiving feast, 187–92
tiger lily buds
    about, 285–6

tiger lily buds (cont.)
    in moo shoo vegetables with
        mandarin pancakes, 144–6
timbales
    leek with white wine sauce, 185–6
    noodle with pesto cream sauce,
        170–71
tofu (bean curd)
    about, 286
    asparagus, and red pepper stir-fried,
        55
    and buckwheat noodles (soba), 37
    fra diavolo with spinach fettuccine,
        90–91
    francese with artichoke hearts,
        178–9
    garlic creamy dressing or dip, 7
    rice, and vegetables, curried, 96–7
    sautéed in french sweet butter and
        vinegar sauce, 138
    and vegetables braised with white
        wine and tarragon, 82
    and vegetables in brandy cream
        sauce, 161–2
    see also bean curd
tomato(es)
    about, 286
    in baked eggplant stuffed with curried
        vegetables, 68
    in braised tempeh napoletano, 4–5
    in braised tofu and vegetables with
        white wine and tarragon, 82
    cream sauce with rolled stuffed
        lasagne with kale, 140–41
    cream sauce with spinach custard
        ring, 150–51
    eggplant, and chickpeas, baked,
        80
    in gazpacho, 202
    in green beans provençale, 121
    in guacamole, 174
        to peel and seed, 286
    plum
        in lima beans baked basque-style,
            94–5
        in polenta puttanesca, 14
    in sautéed tofu in french sweet
        butter and vinegar sauce, 138

tomato(es) (cont.)
    in salsa picante, 70
    sandwiches, open-face, 211
    stuffed, chilled, with white beans and
        pesto, 209
    in tabbouleh, 166
    uncooked, and fresh basil sauce on
        pasta, 197–8
    in vegetable stew with corn
        dumplings, 62–3
    in vegetarian chili, 77
    zucchini, and basil frittata, 24
tomato paste, about, 286
torte
    linzertorte, 142–3
    mocha walnut, 163–4
    peach almond, 196
    raspberry almond, 172–3
tortillas
    in bean tostadas, 17
    in black bean and cream cheese
        enchiladas, 174–5
    in chalupas, 92
    wheat, 277–8
tostadas, bean, 17
tzadziki, 194

vegetable(s)
    about, 286–7
    and bean curd, szechuan braised,
        60–61
    and bulghur in skillet with shredded
        basil, 11
    and kale soup, 244
    kofta, 155–6
    marinated with sesame dressing,
        216–17
    and noodles stir-fried with sesame
        seeds, 74
    and pasta salad, marinated, 203
    pâté, three-layered, with herb
        mayonnaise, 159–61
    slaw, mixed, 93–4
    stew, curried indonesian and coconut
        milk, 47

vegetable(s) *(cont.)*
    stew, fragrant, with corn dumplings,
        62–3
    stock, 267
    and tarragon in bulghur salad, 211
    and tofu braised with white wine and
        tarragon, 82
    and tofu in brandy cream sauce,
        161–2
    tofu, and rice, curried, 96–7
vegetarian
    b'stilla, 182–3
    chili, 77
vermicelli in pasta with uncooked
        tomato and fresh basil sauce,
        197
vinaigrette
    asparagus, 79–80
    on avocado and bread, 10
    basic, 268
    raspberry, with mango and avocado
        salad, 149–50
vinegar
    raspberry, 273
    sauce on sautéed tofu in french sweet
        butter, 138

walnut
    chocolate-chip squares, 130

walnut *(cont.)*
    loaf with burgundy sauce, 188–9
    mocha torte, 163–4
water chestnuts in moo shoo vegetables
        with mandarin pancakes, 144–5
watercress
    and cucumber soup, cold, 208–09
    and jerusalem artichoke salad with
        sweet mustard dressing, 49–50
    in mixed green salad, 21
wheat tortillas, 277–8
white beans and pesto in chilled stuffed
        tomatoes, 209
whole wheat
    biscuits, 261–2
    bread, 252
    bread crumbs, 278
    flour in four-grain bread, 254
whole wheat pastry flour, about,
        282
wild rice and artichoke salad,
        220–21
wine
    "demestica" (greek), 164
    and garlic with braised broccoli, 107
    red, pears poached in, with raisins,
        78
    and strawberries, 69
    white, sauce with leek timbales,
        185–6
    white, and tarragon with braised tofu
        and vegetables, 82

winter fruit salad with apple cider glaze,
    44
Wolfert, Paula, 182

yam soup, elegant, 249
yogurt
    about, 287
    in cacik, 214
    herb cheese, 187–8
    herb dip, 76
    lime sauce with fresh fruit, 72
    sauce, curried, with tempeh, 19
    with sautéed apples and maple syrup,
        15
    with strawberries, 221

zabaglione
    chilled, with honey, 95
    honey sauce with fresh fruit, 108
zucchini
    in crudités, 7
    red pepper, and snow pea sauté,
        171–2
    and shell bean salad, marinated,
        99–100
    tomato, and basil frittata, 24

a note about the author

Jeanne Lemlin was born in New Bedford, Massachusetts, and grew up there. She holds a bachelor's degree in art history. She started giving private cooking classes in Massachusetts, and since 1980 she has been an instructor in vegetarian and vegetable cooking at the New York Cooking Center of the New School for Social Research. She lives in Stockbridge, Massachusetts, with her husband and stepdaughter.

a note on the type

The text of this book was set in Helvetica, a type face designed in the 1950s in Switzerland by Edouard Hoffman and Max Miedinger. Named for its country of origin, and introduced in America in 1963, Helvetica has become one of the most widely accepted and generally acclaimed sans-serif faces because of its unusual clarity, readability, and versatility.

Composed by Superior Type,
Champaign, Illinois
Printed and bound by Halliday Lithographers,
West Hanover, Massachusetts
Designed by Iris Weinstein